"I'm delighted to see *Preaching the truth as it is in Jesus* in print. My delight is threefold. First, Andrew Fuller is one of the greatest but lesser-known Baptists of church history. He merits rediscovery. Second, because this book, as did Andrew Fuller, drips with the gospel of Jesus Christ. Third, this book is another helpful tool in interpreting and applying the text in light of Christ. Kudos to David Prince for assembling this fine work."
   Jason Allen
   President, Midwestern Baptist Theological Seminary

"Andrew Fuller is a hero of mine. He is an example par excellence as a pastor, preacher, theologian, and mobilizer for missions. He and his writings are not as well known as other Christian leaders in his day for whatever reasons. David Prince has set out to correct this problem, and he has succeeded magnificently. Giving his primary attention to Fuller's preaching, Prince explores the brilliance of the man who, as much as William Carey, helped launched the modern missions movement. This book is a treasure. I will consult it again and again with the prayer that I can finish my race like Andrew Fuller finished his."
   Daniel L. Akin
   President, Southeastern Baptist Theological Seminary

"'The gospel is a feast, and you are to invite guests.' Those words and so many others by Andrew Fuller have been beautifully brought to our minds and hearts in this marvelous book by David Prince. More than any other man, God used Andrew Fuller as the theological engine for the modern missionary movement. And while many have heard of the father of modern missions, William Carey, comparatively few have heard of his dear friend and the Secretary of the Baptist Missionary Society, Andrew Fuller. Through this book, Dr. Prince has brought Fuller to life, and through him, we will likewise be challenged to look to Christ and love him earnestly. You will love this book and Andrew Fuller, and you will tell the old, old story all the more. Read and share this book widely!"
   Greg Belser
   Pastor, Morrison Heights Baptist Church

"There has never been a more critical time for pastors to faithfully and boldly preach Christ from the Scriptures than today. This is why *Preaching the truth as it is in Jesus* is a vital resource for pastors. David Prince is both a model of Christ-centered preaching and a lifelong student of the treasures in Andrew Fuller's ministry. This book mines the riches of Fuller's work and offers the choicest resources on the pastoral calling for a new generation. Pastors, don't hesitate to add this book to your library. It will not only make a difference in your preaching; it will minister to your soul."

Daniel Darling
Director, Land Center for Cultural Engagement and Assistant Professor of Faith and Culture at Southwestern Baptist Theological Seminary; bestselling author of several books, including, *The Characters of Christmas*, *A Way With Words*, and *The Dignity Revolution*

"Those of us with an appetite for a return to Christ-centered preaching and theology-driven mission have been ably and amply supplied by David Prince's *Preaching the truth as it is in Jesus*. Prince—who like Fuller is best described as a pastor-theologian—has given us a carefully curated collection from the treasure trove of Andrew Fuller's writings along with introductory essays written with keen pastoral insight. Those who love 'the truth as it is in Jesus' and long to preach more faithfully and fruitfully will benefit immensely from reading this helpful volume."

Barry King
Pastor, Dunstable Baptist Church, Bedfordshire, England
Leader of Grace Baptist Partnership

"*Preaching the truth as it is in Jesus* by David Prince opens up a world of fascination and edification I know almost nothing about but am glad to encounter. How privileged all of us are that the treasures of Andrew Fuller's ministry are here available to us pastors today. We can be strengthened by this faithful testimony from 'the great cloud of witnesses' as we run the race in our generation."

Ray Ortlund
Renewal Ministries, Nashville

"David Prince is a trusted voice in the area of Christ-centered preaching. I have personally benefited from his homiletical thought for a number of years now, and his preaching has edified me on several occasions. So I am thrilled to see *Preaching the truth as it is in Jesus* in print. We don't have enough good material on Fuller on Christ-centered preaching, and so David has given us a double blessing! I plan on adding this book to my current reading list in Christ-centered preaching, and I would encourage other students, professors, and pastors to take up and read, as well!"

Tony Merida
Pastor, Imago Dei Church
Director for Theological Training for Acts 29
Dean and Professor of Pastoral Theology at Grimké Seminary
Author, *The Christ-Centered Expositor*

"Andrew Fuller was a supremely gifted theologian with much to teach us today. As David Prince ably shows, this is because Fuller was not only a first-rate thinker but also a 'sober minded working pastor.' So his work always has a practical thrust. Prince's book is especially noteworthy because it concentrates on the wonderful theme of preaching Christ. Fuller always focused on the Lord Jesus and he helps us to do the same. This book is highly recommended. Pastors and others who preach and teach will benefit from these pages, as will all who simply want to grow in love for Christ and share him more effectively."

Peter J. Morden
Senior Pastor, Cornerstone Baptist Church, leeds, England,
Distinguished Visiting Scholar, Spurgeon's College, London;
Author, *The Life and Thought of Andrew Fuller (1754-1815)*

"David Prince has given the modern day preacher an invaluable gift! *Preaching the truth as it is in Jesus* is part biography, part history, and ALL inspiring! My soul has benefitted by hearing from Andrew Fuller and I pray my preaching might benefit as well. This living historical handbook is a genuine gift to every preacher that loves the hard work of preparing and delivering sermons to the Lord's Church.

Clint Pressley
Pastor, Hickory Grove Baptist Church, Charlotte, NC

"I am thankful to Dr. Prince for introducing me to the life of Andrew Fuller. The work of pastoral ministry can be a lonely work for any man who is not seeking a platform but wants to be faithful in shepherding God's people. If you need motivation to grow deeper in your knowledge of Christ, to soar to new heights in your worship of Christ, and to preach Christ more passionately, then you must read this book."

Victor Sholar
Pastor, Main Street Baptist Church, Lexington, KY

"I am thankful to our Lord for the work of David Prince in bringing the expository preaching ministry of Andrew Fuller back to bear on our generation. This book has been a challenge and an affirmation to me in my own ministry of expository preaching. As iron sharpens iron, so Andrew Fuller has sharpened me in this reader. Especially encouraging to me was "The Nature of the Gospel, and the Manner in Which it Ought to be Preached." Every God-called preacher will be encouraged on to faithful heralding of the Word in this chapter! What a joy and an honor it is to me to be able to recommend this book to you. May it help you preach the truth as it is in Jesus (Eph.4:21)."

Jono Sims
Pastor, Shelbyville Mills Baptist Church

"In a church-world with too many truncated preachers, in truncated pulpits, pastoring and producing truncated Christians, David Prince has served the Church well by giving us a resource commending a Baptist pastor who had a full, not truncated, Christ-honoring spirituality—Andrew Fuller. Pastors and members of Christian congregations will be edified by this primary source (Fuller) and secondary source (Prince)—both working pastors."

Kevin Smith
Executive Director of the Baptist Convention of Maryland/Delaware

"It is sometimes asserted that the Baptist movement, while it has produced great preachers, great missionaries, and great activists, has produced no great theologians. Those who would make such a claim have obviously never read Andrew Fuller, the eighteenth-century British pastor and theologian. In this reader, David Prince has carefully curated some of Fuller's most penetrating writings, not only on the topic of preaching, but also on a range of theological and practical issues. Prince's admiration for Fuller is contagious. His extended introductions to each chapter offer the reader a reliable guide into the riches of Fuller's thought. Those who take up and read this book may well find themselves enraptured by the same vision of Christ that drove Fuller's entire life and career: 'I love his name, and wish to make it the centre in which all the lines of my ministry should meet!'"

R. Lucas Stamps
Associate Professor of Theology, Anderson University

To Greg Belser,
whose faithful expository preaching birthed in my heart a passion for the Scriptures.

To Thom Rainer,
who affirmed my call to preach by trusting me in the pulpit of Green Valley Baptist Church.

To Jeff Noblit,
who helped a young pastor understand that the Scripture is not only sufficient for preaching but also for ordering and shaping congregational life.

To Tom Nettles,
whose enthusiasm for Andrew Fuller helped me discover a historical hero who has been my constant companion in ministry.

To Russell Moore,
whose life, ministry, and friendship has provided me a clear example of preaching "the truth as it is in Jesus" from the church house to the White House.

And, as always, to Judi,
whose love motivates me, makes me better, and teaches me every day that "Two are better than one" (Ecclesiastes 4:9).

PREACHING THE TRUTH AS IT IS IN JESUS

A reader on Andrew Fuller

DAVID E. PRINCE

H&E
Publishing

Preaching the truth as it is in Jesus: A reader on Andrew Fuller

Copyright © 2022 David E. Prince

All rights reserved. This book may not be reproduced, in whole or in part, without written permission from the publishers.

H&E Publishing, Peterborough, Ontario
www.hesedandemet.com

Cover design by Chance Faulkner
Interior font: Equity Text A

Paperback ISBN: 978-1-77484-034-4
Ebook ISBN: 978-1-77484-035-1

Contents

Foreword — i
Michael A.G. Haykin

1. The Truth as It Is in Jesus — 1

The Uniform Bearing of the Scriptures on the Person and Work of Christ — 15

Ministers and Churches Exhorted to Serve One Another in Love — 19

An Essay on Truth — 23

2. Preaching Christ — 29

Faith in the Gospel a Necessary Prerequisite to Preaching it — 43

Preaching Christ — 49

The Nature of the Gospel — 55

Christian Patriotism — 61

Instances, Evil, and Tendency of Delay, in the Concern of Religion — 75

Conformity to the Death of Christ — 87

3. Preparing Sermons to Preach Christ — 99

Reading the Scriptures — 121

Thoughts on Preaching — 123

The Abuse of Allegory in Preaching — 147

The Nature and Importance of Walking by Faith — 151

4. Preparing the Preacher to Preach Christ — 181

The Influence of the Presence of Christ on a Minister — 197

Habitual Devotedness to the Ministry — 201

Affectionate Concern of a Minister — 207

Ministers Should Be Concerned Not to Be Despised — 211

Churches Walking in the Truth and Joy of Ministers — 215

Christian Churches Fellow Helpers with their Pastors — 219

Churches Should Exhibit the Light of the Gospel — 223

An Intimate and Practical Acquaintance with the Word of God   *229*

The Promise of the Spirit   *237*

Acknowledgements   **245**

Scripture Index   **247**

Foreword

In his "Preface" to this reader, which is composed of various texts from the written corpus of Andrew Fuller—an increasingly-famous pastor-theologian of the long eighteenth century—David Prince has rightly noted, "Above all else, Fuller was a gospel preacher." Raised in a genuinely hyper-Calvinist environment—an ambience that afflicted far too many of the Particular Baptist churches of Fuller's denomination and one that Fuller would spend much of his life seeking to dispel—Fuller came to understand the gospel through intense, personal spiritual struggle and through ardent wrestling to understand the Bible aright. That he came to a clear understanding of what the gospel is and how it is to be preached by the close of the 1770s, a few years into his first pastorate at Soham in Cambridgeshire, is of enormous significance for the history of Baptists, and indeed for the global history of Evangelicalism.

If Fuller had remained wandering around the labyrinth of hyper-Calvinism—as he himself once described this insular theological perspective—the history of those stirring days of spiritual awakening and missionary endeavour at the close of the long eighteenth century would have been quite different. For one, William Carey might not have ended up going to India, for Fuller would not have not been there to support him at every step of the way. Yet, as Fuller observed in one place, if such had been the case, God would have raised up others to engage in those world-shaking events in which Fuller and Carey were privileged to participate.

Of course, in our day when the gospel and Evangelicalism—at least in North America—have both been cast in dismal hues by contemporary culture, it is vital that we who love the gospel have a clear idea of what it is and how it should be preached. And it is here that Andrew Fuller is so helpful. I, for one, am deeply grateful to Pastor Prince, himself a pastor-theologian like Fuller, for making this judicious selection from an eminent divine of passages that relate directly to the wholesome preaching of the gospel of grace and life.

Michael A.G. Haykin
Dundas, ON
December 1, 2021.

1
The Truth as It Is in Jesus

Andrew Fuller was born in Wicken, Cambridgeshire, England on February, 6, 1754 and died on May 7, 1815. Charles Haddon Spurgeon said of Fuller, he was "the greatest theologian" of his century.[1] The editor of the standard nineteenth-century collection of Fuller's writings, Joseph Belcher, believed his writings would "go down to posterity side by side with the immortal works of the elder president Edwards, a man truly likeminded with the English writer."[2] Contemporary Baptist historian Thomas J. Nettles writes that Fuller's insights "were of such a timeless nature that every generation of Christians can profit," and pastor John Piper refers to Fuller as "an unusually brilliant theologian."[3] Over two hundred years after his death, the shadow of the great English Baptist pastor and missionary-theologian still casts wide, and I pray it will loom larger still in the days ahead.

Andrew Fuller's seminal work, *The Gospel Worthy of All Acceptation* (1785), influenced William Carey and others and is rightly considered the foundational document that launched the modern missionary movement. Fuller helped found the Baptist Missionary Society and was its leading advocate, fundraiser, and organizer. Piper explains, "The sum of the matter is that Fuller had one great enemy he wanted to defeat—global unbelief in Jesus Christ."[4] It is doubtful William Carey would have ever been sent to India without Andrew Fuller providing the theological foundation for such a mission. William Carey's great grandson and biographer, S. Pearce Carey writes,

---

[1] As cited in Gilbert Laws, *Andrew Fuller: Pastor, Theologian, Ropeholder* (London: Carey Press, 1942), 127.

[2] "Preface to the Complete American Edition," in *The Complete Works of Andrew Fuller: Memoirs, Sermons, Etc.,* J. Belcher, ed., 3 vols. (Harrisonburg: Sprinkle Publications, 1988), 1:viii.

[3] "Andrew Fuller," in *The Particular Baptists: 1638-1910*, Michael A.G. Haykin (Springfield, MO: Particular Baptist Press, 2000), 97; John Piper, *Andrew Fuller: Holy Faith, Worthy Gospel, World Mission* (Wheaton: Crossway, 2016), 16.

[4] John Piper, *Andrew Fuller: Holy Faith, Worthy Gospel, World Mission* (Wheaton: Crossway, 2016), 53.

Preaching the Truth as it is in Jesus

It was fitting that Kettering, Fuller's hometown, should be the mother town of modern British missions. More than anyone else he had rescued the churches from fatalism which had smothered all Christian sense of obligation to carry the Gospel to the unreached world. His sledgehammer had broken the cold reasoning of hyper-Calvinism. He had saved the day, too, at Nottingham, and was to prove to be the unrivaled home captain of the missionary cause.[5]

No other non-biblical author has influenced my thinking as significantly as Andrew Fuller. What draws me to Fuller's life and writings is that he addresses everything with the sober-minded clarity of a working pastor. He spent forty years in pastoral ministry, thirty-two of those years at the Baptist Church of Kettering in Northamptonshire. His work as a theologian, apologist, and missionary never lost sight of Jesus, his church, and his gospel. No topic Fuller addresses is treated in an abstract and hypothetical way, but rather, he treats each subject as having concrete implications for week-by-week gospel preaching, congregational worship, pastoral care, and church governance. On November 21, 1785, Fuller wrote in his diary that he thought one of the devil's devices was "to destroy the good tendency of any truth" by causing adherents to dwell on it while failing to "put it in practice." When that happens "then all is over with us!"[6]

Fuller was consistently concerned about the danger of an empty, ceremonial ministry that possessed the outward appearance of godliness but in practice denied its gospel power (2 Tim. 3:5). In a sermon from 2 Corinthians 4:13 to students at the Bristol Education Society, Fuller exhorts, "We must taste of truth as Christians, before we preach it. Studying it merely as ministers will never do. Believing belongs to us as Christians."[7] In assessing the state of the Baptist church in Northamptonshire in 1814 Fuller warns,

---

[5] S. Pearce Carey, *William Carey* (London: Wakeman Trust, 1993), 81–82.

[6] *The Complete Works of Andrew Fuller: The Diary of Andrew Fuller*, 1780–1801, Michael D. McMullen and Timothy D. Whelan, eds. (Boston: De Gruyter, 2016), 1:158.

[7] Andrew Fuller, "Faith in the Gospel a Necessary Prerequisite to Preaching it," in *The Complete Works of Andrew Fuller: Memoirs, Sermons, Etc.*, ed. and revised Joseph Belcher, 3 vols. (Harrisonburg: Sprinkle Publications, 1988), 1:517.

David E. Prince

We are apt to think, that if we have but made up our minds on the leading points of controversy afloat in the world, and taken the side of truth, we are safe; but it is not so. If we walk not with God, we shall almost be certain in some way to get aside from the gospel, and then the work of God will not prosper in our hands. Ingenious discourses may be delivered, and nothing advanced inconsistent with the gospel, while yet the gospel itself is not preached. We may preach about Christ himself, and yet not "preach Christ." We may pride ourselves in our orthodoxy, and yet be far from the doctrine of the New Testament; may hold with exhortations and invitations to the unconverted, and yet not "persuade men;" may plead for sound doctrine, and yet overlook the things that "become sound doctrine." Finally, we may advocate the cause of holiness, while we ourselves are unholy.[8]

When I first read through Andrew Fuller's *Complete Works*, I was struck by an oft-repeated phrase, which I believe is an excellent way to summarize the distinctiveness of Fuller's life and ministry—and one we would do well to have summarize our own: "the truth as it is in Jesus." He writes concerning this phrase:

With the idea of all divine truth bearing an intimate relation to Christ agrees that notable phrase in Eph. 4:21, "The truth as it is in Jesus." To believe the truth concerning Jesus is to believe the whole doctrine of the Scriptures. Hence it is that in all the brief summaries of Christian doctrine the person and work of Christ are prominent. Such are the following: "Brethren, I declare unto you the gospel which I preached unto you, which also you have received, and wherein ye stand; by which also ye are saved, if ye keep in memory what I preached unto you, unless ye have believed in vain. For I delivered unto you, among the first principles, that which I also received, how that Christ died for our sins according to the Scriptures;"[9] "Great is the mystery of godliness, God was manifest in the flesh, justified in the Spirit, seen of angels, preached unto the Gentiles, believed on in the world, received up into glory;"[10] "This is a faithful saying, and worthy of all acceptation, that Jesus Christ came into the world to save sinners, of

---

[8] Fuller, "State of the Baptist Churches in Northamptonshire [1814]," in *Complete Works*, 3:483.
[9] 1 Corinthians 15:3
[10] 1 Timothy 3:16.

whom I am chief;"[11] "This is the record, that God hath given unto us eternal life, and this life is in his Son;"[12] "He that believeth that Jesus is the Christ is born of God;"[13] "Who is he that overcometh the world, but he that believeth that Jesus is the Son of God?"[14] Fully aware that this golden link would draw along with it the whole chain of evangelical truth, the sacred writers seem careful for nothing in comparison of it. It is on this ground that faith in Christ is represented as essential to spiritual life (John 6:53-56), "Jesus said unto them, Verily, verily, I say unto you, Except ye eat the flesh of the Son of man, and drink his blood, ye have no life in you. Whoso eateth my flesh and drinketh my blood hath eternal life, and I will raise him up at the last day. For my flesh is meat indeed, and my blood is drink indeed. He that eateth my flesh, and drinketh my blood, dwelleth in me, and I in him." We may be Christians by education, may be well versed in Christianity as a science, may be able to converse, and preach, and write, in defence of it; but if Christ crucified be not that to us which food is to the hungry, and drink to the thirsty, we are dead while we live. It is on this ground that error concerning the person and work of Christ is of such importance as frequently to become death to the party. We may err on other subjects and survive, though it be in a maimed state; but to err in this is to contract a disease in the vitals, the ordinary effect of which is death. When Peter confessed him to be the Son of the living God, Jesus answered, "Upon this rock will I build my church, and the gates of hell shall not prevail against it."[15] Upon this principles, as a foundation, Christianity rests; and it is remarkable that, to this day, deviation concerning the person and work of Christ is followed by a dereliction of almost every other evangelical doctrine, and of the spirit of Christianity. How should it be otherwise? If the foundation be removed, the building must fall.[16]

In Ephesians 4:17-24, Paul begins the exhortatory section of his epistle (Eph. 4:17-6:20) and uses the image of "walking" to describe one's lifestyle (Eph. 2:10; 4:1). In contrasting the Christian's life with the unbeliever's life, Paul adopts striking schoolroom language, writing, "But that

---

[11] 1 Timothy 1:5.
[12] 1 John 5:11.
[13] 1 John 5:1.
[14] 1 John 5:5.
[15] Matthew 16:18.
[16] Fuller, "Plan Proposed to Be Pursued," *Complete Works*, 1:691-692

is not the way you learned Christ!" (Eph. 4:20), you "were taught in him, as the truth is in Jesus" (Eph. 4:21). In other words, the content of the teaching is Christ, and all other truths are rightly understood only when their meaning and application is mediated through Christ. Instruction in Christian living begins with Christ, ongoing instruction focuses on Christ, and the end point of the instruction is to learn Christ. Christians are to be pupils of Christ who never graduate. Pursuing the truth as it is in Jesus was Fuller's commitment in life and ministry. On August 21, 1784, Fuller wrote in his diary, "Oh that I might be led into divine truth! 'Christ and his cross be all my theme.' I love his name, and wish to make it the centre in which all the lines of my ministry should meet!"[17]

Fuller was gospel-centered and missional well before that verbiage became vogue in evangelicalism. Michael Haykin observes, "Even where the atoning work of Christ is believed and embraced, Fuller was convinced that the failure to be crucicentric will have its baneful effects."[18] Fuller exhorted, "The army of the Lamb is composed of the whole body of Christians. Every disciple of Jesus should consider himself as a missionary."[19] The commitment of Fuller's life and ministry to knowing and living based on "the truth as it is in Jesus" enabled him to challenge biblical-theological, ecclesial, and missiological errors from all directions. In 1780, Fuller covenanted before the Lord, "Thou hast given me a determination to take up no principle at second-hand; but to search for everything at the pure fountain of thy word."[20] Fuller opposed the errors of his day, not as an end, but always as a means to the end of honoring Jesus, summing up all things in him (Eph. 1:10) and calling the whole world to do the same.

Fuller's ministry friend and partner in the spread of the gospel to the ends of the earth, John Ryland, summarized Fuller's passion and gospel exertions,

> He never seemed to be so much in his element, as when dwelling on the doctrine of the atonement. Like the apostle Paul, he was determined to know nothing but Christ and him crucified. This

---

[17] Fuller, "Diary, August 21, 1784," in *Complete Works*, 1:42.
[18] Michael A.G. Haykin, ed. *The Armies of the Lamb: The Spirituality of Andrew Fuller* (Dundas: Joshua Press, 2001), 39.
[19] Fuller, "Conformity to the Death of Christ," *Complete Works*, 1:315.
[20] Fuller, "Memoir of Mr. Fuller," *Complete Works*, 1:20.

doctrine rejoiced his own soul; and this he used to exhibit to others, as of the greatest importance; comprising all the salvation of a needy sinner, and all the desire of a newborn soul.

Had Mr. Fuller's life been protracted to ever so great a length, he could never have put in execution all the plans he would have laid for attaining his ultimate end; since, as fast as some of his labors had been accomplished, his active mind would have been devising fresh measures for advancing the divine glory, and extending the kingdom of Christ. As it was, he certainly did more for God than most good men could have effected in a life longer by twenty years.[21]

Fuller vigorously rebutted man-centered Arminian theology on one hand, and the doctrinally serious, but evangelistically sterile, anti-missions High Calvinism of his day on the other. He defended the faith against Socinianism (which denied the full deity of Christ, penal substitutionary atonement, and moral inability of man to convert himself), Sandemanianism (which argued that saving faith reduces to mere intellectual assent to a fact or proposition), and Antinomianism (a still-common belief that Christians are under no obligation to obey the laws of ethics and morality). Perhaps one of the greatest reasons Fuller's works are of benefit to modern pastors is the fact that the theological errors Fuller combated have so many contemporary heirs.

According to Fuller "the truth as it is in Jesus" is how the entire Bible must be understood, because to pit the words of Christ against other parts of the Bible would constitute a rejection of the authority of Jesus who taught "Scripture cannot be broken" (John 10:35). Fuller explains, "Every divine truth bears a relation to him: hence the doctrine of the gospel is called 'the truth as it is in Jesus.' In the face of Jesus Christ, we see the glory of the divine character in such a manner as we see it nowhere else."[22] For Fuller "the truth as it is in Jesus" meant not only that evangelical doctrine must be defended, but also that doing so was a matter of both the mind and the heart. Fuller warned pastors, "Beware that you do not preach an unfelt gospel."[23] He explains,

---

[21] John Ryland, *The Work of Faith, the Labor of Love and the Patience of Hope Illustrated in the Life and Death of the Rev. Andrew Fuller* (London: Button and Son, 1818), 364.

[22] Fuller, "The Uniform Bearing of the Scriptures," *Complete Works*, 1:704.

[23] Fuller, "Ministers Should Be Concerned Not to Be Despised," *Complete Works*, 1:489–490.

> The gospel is a feast, and you are to invite guests. You may have many excuses and refusals. But be you concerned to do as your Lord commands. And when you have done your utmost, there will still be room. Dwell on the freeness, and fullness, and all-sufficiency of his grace, and how welcome even the worst of sinners are, who, renouncing all other refuges, flee to him.[24]

"The truth as it is in Jesus" was foundational to Fuller's biblical-theological vision and ministry practice. The phrase is a continual touchstone in the Fuller corpus and holds forth many imperatives for gospel preachers.

We must preach the truth as it is in Jesus

Above all else, Fuller was a gospel preacher. This fact is sometimes obscured because of Fuller's influence and profound contributions in missiology, theology, and apologetics. As Keith S. Grant astutely explains, the evangelical renewal Fuller helped to usher in "did not only take place alongside the local church, but especially in congregational ecclesiology." He continues, "there was a transformation within the pastoral office," it became "very affecting and evangelical."[25] Fuller's pastoral ministry was rooted in expository preaching that was experimental and passionately evangelistic because of a relentless commitment to preaching Christ from the whole Bible. Consider:

> The subject-matter of the apostle's preaching is variously described: it is called "the faith" — "the truth" — "the truth as it is in Jesus" — "Christ crucified" — "the gospel" — "the word of reconciliation," &c. In these descriptions, we see our work.[26]

> Every sermon, more or less, should have some relation to Christ, and bear on his person or work. This is the life of all doctrine, and it will be our own fault if it is dry. Do not consider it as one subject among others, but as that which involves all others, and gives them an interest they could not otherwise

---

[24] Fuller, "Preaching Christ," *Complete Works*, 1:503.
[25] Keith S. Grant, *Andrew Fuller and the Evangelical Renewal of Pastoral Theology* (Eugene: Wipf and Stock, 2013), 2–3.
[26] Fuller, "The Christian Ministry a Great Work," *Complete Works*, 1:515.

possess. Preach not only the truth, but all truth, "as it is in Jesus." However ingenious our sermons may be, unless they bear on Christ, and lead the mind to Christ, we do not preach the faith of the gospel.[27]

We must understand and know doctrinal truth as it is in Jesus

According to Fuller, "Truth is a system, though it is not taught in the Scriptures in a systematic form."[28] He explained that God did not reveal himself to us in an abstract and hyper-systematized fashion, but rather in the context of particular examples in redemptive history. Fuller describes biblical truth as being introduced "incidentally," by which he is not rejecting God's purposeful intention in Scriptural revelation but is noting that God reveals doctrinal truth to us embedded in his historical interaction with his image bearers. Though Fuller does not use the description "Christ-centered biblical theology," that is the label we would attach to what he is advocating.[29] He believed that the biblical writers consider the person and work of Jesus Christ to be "a golden link, that would draw along with it the whole chain of evangelical truth."[30] Consider:

> Be concerned to understand and to teach the doctrine of Christianity—"the truth as it is in Jesus." Be careful, particularly, to be conversant with the doctrine of the cross; if you be right there, you can scarcely be essentially wrong anywhere. Cut off the reproach of dry doctrine, by preaching it feelingly; and of its being inimical to good works, by preaching it practically.[31]

> Truth, we may be certain, is the same thing as what in the Scriptures is denominated "the gospel" — "the common salvation" — "the common faith" — "the faith once delivered to the saints" — "the truth as it is in Jesus," &c.; and what this is may be clearly understood by the brief summaries of the gospel, and of the faith of the primitive Christians, which abound in the New Testament. Of the former, the following are a few of many examples: — "God

---

[27] Fuller, "Faith in the Gospel a Necessary Prerequisite," *Complete Works*, 1:516.
[28] Fuller, "The Deity of Christ," *Complete Works*, 3:695-696.
[29] Fuller, "An Essay on Truth," *Complete Works*, 3:537-540.
[30] Fuller, "An Essay on Truth," *Complete Works*, 3:526.
[31] Fuller, "Ministers and Churches Exhorted," *Complete Works*, 1:544.

so loved the world, that he gave his only begotten Son, that whosoever believeth in him should not perish, but have everlasting life.—The Son of man came to seek and to save that which is lost.—I am the way, the truth, and the life: no man cometh unto the Father but by me.—To him gave all the prophets witness, that through his name whosoever believeth in him shall receive remission of sins. We preach Christ crucified, unto the Jews a stumbling-block, and unto the Greeks foolishness; but unto them which are called, both Jews and Greeks, Christ, the power of God, and the wisdom of God.—I determined not to know anything among you, save Jesus Christ and him crucified.—Moreover, brethren, I declare unto you the gospel which I preached unto you, which also ye have received, and wherein ye stand; by which also ye are saved, if ye hold fast what I preached unto you, unless ye have believed in vain; for I delivered unto you first of all that which I also received, how that Christ died for our sins according to the Scriptures; and that he was buried, and that he rose again the third day, according to the Scriptures.—This is a faithful saying, and worthy of all acceptation, that Christ Jesus came into the world to save sinners, of whom I am chief.—This is the record, that God hath given to us eternal life, and this life is in his Son.—Neither is there salvation in any other; for there is none other name under heaven given among men whereby we must be saved."[32]

Apologetics is explaining and defending the truth as it is in Jesus
Much of Andrew Fuller's writing was born of a sense of pastoral duty rooted in his zealous love for the church of the Lord Jesus Christ. Doctrinal error, particularly error that threatened the message or proclamation of the gospel, was a menace to the church's mission of reaching the globe with gospel truth and must be fought. As a young man, Fuller loved wrestling and his earliest biographer J.W. Morris described him as "tall, stout, and muscular."[33] Morris notes,

> Having been a famous wrestler in his youth, he seldom met with a stout man without making an ideal comparison of strength, and possessing some of his former feelings in reference to its exercise. If necessity required, he was still by no means deficient in courage,

---

[32] Fuller, "An Essay on Truth," *Complete Works*, 3:525–526.
[33] J.W. Morris, *Memoirs of the Life and Writings of the Rev. Andrew Fuller, Late Pastor of the Baptist Church at Kettering, and the First Secretary to the Baptist Missionary Society* (Boston: Lincoln & Edmands, 1830), 306.

of which some evidence was given after he removed to Kettering. When his rest was disturbed by the conduct of disorderly persons, he would sometimes rise in the night, rush alone into the street, half-dressed, and quell the disturbance, without any apprehension of danger.

His nerves were uniformly so firm, that he seemed to be made almost without fear; and such was his invincibility and perfect self-command, that it may be doubted whether he was ever seen in a state of agitation.[34]

As a follower of Christ, Fuller no longer wrestled opponents in hand-to-hand combat for sport, but he never really stopped wrestling. As Haykin observes, "This character trait was turned in a very different direction as he did battle for Christian orthodoxy and resisted vigorously what he saw as distortions of scriptural teaching."[35] In defense of "the truth as it is in Jesus," Fuller wrestled false Calvinism (denied the free offer of the gospel), Sandemanianism (rationalistic faith, bare belief in the bare truth), Deism (God exists but does not interfere in his creation), antinomianism (the moral law is of no use for those with faith), Socianism (anti-Trinitarian), universalism (all will be saved), and Arminianism (man-centered understanding of salvation). Consider:

> In the First Epistle to this church, Paul generously waved a defense of himself and his brethren; being more concerned for the recovery of those to Christ who were in danger of being drawn off from the truth as it is in Jesus, than respecting their opinion of him; yet when the one was accomplished, he undertook the other; not only as a justification of himself and his brethren, but as knowing that just sentiments of faithful ministers bore an intimate connexion with the spiritual welfare of their hearers.[36]

> It becomes those who may be the most firmly established in *the truth as it is in Jesus*, to consider that a portion of the errors of the age, in all probability, attaches to them; and though it were otherwise, yet they are directed to carry it benevolently towards others

---

[34] Morris, *Memoirs of the Life and Writings of the Rev. Andrew Fuller*, 306–307.
[35] Michael A.G. Haykin, "Preface," *At the Pure Fountain of Thy Word: Andrew Fuller as an Apologist*, ed. Haykin (Milton Keynes: Paternoster, 2004), xviiii.
[36] Fuller, "The Gospel Worthy of All Acceptation," *Complete Works*, 2:354.

who may err: "In meekness instructing those that oppose themselves; if God, peradventure, will give them repentance to the acknowledging of the truth."[37]

Is not this a plain proof that neither of these systems is evangelical? That, I say again, is the true gospel which gives to every part of Scripture its fair and full meaning; and if the views we have hitherto entertained will not do this, we ought to conclude that, whatever we may have learned, we have yet to learn "the truth as it is in Jesus."[38]

It teaches us to defend nothing but the truth as it is in Jesus. It also affords presumptive evidence in its favor; for if Christianity itself were false, there is little doubt but that you, or some of your fellow laborers, would be able to prove it so; and this would turn greatly to your account. Your neglecting this, and directing your artillery chiefly against its corruptions and abuses, betray a consciousness that the thing itself, if not invulnerable, is yet not so easy of attack. If Christianity had really been a relic of heathenism, as you suggest, there is little reason to think that you would have so strenuously opposed it.[39]

Christian living is walking in the truth as it is in Jesus

Fuller's spirituality was radically Bible-shaped and cross-centered. He wrote that "if Christ crucified be not that to us which food is to the hungry, and drink to the thirsty, we are dead while we live" because "to err in this is to contract a disease in the vitals, the ordinary effect which is death."[40] Though he believed all truth was revealed to be lived out, he rejected a moralistic approach to spirituality, which is the attempt to obey the ethical commands of the Bible abstracted from the gospel of Jesus Christ. No truth of Scripture is meant to be understood in isolation from the gospel. When ethical and moral imperatives are promoted as sufficient, even abstracted from Jesus, the result is a cross-less Christianity, which Fuller repudiated. For Fuller, the gospel provides the only

---

[37] Fuller, "An Essay on Truth," *Complete Works*, 3:537.
[38] Fuller, "Remarks on Two Sermons by W.W. Horne of Yarmouth," *Complete Works*, 3:583.
[39] Fuller, "The Gospel its Own Witness," *Complete Works*, 2:8.
[40] Fuller, "Letters on Systematic Divinity," *Complete Works*, 1:245.

possible context for genuine obedience: faith. Consider Fuller's reflection on this topic:

> Heartily desiring that every blessing may attend us all, and that we may each be led into the truth as it is in Jesus.[41]

> I have no objection to allowing, however, that if we believe the very truth as it is in Jesus, there can be nothing wanting in the manner of believing it. But though this be true, and though an inquirer after the way of salvation ought to be directed to the saving doctrine of the cross, rather than to the workings of his own mind concerning it, yet there is in the workings of a believer's mind towards it something essentially different from those of the merely nominal Christian; and which, when the inquiry comes to be, "Am I a believer?" ought to be pointed out. He not only believes truths, which the other does not, but believes the same truths in a different manner. In other words, he believes them on different grounds, and with different affections. That which he knows is, in measure, "as he ought to know it." He discerns spiritual things in a spiritual manner; which is the only manner in which they can be discerned as they are.[42]

> O my God, (let not the Lord be angry with his servant for thus speaking,) I have, thou knowest, heretofore sought thy truth. I have earnestly entreated thee that thou wouldest lead me into it; that I might be rooted, established, and built up in it, as it is in Jesus. I have seen the truth of that saying—"It is a good thing to have the heart established with grace;" and now I would this day solemnly renew my prayer to thee, and also enter afresh into covenant with thee.[43]

Aim of a missionary: direct attention to the truth as it is in Jesus

Fuller was elected the first secretary of the Baptist Missionary Society and remained in the unpaid position twenty-three years until his death in 1815. He took upon himself the task of promotion and fundraising for this unpopular venture and faced down considerable political opposition as well, all while faithfully serving as pastor of the Kettering church. His

---

[41] Fuller, "Letter XIII," *Complete Works*, 2:560.
[42] Fuller, "Strictures on Sandemanianism," *Complete Works*, 2:587.
[43] Fuller, "Memoir of Mr. Fuller," *Complete Works*, 1:19.

journals reveal never-ending letters and constant travel to raise support for the missionary cause, which often involved preaching three or four sermons in a day. After his death at age sixty-one, his wife Ann summed up his life of suffering for the world mission when she said, "I am fully persuaded that my dear husband fell a sacrifice to his unremitting application to the concerns of the mission."[44] Fuller's biographer J.W. Morris fittingly wrote, "Fuller lived and died as a martyr to the mission."[45] Consider Fuller's comments on the aim of mission work:

> The truth is, if we wish to convert heathens to ourselves, we must do as the Church of Rome does, set up for infallibility, and withhold the Scriptures from the people, lest they should read and judge for themselves. But if we wish to convert them to Christ, we shall put the Scriptures into their hands, as the only standard of truth, and teach them to consider all other writings as in nowise binding on their consciences, nor even as claiming regard any further than they agree with them. By this rule let them form their judgments of us, and of our differences, should they deem it worthwhile to inquire into them; but the aim of a true missionary will ever be to divert their attention from such things, and to direct it to "the truth as it is in Jesus."[46]

> If "the truth as it is in Jesus" be impressed upon our hearts by the Holy Spirit, whether it be by reading, or hearing, or thinking— whether by any particular passage of Scripture or by some leading truth contained in it occurring to the mind—it will operate to produce humility. To be impressed, for instance, with a sense of the exceeding sinfulness of sin, with the love of God in the gift of his Son, with the love of Christ in dying for the ungodly, with his all-sufficiency and readiness to save to the uttermost all them that come unto God by him, or with the freeness of his grace to the most guilty and unworthy, is the same thing as to be made to feel the influence of that gospel which lays low the pride of man.[47]

Andrew Fuller's combination of a keen critical mind, love for the church, pastoral heart, global gospel burden, clarity of insight, gospel-centered

---

[44] Fuller, "Memoir of Mr. Fuller," *Complete Works*, 1:110.
[45] Morris, *Memoirs of the Life and Writings of the Rev. Andrew Fuller*, 304.
[46] Fuller, "An Apology for Christian Missions," *Complete Works*, 2:826–827.
[47] Fuller, "On Antinomianism," *Complete Works*, 2:741.

practicality, intensity of affections, power of expression, and commitment to spiritual friendships, which are all rooted in "the truth as it is in Jesus," have captivated my mind,stirred my affections, and spurred me on in gospel ministry. I thank God for Andrew Fuller and for leading me to his writings. He has become a vital and constant conversation partner for me in life and ministry, and I have put this reader together in hopes that he will become one to you as well.

The remaining portion of this chapter will be three examples from the Fuller corpus of him working out "the truth as it is in Jesus" as a working pastor and self-taught theologian. In "The uniform bearing of the Scriptures on the person and work of Christ," Fuller contends that the person and work of Christ is the central thread that runs throughout Scripture and gives life to all other facts, truths, and biblical redemptive history. "Ministers and churches exhorted to serve one another in love" is an ordination sermon of Fuller's that directs the pastor and the people to live with one another in cruciform love. Finally, there is an excerpt from Fuller's essay, "On truth," in which Fuller argues that understanding "the truth as it is in Jesus" is essential to avoiding bigotry on the one hand and evangelical compromise on the other.

The Uniform Bearing of the Scriptures on the Person and Work of Christ[1]

In the two preceding letters I have endeavoured to show the necessity of divine revelation, and to give evidence of the Bible's being written by inspiration of God, so as to answer to that necessity; in this I shall add a few thoughts on its uniform bearing on the person and work of Christ.

We need not follow those who drag in Christ on all occasions. To suppose, for instance, that all the Psalms of David refer to him, is to establish the gospel on the ruins of common sense. Still less need we see him prefigured by everything in which a heated imagination may trace a resemblance. This were to go into a kind of spiritual quixotism,[2] finding a castle where others would only find a windmill. Nevertheless, the sacred Scriptures are full of Christ, and uniformly lead to him. The holy book begins with an account of the creation of the world: "In the beginning God created the heavens and the earth."[3] But they elsewhere inform us that, "In the beginning was the Word, and the Word was with God, and the Word was God. All things were made by him, and without him was not anything made that was made."[4] Yea more, that all things were made not only by him, as the first cause, but for him, as the last end. The creation seems to have been designed as a theatre on which he should display his glory, particularly in the work of redemption. Surely it was in this view that he "rejoiced in the habitable parts of the earth, and his delights were with the sons of men."

History

The history contained in the sacred Scriptures is that of the church or people of God; other nations are introduced only in an incidental manner, as being connected with them; and this people were formed for Christ. Him God appointed to be "heir of all things."[5] All that was done

---

[1] Fuller, "The Uniform Bearing of the Scriptures," *Complete Works*, 1:702–704.
[2] A delusional and extravagant undertaking.
[3] Genesis 1:1.
[4] John 1:1.
[5] Hebrews 1:2.

by the patriarchs and prophets, under the Old Testament, was preparatory to his kingdom. It was in his field that they laboured, and therefore his apostles "entered into their labours."[6] God's calling Abraham, and blessing and increasing him, had all along a reference to the kingdom of his Son. He was the principal Seed in whom all the kindreds of the earth were to be blessed. Why did Melchizedek,[7] on meeting Abraham, when he returned from the slaughter of the kings, bless him with so much heart? Was it not as knowing that he had the promises, especially that of the Messiah? Why is Esau's despising his birthright[8] reckoned profaneness, but on account of its referring to something sacred? The promises made to Abraham's posterity chiefly related to things at a great distance; but Esau longed for something nearer at hand, and therefore sold his birthright for a present enjoyment. Why is the reproach which Moses preferred to the treasures of Egypt called "the reproach of Christ,"[9] but that Israel being in possession of the promise of him, and Moses believing it, cast in his lot with them, though in a state of slavery? Were not these the "good things" to which he referred, in persuading Hobab to go with them?[10] All that was done for Israel from their going down into Egypt to their settlement in Canaan, and from thence to the coming of Christ, was in reference to him. The conquest of the seven nations was authorized, and even commanded by Jehovah, for the purpose of re-establishing his government in his own world, from which he had in a manner been driven by idolatry. It was setting up his standard with the design of ultimately subduing the world to the obedience of faith. What but the promise of Christ, as including the covenant that God made with David, rendered it all his salvation and all his desire? It was owing to the bearing which the Old Testament history had on the person and work of Christ that Stephen and Paul, when preaching him to the Jews, made use of it to introduce their subject (Acts 7, 13).

Institutions

The body of the Jewish institutions was but a shadow of good things to

---

[6] John 4:38.
[7] Genesis 14:18.
[8] Genesis 25:29–34; Hebrews 12:16–17.
[9] Hebrews 11:24–26.
[10] Numbers 10:29.

come, of which Christ was the substance. Their priests, and prophets, and kings were typical of him. Their sacrifices pointed to him who "gave himself for us, an offering and a sacrifice to God for a sweet-smelling savour."[11] The manna on which they fed in the wilderness referred to him, as the "bread of God that should come down from heaven."[12] The rock, from whence the water flowed that followed them in their journeys, is said to be Christ, as being typical of him. Their cities of refuge represent him, "as the hope set before us."[13] The whole dispensation served as a foil, to set off the superior glory of his kingdom. The temple was but as the scaffolding to that which he would build, and the glory of which he would bear. The moral law exhibited right things, and the ceremonial law a shadow of good things; but "grace and truth came by Jesus Christ."[14] The Christian dispensation is to that of the Old Testament as the jubilee to a state of captivity. It might be in reference to such things as these that the psalmist prayed, "Open thou mine eyes, that I may behold wonderful things out of thy law!"[15]

Of the prophecies with which the Scriptures abound, the person and work of Christ form the principal theme. "To him gave all the prophets witness,"[16] either in what they wrote or spoke. "The testimony of Jesus is the spirit of prophecy."[17] From the first mention of the woman's seed to his appearance in the flesh, the language of prophecy concerning him became more explicit and distinct. The blessing on Jehovah the God of Shem seems to intimate designs of mercy towards his descendants. The promise to Abraham and his seed is more express. Abraham, understanding it as including the Messiah, believed, and it was counted to him for righteousness. He earnestly desired to see his day; he saw it and rejoiced. Jacob's prophecy is still more explicit and distinct. He foretells his being of the tribe of Judah, and that under his reign the Gentiles should be gathered.[18] After this, the house of David is specified, as that from which the Messiah should spring. The Psalms abound in predictions concerning

---

[11] Ephesians 5:2.
[12] John 6:33, 51.
[13] Hebrews 6:18.
[14] John 1:17.
[15] Psalm 119:18.
[16] Acts 10:43.
[17] Revelation 19:10.
[18] Isaiah 49:6.

him. Isaiah tells of his being miraculously born of a virgin—of his humble and gentle character, "not breaking the bruised reed, nor quenching the smoking flax"[19]—of his sufferings, death, and everlasting kingdom, which implied his resurrection (Acts 13:34). Micah named the town of Bethlehem as the place where he should be born.[20] Zechariah mentioned the beasts on which he should make his public entry into Jerusalem.[21] The Spirit of inspiration in the prophets is called "the Spirit of Christ," because it "testified beforehand the sufferings of Christ, and the glory that should follow."[22] But if the Old Testament had a uniform bearing on the person of Christ, much more the New. This is properly entitled, "The New Testament of our Lord and Saviour Jesus Christ." The one abounds with prophecies; the other relates to their accomplishment. The ordinances of the former were prefigurative; those of the latter are commemorative. But both point to the same object.

Every divine truth bears a relation to him: hence the doctrine of the gospel is called "the truth as it is in Jesus." In the face of Jesus Christ, we see the glory of the divine character in such a manner as we see it nowhere else. The evil nature of sin is manifested in his cross, and the lost condition of sinners in the price at which our redemption was obtained. Grace, mercy, and peace are in him. The resurrection to eternal life is through his death. In him every precept finds its most powerful motive, and every promise its most perfect fulfilment. The Jews possessed the sacred Scriptures of the Old Testament, an "searched them," thinking that in them they had eternal life; but they "would not come to him that they might have it."[23] What a picture does this present to us of multitudes in our own times! We possess both the Old and the New Testament; and it is pleasing to see the zeal manifested of late in giving them circulation. All orders and degrees of men will unite in applauding them. But they overlook Christ, to whom they uniformly bear testimony; and, while thinking to obtain eternal life, will not come to him that they might have it.

---

[19] Isaiah 42:3; Matthew 12:20.
[20] Micah 5:2.
[21] Zechariah 14:4.
[22] 1 Peter 1:11.
[23] John 5:39.

Ministers and Churches Exhorted to Serve One Another in Love[1]

[Ordination Sermon, addressed to both Pastor and People]

"By love serve one another." Galatians 5:13

My brethren, having been requested on this solemn occasion to address a word of exhortation to both pastor and people, I have chosen a subject equally suitable for both.

Charge to the Pastor

I shall begin by addressing a few words to you, my brother, the pastor of this church.

The text expresses your duty—to "serve" the church; and the manner in which it is to be performed: "in love." Do not imagine there is anything degrading in the idea of being a servant. Though you are to serve them, and they you, yet neither of you are to be masters of the other. You are fellow servants, and have each "one Master, even Christ."[2] It is a service, not of constraint, but of love; like that which your Lord and Master himself yielded: "I have been among you as one that serveth."[3] Let the common name of minister remind you of this: the authority you exercise must be invariably directed to the spiritual advantage of the church. You are invested with authority; you are to have the rule over them in the Lord; but not as a "lord over God's heritage." Nor are you invested with this authority to confer dignity on you, or that you may value yourself as a person of consequence; but for the good of the church. This is the end of office: "Whosoever will be great among you, let him be your minister; and whosoever will be chief among you, let him be your servant. Even as the Son of man came not to be ministered unto, but to

---

[1] Fuller, "Ministers and Churches Exhorted," *Complete Works*, 1:544–545.
[2] Matthew 23:10.
[3] Luke 22:27.

minister."[4] ... But, more particularly:

Feed the flock
You must serve the church of God, by feeding them with the word of life. This is the leading duty of a minister. "Preach the word; be instant in season, and out of season."[5] This will be serving them, as it will promote their best interests. For this end you must be familiar with the word: "Meditate on these things: give thyself wholly to them."[6] It is considered a fine thing with some to have a black coat, to loiter about all the week, and to stand up to be looked at and admired on the sabbath. But truly this is not to serve the church of God. Be concerned to be "a scribe well instructed in the things of the kingdom."[7] Be concerned to have treasures, and to bring them forth. I would advise that one service of every sabbath consist of a well-digested exposition, that your hearers may become Bible Christians. Be concerned to understand and to teach the doctrine of Christianity — "the truth as it is in Jesus." Be careful, particularly, to be conversant with the doctrine of the cross; if you be right there, you can scarcely be essentially wrong anywhere. Cut off the reproach of dry doctrine, by preaching it feelingly; and of its being inimical to good works, by preaching it practically.

And do all this in love. Your love must be, first, to Christ, or you will not be fitted for your work of feeding the church (John 21:15-17). Also to the truth, or your services will be mischievous, rather than useful. And to Christians, for Christ's sake (Acts 20:28). And to the souls of men, as fellow men and fellow sinners. If love be wanting, preaching will be in vain.

Watch over the flock
You must feed the church of God, by watching over them. "Be instant in season, and out of season; reprove, rebuke, exhort with all long-suffering and doctrine."[8] Watch over them, not as a vulture, to destroy them: but

---

[4] Mark 10:45.
[5] 2 Timothy 4:2.
[6] 1 Timothy 4:15.
[7] Matthew 13:52.
[8] 2 Timothy 4:2.

as a good shepherd, who cares for the sheep. If you are compelled to reprove, beware that your reproof be conveyed, not in ill temper, but in love; not to gratify self, but to do your brother good.

Lead the flock
You must serve them, by leading them on in all spiritual and holy exercises. Lead them by your example. "Be thou an example of the believers, in word, in conversation, in charity, in spirit, in faith, in purity."[9] Visit them. You have as much need to pray with them and for them in private, as to preach to them in public. And you must do all this in love. An affectionate example and deportment will draw them on.

Charge to the Church
Let me now address myself to the church. You also must serve your pastor, as well as he you, and this in love. You must seek his good, as well as he yours.

Make him happy
Be assiduous to make him happy in his mind. If he discharges his work with grief, it will be unprofitable for you. If you be touchy, and soon offended, or cold and distant, it will destroy his happiness. Do not be content with a merely negative respect. Be free, open, kind, inviting to friendly and Christian intercourse and conversation; and be early and constant in your attendance on public worship.

Care for him
Be concerned to render him as easy in his circumstances as possible. If he serves you in spiritual things, is it such a great thing that he partake of your carnal things? I hope he does not covet a haughty independence of you; but neither let him sink into an abject dependence. Worship not with—offer not to God—that which costs you nothing. It is the glory of dissenting churches, if they voluntarily make sacrifices for the maintenance of the true religion among them.

---

[9] 1 Timothy 4:12.

Correct him in private
If there be anything apparently wrong in his conduct or his preaching, do not spread it abroad, but tell him of it alone. You may have mistaken him, and this will give him an opportunity of explaining, or, if he be in fault, this will give him an opportunity of correcting himself.

Do everything in love
And do everything in love. Love will dictate what is proper on most occasions. It will do more than a thousand rules; and all rules without it are nothing.

To the deacons let me say: be you helpers in everything—whether agreeable or disagreeable.

Conclusion
To the congregation generally, I would say, you also have an interest in the proceedings of this day. My brother considers you as part of his charge. His appointment by the church is with your approbation. He will seek the good of you and your children. Then teach them to respect and love him.

An Essay on Truth[1]

The multifarious and discordant sentiments which divide mankind afford a great temptation to skepticism, and many are carried away by it. The open enemies of the gospel take occasion from hence to justify their rejection of it; and many of its professed friends have written as if they thought that to be decided amidst so many minds and opinions were almost presumptuous. The principal, if not the only, use which they would make of these differences is to induce a spirit of moderation and charity, and to declaim against bigotry.

To say nothing at present how these terms are perverted and hackneyed in a certain cause, let two things be seriously considered:

The apostolic example

First, whether this was the use made by the apostles of the discordant opinions which prevailed in their times, even among those who "acknowledged the Divinity of our Saviour's mission?" In differences among Christians which did not affect the kingdom of God, nor destroy the work of God, it certainly was; such were those concerning meats, drinks, and days, in which the utmost forbearance was inculcated. But it was otherwise in differences which affected the leading doctrines and precepts of Christianity. Forbearance in these cases would, in the account of the sacred writers, have been a crime. Paul "would they were even cut off"[2] who troubled the Galatian churches by corrupting the Christian doctrine of justification. And it is recorded to the honour of the church at Ephesus, that it "could not bear" them that were evil; but "had tried them who said they were apostles and were not, and found them liars" (Gal. 5:12; Rev. 2:2).

Standing for truth is not bigotry

Secondly, whether an unfavourable opinion of those who reject what we

---

[1] Fuller, "An Essay on Truth," *Complete Works*, 3:524–532; see also Andrew Fuller, *What Is Truth?* (Peterborough, ON: H&E Publishing, 2018).
[2] Galatians 5:12.

account the leading principles of Christianity, supposing it to be wrong, be equally injurious with a contrary opinion, supposing that to be wrong? To think unfavourably of another does not affect his state towards God. If, therefore, it should prove to be wrong, it only interrupts present happiness. We have lately been told indeed, but from what authority I cannot conceive, that "the readiest way in the world to thin heaven, and to replenish the regions of hell, is to call in the spirit of bigotry." Far be it from me to advocate the cause of bigotry, or to plead for a bitter, censorious spirit, a spirit that would confine the kingdom of heaven to a party; but I do not perceive how this spirit, bad as it is, is productive of the effects ascribed to it. If, on the other hand, through an aversion to bigotry, we treat those as Christians to whom an apostle would at least have said, "I stand in doubt of you," we flatter and deceive them; which is really "the readiest way in the world to thin heaven, and to replenish the regions of hell."

Surely there is a medium between bigotry and esteeming and treating men as Christians irrespective of their avowed principles. Certainly, a benevolent and candid treatment is due to men of all denominations; but to consider all principles as equally safe is to consider truth as of no importance.

Let us candidly inquire, Christian reader, whether, notwithstanding the diversity of sentiments in the Christian world, truth may not be clearly ascertained? Whether it be not of the utmost importance? Whether the prevalence of error may not be accounted for? And lastly, Whether the wisdom as well as the justice of God may not be seen in his permitting it?

What is truth?
In attempting to answer this question, I desire to take nothing for granted but that Christianity is of God, and that the Scriptures are a revelation of his will. If Christianity be of God, and he has revealed his will in the holy Scriptures, light has come into the world, though the dark minds of sinful creatures comprehend it not. It does not follow, because many wander in mazes of fruitless speculation, that there is not a way so plain that a wayfaring man, or one who "walketh in the truth,"[3] though a fool, shall not

---

[3] Isaiah 35:8.

err. The numerous sects among the Greeks and Romans, and even among the Jews at the time of our Saviour's appearing, did not prove that there was no certain knowledge to be obtained of what was truth. Our Lord considered himself as speaking plainly, or he would not have asked the Jews as he did, "Why do ye not understand my speech?"[4] The apostles and primitive believers saw their way plainly; and though we cannot pretend to the extraordinary inspiration which was possessed by many of them, yet if we humbly follow their light, depending on the ordinary teachings of God's Holy Spirit, we shall see ours.

Truth, we may be certain, is the same thing as what in the Scriptures is denominated "the gospel,"[5] "the common salvation,"[6] "the common faith,"[7] "the faith once delivered to the saints,"[8] "the truth as it is in Jesus,"[9] etc.; and what this is may be clearly understood by the brief summaries of the gospel, and of the faith of the primitive Christians, which abound in the New Testament. Of the former, the following are a few of many examples:

- "God so loved the world, that he gave his only begotten Son, that whosoever believeth in him should not perish, but have everlasting life."[10]
- "The Son of man came to seek and to save that which is lost."[11]
- "I am the way, the truth, and the life: no man cometh unto the Father but by me."[12]
- "To him gave all the prophets witness, that through his name whosoever believeth in him shall receive remission of sins."[13]
- "We preach Christ crucified, unto the Jews a stumbling-block, and unto the Greeks foolishness; but unto them which are

---

[4] John 8:43.

[5] Matthew 4:23, 9:35; Mark 1:1; 14–15; 10:29; 13:10; 14:9; 16:15; Luke 9:6; 20:1; Acts 8:26, 40; 14:7, 21; 15:7; 16:10; 20:24; Romans 1:9, 15–16; 10:16; 11:28; 15:16, 19–20; 1 Corinthians 1:17; 4:15; 9:12, 14, 16, 18; 9:23; 15:1; 2 Corinthians 2:12; 4:4; 8:18; 9:13; 10:14, 16; Galatians 1:7, 11; 2:2, 5, 7, 14; 3:8, 4:13; Ephesians 1:13; 3:6; 6:15, 19; Philippians 1:5, 7, 12, 16, 27; 2:22; 4:3, 15; Colossians 1:5, 23; 1 Thessalonians 2:2, 4, 8–9; 3:2; 2 Thessalonians 1:8; 1 Timothy 1:11; 2 Timothy 1:8, 10; Philemon 13; 1 Peter 4:6, 17.

[6] Jude 3.

[7] Titus 1:4.

[8] Jude 3.

[9] Ephesians 4:21.

[10] John 3:16.

[11] Luke 19:10.

[12] John 14:6.

[13] Acts 10:43.

called, both Jews and Greeks, Christ, the power of God, and the wisdom of God."[14]
- "I determined not to know anything among you, save Jesus Christ and him crucified."[15]
- "Moreover, brethren, I declare unto you the gospel which I preached unto you, which also ye have received, and wherein ye stand; by which also ye are saved, if ye hold fast what I preached unto you, unless ye have believed in vain; for I delivered unto you first of all that which I also received, how that Christ died for our sins according to the Scriptures; and that he was buried, and that he rose again the third day, according to the Scriptures."[16]
- "This is a faithful saying, and worthy of all acceptation, that Christ Jesus came into the world to save sinners, of whom I am chief."[17]
- "This is the record, that God hath given to us eternal life, and this life is in his Son."[18]
- "Neither is there salvation in any other; for there is none other name under heaven given among men whereby we must be saved."[19]

If language has any determinate meaning, it is here plainly taught that mankind are not only sinners, but in a lost and perishing condition, without help or hope but what arises from the free grace of God, through the atonement of his Son; that he died as our substitute; that we are forgiven and accepted only for the sake of what he hath done and suffered; that in his person and work all evangelical truth concentrates; that the doctrine of salvation for the chief of sinners through his death was so familiar in the primitive times as to become a kind of Christian proverb, or saying; and that on our receiving and retaining this depends our present standing and final salvation. If this doctrine be received, Christianity is received; if not, the record which God hath given of his Son is rejected, and he himself treated as a liar.

When this doctrine is received in the true spirit of it, which it never

---

[14] 1 Corinthians 1:23.
[15] 1 Corinthians 2:2.
[16] 1 Corinthians 15:1–3.
[17] 1 Timothy 1:15.
[18] 1 John 5:11.
[19] Acts 4:12.

is but by a sinner ready to perish, all those fruitless speculations which tend only to bewilder the mind will be laid aside; just as malice, and guile, and envies, and evil speakings are laid aside by him who is born of God. They will fall off from the mind, like the coat of the chrysalis, of their own accord. Many instances of this are constantly occurring. Persons who, after having read and studied controversies, and leaned first to one opinion and then to another, till their minds have been lost in uncertainty, have at length been brought to think of the gospel, not as a matter of speculation, but as that which seriously and immediately concerns them; and, embracing it as good news to them who are ready to perish, have not only found rest to their souls, but all their former notions have departed from them as a dream when one awakes.

Corresponding with the brief summaries of the gospel are the concise accounts given of the faith of the primitive Christians:

- "Whosoever believeth that Jesus is the Christ is born of God."[20]
- "Who is he that overcometh the world, but he that believeth that Jesus is the Son of God?"[21]
- "If thou shalt confess with thy mouth the Lord Jesus, and believe in thine heart that God hath raised him from the dead, thou shalt be saved."[22]

The sacred writers did not mean, by this language, to magnify the belief of one or two divine truths at the expense of others; but to exhibit them as bearing an inseparable connection; so that if these were truly embraced, the other would be certain to accompany them. They considered the doctrine of the person and work of Christ as a golden link, that would draw along with it the whole chain of evangelical truth. Hence we perceive the propriety of such language as the following:

- "He that hath the Son hath life; and he that hath not the Son hath not life."[23]

---

[20] 1 John 5:1.
[21] 1 John 5:5.
[22] Romans 10:9.
[23] 1 John 5:12.

- "Whosoever denieth the Son, the same hath not the Father."[24]

The doctrine and the faith of the primitive Christians were summarily avowed every time they celebrated the Lord's supper. The leading truth exhibited by that ordinance is the same which John calls "the record;" namely, that "God hath given unto us eternal life, and this life is in his Son."[25] Under the form of a feast, of which we are invited to take, to eat, and to drink, are set forth the blessings of the New Testament, or covenant, and the medium through which they were obtained; namely, "the blood of Jesus, shed for many for the remission of sins; and the way in which they must be received; that is to say, as a free gift, bestowed on the unworthy for his sake."[26] If this simple doctrine were believed with the spirit of a little child, and lived upon as our meat and drink, we might take an everlasting leave of speculations on things beyond our reach; and that without sustaining the loss of anything but what were better lost than retained.

---

[24] 1 John 2:23.
[25] 1 John 5:11.
[26] Matthew 26:28.

2
Preaching Christ

Historian, Peter J. Morden, describes Andrew Fuller's seminal book, *The Gospel Worthy of All Acceptation* (1785), as the "theological motor" of the Baptist Missionary Society (1792), which is credited with launching the modern missionary movement.[1] In fact, it seems that Fuller's plea in *The Gospel Worthy* was the theological motor of every aspect of his life and ministry, especially his pulpit ministry. Fuller explains that his convictions expressed in *The Gospel Worthy* were a rejection of his formative church influences,

> My father and mother were Dissenters, of the Calvinistic persuasion, and were in the habit of hearing Mr. Eve, a Baptist minister, who being what is here termed high in his sentiments, or tinged with false Calvinism, had little or nothing to say to the unconverted. I therefore never considered myself as any way concerned in what I heard from the pulpit.[2]

Before his conversion, Fuller had an agonizing spiritual struggle exacerbated by what he later came to label false Calvinism. The false Calvinists of Fuller's day explained the sovereignty of God in a way that minimized human responsibility. According to the false Calvinists that Fuller had encountered, human depravity was so complete that no one had a duty to believe in Christ, because it was not possible for the sinner to do so. Thus, they denied that there could be any sincere free offer of the gospel to sinners and focus was redirected toward individual introspection in determining if one was of the elect. Fuller explains,

> I was not then aware that any poor sinner had a warrant to believe in Christ for the salvation of his soul; but supposed there must be some kind of qualification to entitle him to do it; yet I was aware

---

[1] Peter J. Morden, "Andrew Fuller and The Gospel Worthy of All Acceptation" in *Pulpit and People: Studies in Eighteenth-Century Baptist Life and Thought* (Eugene: Wipf and Stock Publishers, 2009), 129.

[2] Andrew Gunton Fuller, "Memoir," in *The Complete Works of the Rev. Andrew Fuller*, ed. Joseph Belcher, 3 vols (Harrisonburg: Sprinkle Publications, 1845), 1:2.

that I had no qualifications.

I must—I will—yes, I will trust my soul—my sinful lost soul—in his hands. If I perish, I perish! Such in substance were my resolutions. In this state of mind I continued nearly an hour, weeping and supplicating mercy for the Savior's sake; (my soul hath it still in remembrance, and is humbled in me!) And as the eye of my mind was more and more fixed on him, my guilt and fears were gradually and insensibly removed.

I now found a rest for my troubled soul, and I reckon that I should've found it sooner, if I had not entertained the notion of my having no warrant to come to Christ, without some previous qualification. This notion was a bar that kept me back for a time, though, through divine drawings, I was enabled to overleap it. ... I mention this because it may be the case with others, who may be kept in darkness and despondency by erroneous views of the gospel much longer than I was.³

Fuller described the joy of his conversion, "But, having found rest for my soul in the cross of Christ, I was now conscious of my being the subject of repentance, faith, and love."⁴ Andrew Fuller was baptized by Pastor Eve on April 1770, becoming a member of the church in Soham. In 1771, the church in Soham forced pastor Eve to resign. The congregation did not consider Eve's Calvinism to be high enough because he suggested that sinners could obey the will of God as to outward action though they could do themselves no spiritual good. By 1775, Fuller became the pastor of the Soham church and the church joined the Northamptonshire Association of Particular Baptist churches. During his pastorate, Fuller began to publicly move away from false Calvinism and to make direct gospel appeals to the unconverted. He wrote, "But as I perceived this reasoning would affect the whole tenor of my preaching, I moved on with slow and trembling steps; and, having to feel my way out of a labyrinth, I was a long time ere I felt satisfied."⁵

In 1782, Fuller became the pastor of the Baptist church at Kettering,

---

³ J.W. Morris, *Memoirs of the Life and Writings of the Rev. Andrew Fuller, Late Pastor of the Baptist Church at Kettering, and First Secretary to the Baptist Missionary Society* (Boston: Lincoln and Edmands, 1830), 19-20.

⁴ John Ryland Jr., *The Work of Faith, the Labor of Love, and the Patience of Hope Illustrated in the Life and Death of the Rev. Andrew Fuller* (London: Button and Son, 1818), 19-20.

⁵ Fuller, "Memoir," *Complete Works*, 1:13.

where he served as pastor until his death in 1815. Grasping Fuller's spiritual biography is necessary for understanding his uncompromising commitment to preach Christ and call all sinners in all places to faith and repentance. In assuming his duties at the church in Kettering Fuller provided a personal statement of his principles, which included his conviction to preach Christ,

> I believe, it is the duty of every minister of Christ plainly and faithfully to preach the gospel to all who will hear it; and, as I believe the inability of men to spiritual things to be wholly of the moral, and, therefore, of the criminal kind—and that it is their duty to love the Lord Jesus Christ, and trust him for salvation, though they do not; I, therefore, believe free and solemn addresses, invitations, calls, and warnings to them, to be not only consistent, but directly adapted, as means, in the hand of the Spirit of God, to bring them to Christ. I consider it as a part of my duty, which I could not omit without being guilty of the blood of souls.[6]

In *The Gospel Worthy*, Fuller's primary aim is to argue that it is the duty of sinners to believe in Christ for salvation and that they are commanded, exhorted, and invited to do so in the Scripture. Fuller explains,

> the proper object of saving faith is not our being interested in Christ, but the glorious gospel of the ever-blessed God (which is true, whether we believe it or not), a contrary inference must be drawn; for it is admitted, on all hands, that it is the duty of every man to believe what God reveals.[7]

Fuller continues, "The gospel is a feast freely provided, and sinners of mankind are freely invited to partake of it."[8] Fuller's commitment to the truth as it is in Jesus birthed his conviction to preach Christ in every sermon: "Let Christ be not only the theme of my remaining ministry, but the exaltation of him and the enlargement of his kingdom the great end of my life! If I forget thee, O my Saviour, let my right hand forget; if I do

---

[6] Fuller, "Memoir," *Complete Works*, 1:68.
[7] Andrew Fuller, "Gospel Worthy of All Acceptation" in *The Complete Works of the Rev. Andrew Fuller*, ed. Joseph Belcher, 3 vols (Harrisonburg: Sprinkle Publications, 1845), 2:333; *Complete Works*, 2:333.
[8] Fuller, "Gospel Worthy of All Acceptation," *Complete Works*, 2:338.

not remember thee, let my tongue cleave to the roof my mouth!"[9]

Fuller's understanding of the gospel shaped his convictions about preaching. Not only was he determined to preach Christ in every sermon, but according to Fuller, every sermon must be guided by the following emphases.

Every sermon must have a gospel errand

According to Fuller, every sermon must have a gospel "errand." Fuller turns to this descriptive language to communicate the fact that sermons must be purposeful about the gospel. An errand is a purposeful act to attend to some specific responsibility. We deny the Spirit-intended purpose of a particular text of Scripture if we neglect to understand its meaning in the overall story of redemptive history in the Bible. Charles Bridges spoke in a manner similar to Fuller when he wrote, "Many important truths of the gospel may be preached in a disjointed manner; and yet the gospel itself, truly speaking, not be preached."[10] For Fuller, true preaching, no matter the text or the topic is always on a gospel errand. Consider:

> If you look over the New Testament, you will find the subject-matter of your preaching briefly yet fully expressed in such language as the following: "Preach the word.[11]—Preach the gospel.[12]—Preach the gospel to every creature.[13]—Thus it is written, and thus it behoved Christ to suffer, and to rise from the dead the third day, and that repentance and remission of sins should be preached in his name, among all nations, beginning at Jerusalem.[14]—I declare unto you the gospel which I preached unto you, which also ye have received, and wherein ye stand, if ye keep in memory what I preached unto you, unless ye have believed in vain. For I delivered unto you, first of all, that which I also received, how that Christ died for our sins according to the Scriptures; and that he was bur-

---

[9] Fuller, "Preaching Christ," *Complete Works*, 1:504.

[10] Charles Bridges, *The Christian Ministry* (Carlisle: The Banner of Truth Trust, 1991), 253-254.

[11] 2 Timothy 4:2.

[12] Luke 9:6, 20:1; Acts 8:25, 40; 14:7, 21; 16:10; Romans 1:15; 15:20; 16:25; 1 Corinthians 1:17; 9:16, 18; 15:1; Galatians 1:8, 9, 11; 3:8; 4:13; 2 Timothy 2:8; 1 Peter 4:6.

[13] Mark 16:15.

[14] Luke 24:47.

ied, and that he rose again on the third day according to the Scriptures.[15]—We preach Christ crucified.[16]—I am determined to know nothing among you but Jesus Christ and him crucified.—This is the record, that God hath given unto us eternal life, and this life is in his Son.[17]—We are ambassadors for Christ, as though God did beseech men by us, we pray them in Christ's stead, saying, Be ye reconciled unto God.[18]—For he hath made him to be sin for us who knew no sin, that we might be made the righteousness of God in him.[19]—I have kept back nothing that was profitable unto you, but have showed you, and have taught you publicly, and from house to house, testifying both to the Jews, and also to the Greeks, repentance toward God, and faith toward our Lord Jesus Christ."[20]

Such, my brother, is the concurrent language of the New Testament. Every one of the foregoing passages contains an epitome of the gospel ministry. You will not expect me to expatiate upon their various connexions: I may, however, notice three or four particulars, which follow from them.

First, *In every sermon we should have an errand; and one of such importance that if it be received or complied with it will issue in eternal salvation.* I say nothing of those preachers who profess to go into the pulpit without an errand, and to depend upon the Holy Spirit to furnish them with one at the time. I write not for them, but for such as make a point of thinking before they attempt to preach. Even of these I have heard some who, in studying their texts, have appeared to me to have no other object in view than to find something to say, in order to fill up the time. This, however, is not preaching, but merely talking about good things. Such ministers, though they think of something beforehand, yet appear to me to resemble Ahimaaz, who ran without tidings.[21] I have also heard many an ingenious discourse, in which I could not but admire the talents of the preacher; but his only object appeared to be to correct the grosser vices, and to form the manners of his audience, so as to render them useful members of civil society. Such ministers have an errand; but not of such importance as to save those who

---

[15] 1 Corinthians 15:1-3.
[16] 1 Corinthians 1:23.
[17] 1 Corinthians 2:2.
[18] 2 Corinthians 5:20.
[19] 2 Corinthians 5:21.
[20] Acts 20:20.
[21] 1 Samuel 18:22.

receive it, which sufficiently proves that it is not the gospel.[22]

It is of the first importance to a messenger to know his errand. Without this, whatever be our talents, natural or acquired, we are unqualified for the Christian ministry. Without this, the most fascinating eloquence is in danger of becoming an engine of mischief. The subject-matter of the apostle's preaching is variously described: it is called "the faith"—"the truth"—"the truth as it is in Jesus"—"Christ crucified"—"the gospel"—"the word of reconciliation," &c. In these descriptions, we see our work.[23]

Consider the subject-matter of his ministry: "The gospel of God." It is a blessed errand to go on. Good news to a lost world. Angels were visited with wrath, but men with the cup of salvation. There is a pleasure in being an almoner, even of earthly blessings: but you have the unsearchable riches of Christ to impart; you are the herald of peace, and pardon, and reconciliation. How a man, bearing such tidings from an earthly sovereign, would be hailed by a number of convicts![24]

Every sermon must preach the doctrine of the cross

For Fuller, following Paul when he declared, "For I have decided to know nothing among you except Jesus Christ and him crucified" (1 Cor. 2:2) was not simply a matter of tacking Jesus onto the end of the sermon or finding a way to fit Christ into the sermon. Jesus and his atoning death were not an addition to the message of a biblical text. Rather, Christ crucified is the reason every text is meaningful and powerful. In referencing 1 Corinthians 2:2, Fuller avers, "in his person and work all evangelical truth concentrates."[25] Elsewhere Fuller asserts, "That which food is to the body, the doctrine of Christ crucified is to the mind."[26] In summary fashion Fuller also declared "The doctrine of the cross is the Christian doctrine."[27] Consider:

---

[22] Fuller, "Letter II, Sermons—Subject-Matter of Them," *Complete Works*, 1:715.
[23] Fuller, "The Christian Ministry a Great Work," *Complete Works*, 1:515.
[24] Fuller, "Affectionate Concern of a Minister for the Salvation of His Hearers," *Complete Works*, 1:509.
[25] Fuller, "An Essay on Truth," *Complete Works*, 3:526.
[26] Fuller, "Sermon XLIV: Individual and Social Religion," *Complete Works*, 1:433.
[27] Fuller, "Conformity to the Death of Christ," *Complete Works*, 1:310.

Every sermon should contain a portion of the doctrine of salvation by the death of Christ. If there be any meaning in the foregoing passages, this is emphatically called the gospel. A sermon, therefore, in which this doctrine has not a place, and I might add, a prominent place, cannot be a gospel sermon. It may be ingenious, it may be eloquent; but a want of the doctrine of the cross is a defect which no pulpit excellence can supply.[28]

I do not know how it may prove on trial, but I wish to begin with the centre of Christianity—the doctrine of the cross, and to work round it; or with what may be called the heart of Christianity, and to trace it through its principal veins or relations, both in doctrine and practice. If Christianity had not been comprehended in this doctrine, the apostle, who shunned not to declare the whole counsel of God, could not have determined to know nothing else in his ministry. The whole of the Christian system appears to be presupposed by it, included in it, or to arise from it: if, therefore, I write anything, it will be on this principle.[29]

In fine, the doctrine of the cross is the central point in which all the lines of evangelical truth meet and are united. What the sun is to the system of nature, that the doctrine of the cross is to the system of the gospel; it is the life of it.[30]

We may preach about the gospel without preaching the gospel

According to Fuller, sermons that fail to exposit the text in view of Jesus vis-à-vis the Bible's storyline of redemptive history are not preaching Christ—no matter how frequently they mention him. Simply mentioning Jesus or preaching about an encounter in the life of Christ does not constitute preaching Christ. Whenever one makes the jump from the biblical text straight to an application for modern readers, we are guilty of treating the Bible as if it is all about us instead of all about Jesus. Moralistic, atomistic sermons that abstract moral principles apart from the Gospel of Jesus Christ are anti-Christ even when the principles are drawn from a particular episode in the life of Christ. Preaching Christ from the Gospels means never taking the Gospel for granted. Consider:

---

[28] Fuller, "Letter II, Sermons—Subject-Matter of Them," *Complete Works*, 1:716.
[29] Fuller, "A Plan to Be Pursued," *Complete Works*, 1:690.
[30] Fuller, "Charity: In Which Is Considered the Charge of Bigotry," *Complete Works*, 2:182.

Besides this, there are many ways by which a minister may get beside the gospel without falling into any palpable errors. There may be nothing crooked, yet much wanting. We may deliver an ingenious discourse, containing nothing inconsistent with truth, and yet not preach that truth "in which believers stand, and by which they are saved."[31] We may preach about the gospel, and yet not preach the gospel, so as to "show unto men the way of salvation."[32] And if we get into a vain, carnal, and worldly frame of mind, this is almost certain to be the case. It is no breach of charity to say, of hundreds of sermons that are ordinarily delivered by those who are reputedly orthodox, that they are not the gospel which Jesus commissioned his servants to preach; and if it be thus among preachers, is it marvelous that a large proportion of religious people are not strictly evangelical, but imbibe another spirit? And if the doctrine of Christ be neglected (not to say corrupted), the effects will appear in a neglect of faithful discipline, in a worldly spirit, and in a gradual disregard of a watchful, circumspect, and holy individual conduct.[33]

Preach Christ—not moralism

Andrew Fuller frequently speaks of his appreciation for the ministry of missionary David Brainerd. The preface of *The Gospel Worthy* explains, "Reading the lives and labours of such men as Elliot, Brainerd, and several others, who preached Christ with so much success to the American Indians, had an effect upon him."[34] Fuller, like Brainerd, preached with the conviction that "morality, sobriety, and external duties" are best "promoted by preaching Christ crucified." Both men believed that external duties of Christianity flow from the internal power of genuinely embracing divine grace in Christ. The proper relationship between the gospel indicative and imperative is not to pit one against the other. Rather, it is to understand that their relationship is irreversible. The imperative rests on the foundational gospel indicative and is consequential. Thus, true morality is only promoted through preaching Christ. Brainerd

---

[31] Matthew 24:13.
[32] Acts 16:17.
[33] Fuller, "Irremediable Evils," *Complete Works*, 1:467.
[34] Fuller, "Gospel Worthy of All Acceptation," *Complete Works*, 2:329.

insisted, "I have been naturally and easily led to Christ as the substance of every subject."[35] He explains,

> I have been drawn in a way not only easy and natural, proper and pertinent, but almost unavoidable, to discourse of him, either in regard of his undertaking, incarnation, satisfaction, admirable fitness for the work of man's redemption, or the infinite need that sinners stand in of an interest in him; which has opened the way for a continual strain of gospel-invitation to perishing souls, to come empty and naked, weary and heavy laden, and cast themselves upon them. ... And God was pleased to give these divine truths such a powerful influence upon the minds of these people, and so to bless them for the effectual awakening of numbers of them, that their lives were quickly reformed, without my insisting upon the precepts of morality, and spending time in repeated harangues upon external duties.[36]

Brainerd believed that according to Christ and his apostles, "smooth and plausible harangues upon moral virtues and external duties, at best are likely to do no more than lop off the branches of corruption, while the root of all vice remains still untouched" and the only way to get to the root of the sin problem was by the gospel of sovereign grace in Christ.[37] Fuller explains it this way, "It is one of the devices of Satan to alarm the sinner, and fill him with anxiety for the healing of outward eruptions of sin; while the inward part is overlooked, though it be nothing but sin."[38] Neither Brainerd nor Fuller opposed the preaching of morality, but rather insisted that morality must be preached as a consequence of faith in the gospel, and not abstracted from the gospel. Consider:

> And as Christ and his apostles never appear to have exhorted the unconverted to anything which did not include or imply repentance and faith, so in all their explications of the divine law, and preaching against particular sins, their object was to bring the sinner to this issue. Though they directed them to no means, in order to get a penitent and believing heart, but to repentance and faith

---

[35] David Brainerd as quoted in, *The Works of Jonathan Edwards* (Edinburgh: Banner of Truth Trust, 1974), 2:416–418.
[36] Brainerd as quoted in *Works of Jonathan Edwards*, 2:416–418.
[37] Brainerd as quoted in *Works of Jonathan Edwards*, 2:416–418.
[38] Fuller, "Gospel Worthy of All Acceptation," *Complete Works*, 2:329.

themselves; yet they used means with them for that purpose. Thus our Lord expounded the law in his sermon on the mount, and concluded by enforcing such a "hearing of his sayings and doing them" as should be equal to "digging deep, and building one's house upon a rock." And thus the apostle Peter, having charged his countrymen with the murder of the Lord of glory, presently brings it to this issue: "Repent ye, therefore, and be converted, that your sins may be blotted out."[39]

Some years ago I met with a passage in Dr. [John] Owen on this subject, which, at that time, sunk deep into my heart; and the more observation I have since made, the more just his remarks appear. "It is the duty of ministers," says he, "to plead with men about their sins; but always remember that it be done with that which is the proper end of law and gospel; that is, that they make use of the sin they speak against to the discovery of the state and condition wherein the sinner is, otherwise, haply, they may work men to formality and hypocrisy, but little of the true end of preaching the gospel will be brought about. It will not avail to beat a man off from his drunkenness into a sober formality. A skillful master of the assemblies lays his axe at the root, drives still at the heart. To inveigh against particular sins of ignorant, unregenerate persons, such as the land is full of, is a good work; but yet, though it may be done with great efficacy, vigor, and success, if this be all the effect of it, that they are set upon the most sedulous endeavors of mortifying their sins preached down, all that is done is but like the beating of an enemy in an open field, and driving him into an impregnable castle not to be prevailed against. Get you, at any time, a sinner at the advantage on the account of any one sin whatever; have you any thing to take hold of him by, bring it to his state and condition, drive it up to the head, and there deal with him. To break men off from particular sins, and not to break their hearts, is to deprive ourselves of advantages of dealing with them."

When a sinner is first seized with conviction, it is natural to suppose that he will abstain from many of his outward vices, though it be only for the quiet of his own mind: but it is not for us to administer comfort to him on this ground; as though, because he had "broken off" a few of "his sins," he must needs have broken them off "by righteousness," and either be in the road to life, or at least in a fair way of getting into it. It is one of the devices of Satan to alarm the sinner, and fill him with anxiety for the healing of outward eruptions of sin; while the inward part is overlooked,

---

[39] Acts 3:19.

though it be nothing but sin. But we must not be aiding and abetting in these deceptions, nor administer any other relief than that which is held out in the gospel to sinners as sinners.[40]

Let them equally beware of so dwelling upon the preceptive part of Scripture, as to forget the grand principles on which alone it can be carried into effect. We may contend for practical religion, and yet neglect the practice of religion.[41]

Fuller was not content merely to preach Christ in every sermon, he believed that he had a responsibility to define and promote Christ-centered preaching to all who would listen. According to him, "Preach Christ, or you had better be anything than a preacher."[42] In an ordination charge Fuller exhorted,

Make a point, then, of distinctly and habitually preaching the gospel. Do not suppose your people are so good, and so well informed, as not to need this. Visit the sick, and you will be astonished how little they know, compared with what it might reasonably be expected they should know. Many sermons are ingenious essays; but if they bear not on this great object, they are not the gospel. Woe unto you if you preach not the gospel! Do not suppose I have any particular suspicion that you will not. But I feel the importance of the exhortation, "Preach the gospel." Study the gospel—what it implies, what it includes, and what consequences it involves. I have heard complaints of some of our young ministers, that though they are not heteredox, yet they are not evangelical; that though they do not propagate error, yet the grand, essential, distinguishing truths of the gospel do not form the prevailing theme of their discourses.[43]

Providing adequate samples of Fuller's preaching is challenging because, as we will see in the next chapter, he believed in extemporaneous preaching without using extensive notes. As historian and Fuller biog-

---

[40] Fuller, "Gospel Worthy of All Acceptation," *Complete Works*, 2:390–391.
[41] Andrew Fuller, "Letter to John Ryland at the Baptist Academy at Bristol, April 5, 1799," in Ryland, *Work of Faith, the Labor of Love*, 234.
[42] Fuller, "Preaching Christ," *Complete Works*, 1:503.
[43] Fuller, "Affectionate Concern of a Minister," *Complete Works*, 1:509.

rapher Peter Morden explains, many of Fuller's sermon notes were written in his own self-styled shorthand and simply provided a text and some key words.[44] Volume one, of Fuller's *Complete Works*, contains ninety-two sermons and sermon sketches, most of which are probably little more than his notes minimally expanded. Biographer J.W. Morris wrote,

> The composition of a sermon seldom cost Mr. Fuller much trouble; owing to his constant habits of thinking, it was generally the easiest part of all his labours ... He never filled up any written discourse, except when it is intended for press, and after it had been delivered.[45]

The Fuller readings in this chapter have been chosen to reveal his pervasive commitment to preaching Christ in all the Scripture and his incessant admonition for others to do the same. Fuller's sermon, "Faith in the Gospel A Necessary Prerequisite to Preaching It" was an address to ministry students at the Bristol Baptist Academy and reflects a persistent theme of Fuller's that the preacher must labor as a Christian and not merely as a minister. The sermon, "Preaching Christ," deals directly with the topic of this chapter and reveals that Fuller believed contemporary preachers could and should follow the Christ-centered preaching model of the apostles. "The Nature of the Gospel, and the Manner in which it Ought to be Preached," is an ordination sermon preached by Fuller. His sermon on "Christian Patriotism," was preached at Kettering, in 1803, at a time of threatened invasion by France and shows how Fuller addresses a contemporary ethical issue through the lens of Christ and his gospel. "Instances, Evil, and Tendency of Delay, in the Concerns of Religion" was preached by Fuller at a Ministers' Meeting, held at Clipstone, April 27, 1791 and is one of his most famous sermons. In the sermon, he confronts what he refers to as a "procrastinating spirit" and called for active engagement in global missions. J.W. Morris writes that the sermon "gave an impetus to the missionary spirit that was already

---

[44] Peter J. Morden, *The Life and Thought of Andrew Fuller 1754-1815* (Milton Keynes: Paternoster, 2015), 77.

[45] J.W. Morris, *Memoirs of the Life and Writings of the Rev. Andrew Fuller, Late Pastor of the Baptist Church at Kettering, and First Secretary to the Baptist Missionary Society* (Boston: Lincoln and Edmands, 1830), 70.

afloat."[46] Finally, in "Conformity to the Death of Christ," Fuller argues, "There is not an important truth, but what is presupposed by [the death of Christ], included in it, or arises out of it; nor any part of practical religion but what hangs upon it."[47]

---

[46] Morris, *Memoirs*, 166.
[47] Fuller, "Conformity to the Death of Christ," *Complete Works*, 1:310.

Faith in the Gospel a Necessary Prerequisite to Preaching it[1]

[Addressed to the Students of the Bristol Education Society]

"We believe, and therefore speak" 2 Corinthians 4:13.

The words immediately preceding those on which I shall found a few observations on the important work of the ministry are a quotation from the 116th Psalm. David, under his troubles, believed in God, and therefore spoke. And the apostles, under persecutions and reproaches, believed in the gospel, and therefore spoke. They spoke boldly in the name of Jesus, whatever might be the consequence. They might be slain, as Christ was. But then like him, too, they would be raised (verse 14). If they suffered with him, they would also reign with him.

I shall comprise what I have to offer under two heads of discourse—the subject-matter of the Christian ministry, and the necessity of believing it.

The subject matter of the Christian minister

It is that which we have believed. It is of the first importance to a messenger to know his errand. Without this, whatever be our talents, natural or acquired, we are unqualified for the Christian ministry. Without this, the most fascinating eloquence is in danger of becoming an engine of mischief. The subject-matter of the apostle's preaching is variously described: it is called "the faith,"[2] "the truth,"[3]—"the truth as it is in Jesus," "Christ crucified,"[4] "the gospel,"[5] "the word of reconciliation,"[6] &c. In these descriptions, we see our work.

It does not follow that the dictates of reason and conscience are to be rejected or disused in preaching. The light of nature itself teaches some

---

[1] Fuller, "Faith in the Gospel a Necessary Prerequisite," *Complete Works*, 1:515–518.
[2] Galatians 1:23.
[3] 1 Timothy 2:7.
[4] Ephesians 4:21.
[5] 1 Corinthians 1:23.
[6] 2 Corinthians 5:19.

truth—such as the being of God, the accountableness of man, the fitness of doing to others as we would they should do to us, our being sinners, or what we ought not to be. These are truths which the gospel supposes, and which require to be enforced in subserviency to it.

But several important particulars do follow; as,

1. That we must not deal in curious speculations, which have no foundation in the Scriptures. Some have been turned aside by such an indulgence to false hypotheses, and made shipwreck of faith and a good conscience. A large proportion of the objections to divine truth are of this kind: How can a man be born when he is old? How are the dead raised, and with what body? How can one be three, and three one? How could Christ be both God and man? How can the certain efficaciousness of grace consist with free agency and the accountableness of man? Paul would not answer such questions as these by opposing conjecture to conjecture, but in the spirit of the text—"We believe, and therefore speak."

2. That we must not deal in private impulses or impressions, which have no foundation in the Scriptures. One founds a doctrine on his own experience; but experience ought to be judged by the Bible, not the Bible by experience. "The prophet that hath a dream, let him tell a dream; and he that hath my word, let him speak my word faithfully. What is the chaff to the wheat? saith the Lord." Another swears that, as God liveth, such a thing is true; but what does this prove, save the impudence and profanity of the preacher?

3. That the person and work of Christ must be the leading theme of our ministry. In this, if we be Christians, we have believed; and this we must preach to others. For example: We must preach him as divine. How else could we know whom we had believed? We must preach him as having assumed our nature, and thereby qualified himself to be our Saviour (Heb 2:14, 15). We must preach him as dying for our sins, &c. (1 Cor. 15:1-4). We must preach him as the Saviour of the lost, taking the place of the chief of sinners. We must preach him as the only way of acceptance with God. "Being justified freely by his grace, we have peace with God, through our Lord Jesus Christ." In short, he is suited to all our wants. To whom else shall we go? He hath the words of eternal life. So preach Christ.

Every sermon, more or less, should have some relation to Christ, and bear on his person or work. This is the life of all doctrine, and it will be our own fault if it is dry. Do not consider it as one subject among others, but as that which involves all others, and gives them an interest they could not otherwise possess. Preach not only the truth, but all truth, "as it is in Jesus." However ingenious our sermons may be, unless they bear on Christ, and lead the mind to Christ, we do not preach the faith of the gospel.

As all doctrinal religion meets here, so does all practical. The Scriptures draw everything from the dying love of Christ.

- "Feed the church of God, which he hath purchased with his own blood."[7]
- "Be ye kind one to another, tender-hearted, forgiving one another, even as God for Christ's sake hath forgiven you."[8]
- "Ye know the grace of our Lord Jesus Christ, that though he was rich, yet for your sakes he became poor, that ye through his poverty might be rich."[9]
- "Let this mind be in you which was in our Lord Jesus Christ."[10]
- "Hereby perceive we the love of God, because he laid down his life for us: and we ought to lay down our lives for the brethren."[11]
- "Husbands, love your wives, *as* Christ also loved the church."[12]

The same may be said of experience. Christian experience clings to Christ and his gospel. The religion of some, who talk of experience, goes to idolize their own feelings and admire their supposed graces. But true Christian experience thinks little of self, and much of Christ (John 6:68).

The necessity of believing the gospel before we preach it
"We believe, and therefore speak." It does not follow that every believer should be a preacher; but every preacher ought to be a believer; for,

1. This is the only motive that will render preaching a delight. How can we discourse on subjects which we do not believe? If we have not

---

[7] Acts 20:28.
[8] Ephesians 4:32.
[9] 2 Corinthians 8:9.
[10] Philippians 2:5.
[11] 1 John 3:16.
[12] Ephesians 5:25.

tasted the grace of God, we shall feel no pleasure in proclaiming it to others. Is it any wonder that faithless preachers call preaching "doing duty?" or that they preach other men's sermons, and that in delivering them they are uninterested by them? But if we speak because we believe, our preaching will be the utterance of a full heart, and our work its own reward. We must taste of truth as Christians, before we preach it. Studying it merely as ministers will never do. Believing belongs to us as Christians.

2. It affords ground to hope for usefulness to others. What effect will the sermons of those ministers have, who, by their frothy conversation, loose deportment, or avaricious spirit, are always counteracting them? The hearers will say, and say truly, "He does not believe his own doctrine. He may talk of truth, or of holiness and practical religion; but all is vain." If, on the other hand, we feel and practise what we preach, this must at least recommend it to the conscience; and it often does more. The one resembles a man persuading you to embark on board his vessel, assuring you it is safe, while he himself stands on the shore. The other has embarked himself and all he has; and, like Moses to Hobab, invites you to accompany him.

3. It will render the work of the ministry compatible with common honesty. The world has long accused ministers with being hypocrites. This is malicious enough; but while men engage in this work from indolence, avarice, pride, or any other worldly motive, rather than from the principle expressed in the text, they are furnished with a pretext for such reproaches. If we believe not ere we speak, we only deceive, and the sooner we throw off the deception the better.

4. No other motive will bear the test. What an account will faithless ministers have to give when asked, "What hast thou to do to declare my statutes, or that thou shouldest take my covenant in thy mouth?" One may have to answer, "The vanity of my parents led them to educate me for the ministry, and when I grew up I was fit for nothing else." Another may have to answer, "My own vanity influenced me: having a taste for learning, and public speaking, and esteeming it a reputable and genteel mode of life, I took to it." Another may have to say, "It was my own conceit and arrogance: having a large portion of native effrontery, I made my way, and was caressed by the people." Oh how different these from the apostles! — "We have believed, and therefore speak."

Carry on the work

But why do I thus speak? I am not addressing a society which pretends to train graceless characters for the ministry, or to make men ministers by mere education. They are aware of the necessity of their pupils being believers; and if any of them prove otherwise, they have deceived their patrons. They do not so much as pretend to impart gifts; but merely to improve those which Christ appears to have imparted. They wish to enable the aged and experienced part of our ministers, like Aquila and Priscilla, to expound to the younger brethren the way of the Lord more perfectly.

And as to you, my young brethren, I have no particular jealousy of you; only as we ought to be jealous with a godly jealousy, "looking lest anyone fail of the grace of God."[13] You are likely, another day, to occupy stations of much greater importance than if each were a minister of state. Our churches look to you. Many aged ministers are gone. Those that remain will soon follow. God has begun a great work in our day. May you take it up, and carry it on. It is but the other day since *we* were youths, looking up to those who are now no more. Now the load lies on us. Soon it must lie on you, or on some others. Should you prove yourselves unworthy, God will find others. Deliverance will arise from some other quarter. O men of God, "Flee youthful lusts, and follow after righteousness, faith, charity, peace, with them that call on the Lord out of a pure heart!"

I ought not to conclude without recommending to the audience that Saviour whom we have believed. We have found rest for our souls. Come ye. Forsake the world and your own righteousness. We have worn his yoke, some of us for forty years, and it has never galled us. Take his yoke, and learn of him, and you shall find rest for your souls. His yoke is easy, and his burden is light.

---

[13] Hebrews 12:15.

Preaching Christ[1]

> "We preach not ourselves, but Christ Jesus the Lord;
> and ourselves your servants for Jesus' sake." 2 Corinthians 4:5

A remark, which I once heard from the lips of that great and good man, the late Mr. Abraham Booth, has often recurred to my recollection. "I fear," said he, "there will be found a larger proportion of wicked ministers than of any other order of professing Christians!" It did not appear to me at the time, nor has it ever appeared since, that this remark proceeded from a want of charity, but rather from a deep knowledge of the nature of Christianity, and an impartial observation of men and things. It behooves us, not only as professing Christians, but as ministers, to "examine ourselves, whether we be in the faith." It certainly is possible, after we have preached to others, that we ourselves should be cast away! I believe it is very common for the personal religion of a minister to be taken for granted; and this may prove a temptation to him to take it for granted too. Ministers, being wholly devoted to the service of God, are supposed to have considerable advantages for spiritual improvement. These they certainly have; and if their minds be spiritual, they may be expected to make greater proficiency in the divine life than their brethren. But it should be remembered, that if they are not spiritual, those things which would otherwise be a help would prove a hinderance. If we study divine subjects merely as ministers, they will produce no salutary effect. We may converse with the most impressive truths, as soldiers and surgeons do with blood, till they cease to make any impression upon us. We must meditate on these things as Christians, first feeding our own souls upon them, and then imparting that which we have believed and felt to others; or, whatever good we may do to them, we shall receive none ourselves. Unless we mix faith with what we preach, as well as with what we hear, the word will not profit us. It may be on these accounts that ministers, while employed in watching over others, are so solemnly warned against

---

[1] Fuller, "Preaching Christ," *Complete Works*, 1:501-504; See also Andrew Fuller, *Preaching* (Peterborough: H&E Publishing, 2019).

neglecting themselves: "Take heed unto yourselves and to all the flock,"[2] "Take heed unto thyself, and unto the doctrine; continue in them; for in doing this thou shalt both save thyself and them that hear thee."[3]

Preaching the gospel is not the only work of a Christian minister; but it is a very important part of his duty, and that which, if rightly attended to, will be followed by other things. To this, therefore, I shall request your attention.

You cannot have a better model than that which is here held up to you. The example of the apostles and primitive ministers is for our imitation. Three things are here presented to our notice: what they did not preach—what they did preach—and what they considered themselves.

What the apostles did not preach
"We preach not ourselves." It might be thought that this negative was almost unnecessary; for, except a few gross impostors, who would ever think of holding up themselves as saviours, instead of Christ? "Was Paul crucified for you? or were ye baptized into the name of Paul?" Very true, in this gross sense, few men in the present day will be found to preach themselves. But self may be an object of preaching without being expressly avowed, and even while with the tongue Christ is recommended. And there is little doubt that self is the great end of numbers who engage in the Christian ministry. For example:

Worldly advantage
If worldly advantage be our object, we preach ourselves. It is true there is but little food for this appetite in our congregations. Yet there are cases where it is otherwise. Men have made their fortunes by preaching. And if this have been their object, they have had their reward. If this had not been a possible case, Paul would not have disavowed it as he does: "Not for a cloak of covetousness, God is witness."

A life of ease and indolence
If we make the ministry subservient to a life of ease and indolence, we

---

[2] Acts 20:28.
[3] 1 Timothy 4:16.

preach ourselves rather than Christ. We may get but little for our labour, and yet, being fond of a life of sloth (if a life it can be called), it may be more agreeable to us than any other pursuit. It is from this disposition that many ministers have got into the habit of spending a large part of every week in gossiping from house to house; not promoting the spiritual good of the people, but merely indulging themselves in idle talk. I might add, it is from this disposition and practice that a large proportion of the scandals among ministers have arisen. Had there been no danger from these quarters, we should not have met with another of Paul's solemn disavowals: "Our exhortation was not of uncleanness."[4] Such a declaration as this was not without meaning. It describes the false teachers of those times, and of all times.

Seeking the applause of hearers
If the applause of our hearers be the governing principle of our discourses, we preach ourselves, and not Christ. To be acceptable is necessary to being useful, and an attention to manner with this end in view is very proper; but if the love of fame be our governing principle, our whole ministry will be tainted by it. This subtle poison will penetrate and pervade our exercises, till everyone perceives it, and is sickened by it, except ourselves. It will inflate our composition in the study, animate our delivery in the pulpit, and condescend to fish for applause when we have retired. It will even induce us to deal in flattering doctrine, dwelling on what are known to be favourite topics, and avoiding those which are otherwise. It is a great matter to be able to join with the apostle in another of his solemn disavowals: "For neither at any time used we flattering words, as ye know, nor of men sought we glory."[5]

Making converts to ourselves
If our aim be to make proselytes to ourselves, or to our party, rather than converts to Christ, we shall be found to have preached ourselves, and not him. We certainly have seen much of this species of zeal in our times— "Men speaking perverse things, to draw away disciples after them."[6]

---

[4] 1 Thessalonians 2:3.
[5] 1 Thessalonians 2:5.
[6] Acts 20:30.

Preaching Christ

Nor do I refer merely to men who would be thought singularly evangelical, and even inspired of God—who are continually holding up themselves as the favourites of heaven and the darlings of providence and denouncing judgments on all who oppose them; and the tenor of whose preaching is to persuade their admirers to consider themselves as the dear children of God, and all who disapprove of them as poor blind creatures, knowing nothing of the gospel. Of them and their followers I can only say, "If any man be ignorant, let him be ignorant" (1 Cor. 14:38). But men who have paid great attention to the Scriptures, and who have preached and written many things on the side of truth, have nevertheless given but too evident proof that the tenor of their labours has been to make proselytes to themselves, or to their party, rather than converts to Christ.

What the apostles did preach

We preach "Christ Jesus the Lord." This is the grand theme of the Christian ministry. But many have so little of the Christian minister about them, that their sermons have scarcely any thing to do with Christ. They are mere moral harangues. And these, forsooth, would fain be thought exclusively the friends of morality and good works! But they know not what good works are, nor do they go the way to promote them. "This is the work of God, that ye believe on him whom he hath sent."[7] Preach Christ, or you had better be anything than a preacher. The necessity laid on Paul was not barely to preach, but to preach Christ. "Woe unto me if I preach not the gospel!"[8] Some are employed in depreciating Christ. But do you honour him. Some who talk much about him, yet do not preach him, and by their habitual deportment prove themselves enemies to his cross. If you preach Christ, you need not fear for want of matter. His person and work are rich in fullness. Every divine attribute is seen in him. All the types prefigure him. The prophecies point to him. Every truth bears relation to him. The law itself must be so explained and enforced as to lead to him. Particularly,

---

[7] John 6:29.
[8] 1 Corinthians 9:16.

His divinity and glorious character
Exhibit his divinity and glorious character. The New Testament dwells much on his being the Son of God—equal with God. It was this that heightened the gift of him (John 3:16). Hence the efficacy of his blood (1 John 1:7). Hence the condescension of his obedience, and the dignity of his priesthood (Heb. 4:14–16). Hence the greatness of the sin of rejecting him (John 3:18); and of apostasy (Heb. 10:29).

His atonement and mediation
Hold up his atonement and mediation as the only ground of a sinner's hope. It is the work of a Christian minister to beat off self-righteous hope, which is natural to depraved man, and to direct his hearers to the only hope set before them in the gospel. Be not concerned merely to form the manners of your congregation, but bring them to Christ. That will best form their manners. The apostles had no directions short of this: "Repent, and believe the gospel."[9] They never employed themselves in lopping off the branches of sin; but laid the axe to the root. Your business with the sins of mankind is, to make use of them to convince your hearers of the corruption of their nature, and their need of a radical cure.

His salvation, even for the chief of sinners
Hold up the blessings of his salvation for acceptance, even to the chief of sinners: "This is a faithful saying, and worthy of all acceptation, that Christ Jesus came into the world to save sinners, of whom I am chief."[10] The gospel is a feast, and you are to invite guests. You may have many excuses and refusals. But be you concerned to do as your Lord commands. And when you have done your utmost, there will still be room. Dwell on the freeness, and fullness, and all-sufficiency of his grace, and how welcome even the worst of sinners are, who, renouncing all other refuges, flee to him.

His lordship
Preach him as "the Lord," or Lawgiver, of his church, no less than as a

---

[9] Mark 1:15.
[10] 1 Timothy 1:15.

Saviour. Christ's offices must not be divided. Taking his yoke, and learning his spirit, are connected with coming to him. Believers are "not without law unto God, but under the law to Christ."

The preaching of Christ will answer every end of preaching. This is the doctrine which God owns to conversion, to the leading of awakened sinners to peace, and to the comfort of true Christians. If the doctrine of the cross be no comfort to us, it is a sign we have no right to comfort. This doctrine is calculated to quicken the indolent, to draw forth every Christian grace, and to recover the backslider. This is the universal remedy for all the moral diseases of all mankind. We proceed to notice,

In what light the apostles considered themselves
"Your servants for Jesus' sake." Ministers are not the servants of the people in such a sense as implies inferiority, or their having an authority over them. On the contrary, what authority there is, is on the other side: "Obey them that have the rule over you."[11] Nor are ministers the servants of the people in such a sense as to be directed by them what to preach. In these respects one is their Master, even Christ. But ministers are the servants of their people, inasmuch as their whole time and powers require to be devoted to their spiritual advantage—to know them, caution, counsel, reprove, instruct, exhort, admonish, encourage, stimulate, pray, and preach. Study to promote their spiritual interests as individuals, and their prosperity as a people.

Nor should ministers think it too much to lay themselves out in this work. They do it "for Jesus' sake." This was the motive addressed to Peter. "Lovest thou me?—Feed my sheep. Feed my lambs,"[12] "Feed the church of God, which he hath purchased with his own blood."[13] Let Christ be not only the theme of my remaining ministry, but the exaltation of him and the enlargement of his kingdom the great end of my life! If I forget thee, O my Saviour, let my right hand forget; if I do not remember thee, let my tongue cleave to the roof my mouth!

---

[11] Hebrews 13:17.
[12] John 21:15.
[13] Acts 20:28.

The Nature of the Gospel, and the Manner in Which it Ought to Be Preached[1]

> "Praying for us, that God would open unto us a door of utterance, to speak the mystery of Christ, that I may make it manifest, as I ought to speak." Colossians 4:3–4

My dear brother,

I have chosen this passage, on the present occasion, as expressing not the whole of your work, but an important part of it—preaching the gospel. For the discharge of this, an apostle besought the prayers of his brethren, and so should we.

The words imply that, to do justice to the gospel, or to preach it as it ought to be preached, we need a special divine influence, and consequently the prayers of our brethren. I wish at this time to call your attention to the work itself—the manner in which the gospel ought to be preached; and then to offer a few motives to your consideration.

The manner

I shall call your attention to the manner in which the gospel ought to be preached.

It is not my wish to dismay your spirit, but yet I desire to impress you with a sense of the importance of the work of the ministry, that, like the apostle, you may cry to him who alone can give you strength to discharge it. That we may form some idea of the manner in which the gospel ought to be preached, it is necessary to consider some of its leading properties. We may mention four or five:

Requires faithfulness

The gospel is a message which implies a disagreeable and heavy charge against those to whom it is addressed, and therefore requires great faithfulness. It supposes that all mankind are the enemies of God, and exposed

---

[1] Fuller, "The Nature of the Gospel," *Complete Works*, 1:494–496.

to his righteous displeasure. You will have to do with the wicked as well as with the righteous, and you must not flatter them. It is at your peril to say anything soothing to the wicked. It will be very painful to keep them at a distance, and to exhibit to them the threatenings of God's word against them. They will be trying to shift the blame, and to invent excuses; but you must follow up your charges. Their hearts may rise against you, and they may be displeased with your preaching; but you must not desist.

If we could go with a message of approbation and applause—if we could tell our auditory that they are amiable and virtuous beings, with only a few imperfections, which God will doubtless overlook—it might be much more pleasing and agreeable to ourselves as men. We can feel no pleasure in accusing our species. But woe unto us if we speak not the truth! The wicked will perish, and their blood will be required at our hand! (Ezek. 3:16–21). Then beware of softening matters, either with the unconverted or the backslider. Beware of giving up the authority of God over the heart, and of allowing either that the heartless services of the unconverted are pleasing to him, or if not, that the fault is not in them. Beware of countenancing their own views of themselves, that they are poor pitiable creatures instead of sinners. The wound must be probed, or your patient will be lost! O, if we preach the gospel as we ought to preach it, what fidelity is here required! You must my brother, side with God against an ungodly world. You must follow the windings of their evil hearts; you must detect them in all their refuges of lies, that they may flee to the only refuge set before them in the gospel. However it may pain you, or offend your hearers, if you would preach the gospel as you ought to preach it—you must be faithful.

Firm and fearless of consequences
The gospel is a message in which we have truth and justice on our side; and therefore we ought to be firm and fearless of consequences. Speak boldly (Eph. 6:19). If a man's cause be bad, it must render him timid; but to be timid in the cause of God and truth is unworthy. When, however, I recommend boldness, I do not mean that which is opposed to modesty and respectful feeling, nor yet that dogmatical rant which deals in assertion without evidence; but that which is opposed to mercenary fear and cowardice. You must not calculate consequences as they respect this life.

David E. Prince

If you would preach the gospel as you ought to preach it, the approbation of God must be your main object. What if you *were* to lose your friends and diminish your income; nay, what if you lose your liberty, or even your life—what would this all be, compared with the loss of the favour and friendship of God? Woe unto us, if we shun to declare any part of the counsel of God! He that is afraid or ashamed to preach the whole of the gospel, in all its implications and bearings, let him stand aside; he is utterly unworthy of being a soldier of Jesus Christ. Sometimes, if you would speak the whole truth, you may be reproached as unsound and heterodox. But you must not yield to popular clamour. If you have truth on your side, stand firm against all opposition.

Earnest

The gospel is a message full of importance, and therefore you must be in earnest. If your message respected the health of your hearers, or their temporal interest, or their reputation, it would be thought important. But what are these compared with the salvation of their souls! Salvation by Jesus Christ is God's last remedy—his ultimatum with a lost world (Mark 16:16; Acts 4:12). There remains no other sacrifice for sins. Then do not trifle on such subjects as these, lest you lose your own soul. What can be thought of you if you employ your time in making pretty speeches, and turning elegant periods, instead of endeavouring to "save yourself and them that hear you."[2] What if, instead of beseeching sinners to be reconciled to God, you should crack jokes before them, to excite a laugh! What can be thought of you if you trifle with principles, and join the sneer of the poet, when he says,

> For modes of faith let graceless zealots fight:
> He can't be wrong whose life is in the right![3]

Your hearers will doubtless conceive that you are insincere, and that you do not believe the message you are appointed to deliver.

---

[2] 1 Timothy 4:16.
[3] Alexander Pope, *An Essay on Man* (London: Cassell & Company, 1891), 35.

Preaching Christ

Plainness of speech

The gospel is a message that abounds with deep wisdom, and therefore we ought to possess a deep insight into it, and to cultivate great plainness of speech. The gospel is "a mystery," and a mystery that requires to be made manifest. A mystery is something hidden, or secret. Such are the great things of God. They are "hid from the wise and the prudent, and revealed unto babes,"[4] "Unto you it is given to know the mysteries of the kingdom of God."[5] Much of it, indeed, was hidden from Old Testament believers (Eph. 3:5). Nor is it known even to New Testament believers but by the Spirit (1 Cor. 2:7). Nor is it fully comprehensible to any; for it is called "unsearchable riches."[6] "Great is the mystery of godliness."[7] Even angels make it their study. Then to make these things manifest must require great insight into them, and great plainness of speech. Do not be content with superficial views of the gospel. Read and think for yourself on every subject. Read the Bible, not merely for texts, but for Scriptural knowledge. Truth attained in this way is like property—it will wear the better for having been acquired by dint of industry. To preach the gospel as we ought to preach it requires, not the subtilty of the metaphysician, but the simplicity of the Christian.

Gospel preached with affection

The gospel is a message of love, and therefore it ought to be preached with great affection. Never were such messages of love announced to the world before. "God so loved the world,"[8] "Come ye out from them, be ye separate,"[9] &c. This is fitly called "the glorious gospel of the blessed God."[10] It is an overflow of his blessedness. To preach these things with an unfeeling heart is not to preach "as we ought"[11] to preach. Cultivate the affectionate. Not indeed an affectation of feeling, but genuine feeling. Christ wept over sinners, and so must we. If we trifle with men, or be careless about their salvation, or deal forth damnation with an unfeeling

---

[4] Matthew 11:25.
[5] Matthew 13:11.
[6] Ephesians 3:8.
[7] 1 Timothy 3:16.
[8] John 3:16.
[9] 2 Corinthians 6:17.
[10] 1 Timothy 1:11.
[11] Colossians 4:4.

heart, we do not preach "as we ought."

Motives

Let me offer a few motives to this duty of preaching the gospel as it ought to be preached.

Consider the examples held up for your imitation. You have Peter ... Paul ... John ... in each of whom these things are exemplified. Nay, more—you have Christ. Nor have you examples in distant ages only; but you have seen some, even among you. ... [Samuel] Pearce!

Consider the examples exhibited for your warning. Some have sunk into indolence and self-indulgence; sauntering about and gossiping, instead of preaching, from house to house; and there has been an end of them. Some have risen into pride and priestly insolence, and there has been an end of them. Some have trifled with the truth, and God has given them up to destructive error. Others have plunged into political speculations, which have eaten up all their religion: aiming to govern the world, they have lost the government of their own souls, and of their peculiar charge.

Consider the effects that may follow. If you were deputed to negotiate a peace between the contending powers of Europe, you would tremble lest the curses of many should fall upon you. My brother, be faithful, and you shall receive a crown. If you be not, the eternal curse of God awaits you!

Christian Patriotism[1]

[Delivered at Kettering, in 1803, at a time of threatened invasion]

> "And seek the peace of the city whither I have caused you to be carried away captives, and pray unto the Lord for it; for in the peace thereof shall ye have peace" Jeremiah 29:7.

In the course of human events, cases may be expected to occur in which a serious mind may be at a loss with respect to the path of duty. Presuming, my brethren, that such may be the situation of some of you, at this momentous crisis—a crisis in which your country, menaced by an unprincipled, powerful, and malignant foe, calls upon you to arm in its defence—I take the liberty of freely imparting to you my sentiments on the subject.

When a part of the Jewish people were carried captives to Babylon, ten years, or thereabouts, before the entire ruin of the city and temple, they must have felt much at a loss in determining upon what was duty. Though Jeconiah, their king, was carried captive with them, yet the government was still continued under Zedekiah; and there were not wanting prophets, such as they were, who encouraged in them the hopes of a speedy return. To settle their minds on this subject, Jeremiah, the prophet, addressed the following letter to them, in the name of the Lord:

> Thus saith the Lord of hosts, the God of Israel, unto all that are carried away captives, whom I have caused to be carried away from Jerusalem unto Babylon: Build ye houses, and dwell in them; and plant gardens, and eat the fruit of them; take ye wives, and beget sons and daughters; and take wives for your sons, and give your daughters to husbands, that they may bear sons and daughters; that ye may be increased there, and not diminished: and seek the peace of the city whither I have caused you to be carried away captives, and pray unto the Lord for it; for in the peace thereof shall ye have peace.[2]

---

[1] Fuller, "Christian Patriotism," *Complete Works*, 1:202-209.
[2] Jeremiah 29:4-7.

I do not suppose that the case of these people corresponds exactly with ours; but the difference is of such a nature as to heighten our obligations. They were in a foreign land; a land where there was nothing to excite their attachment, but everything to provoke their dislike. They had enjoyed all the advantages of freedom and independence, but were now reduced to a state of slavery. Nor were they enslaved only: to injury was added insult. They that led them captive required of them mirth, saying, "Sing us one of the songs of Zion!" Revenge, in such circumstances, must have seemed natural; and if a foreign invader, like Cyrus, had placed an army before their walls, it had been excusable, one would have thought, not only to have wished him success, but if an opportunity had offered, to have joined an insurrection in aid of him: yet nothing like this is allowed. When Cyrus actually took this great city, it does not appear that the Jews did anything to assist him. Their duty was to seek the welfare of the city, and to pray to the Lord for it, leaving it to the great Disposer of all events to deliver them in his own time; and this not merely as being right, but wise: "In their peace ye shall have peace."[3]

Now if such was the duty of men in their circumstances, can there be any doubt with respect to ours? Ought we not to seek the good of our native land; the land of our fathers' sepulchres: a land where we are protected by mild and wholesome laws, administered under a paternal prince; a land where civil and religious freedom are enjoyed in a higher degree than in any other country in Europe; a land where God has been known for many centuries as a refuge; a land, in fine, where there are greater opportunities for propagating the gospel, both at home and abroad, than in any other nation under heaven? Need I add to this, that the invader was to them a deliverer; but to us, beyond all doubt, would be a destroyer?

Our object, this evening, will be, partly to inquire into the duty of religious people towards their country, and partly to consider the motive by which it is enforced.

Inquire into the duty of religious people towards their country
Though, as Christians, we are not of the world, and ought not to be conformed to it; yet, being in it, we are under various obligations to those

---

[3] Jeremiah 29:7.

about us. As husbands, wives, parents, children, masters, servants, &c., we cannot be insensible that others have a claim upon us, as well as we upon them; and it is the same as members of a community united under one civil government. If we were rulers, our country would have a serious claim upon us as rulers; and, as we are subjects, it has a serious claim upon us as subjects. The manner in which we discharge these relative duties contributes not a little to the formation of our character, both in the sight of God and man.

The directions given to the Jewish captives were comprised in two things; "seeking the peace of the city," and "praying to the Lord for it." These directions are very comprehensive; and apply to us, as we have seen, much more forcibly than they did to the people to whom they were immediately addressed. Let us inquire, more particularly, what is included in them.

Seek the peace of the city

The term here rendered *peace* (שלם) signifies not merely an exemption from wars and insurrections, but prosperity in general. It amounts, therefore, to saying, Seek the *good* or *welfare* of the city. Such, brethren, is the conduct required of us, as men and as Christians. We ought to be patriots, or lovers of our country.

To prevent mistakes, however, it is proper to observe that the patriotism required of us is not that love of our country which clashes with universal benevolence, or which seeks its prosperity at the expense of the general happiness of mankind. Such was the patriotism of Greece and Rome; and such is that of all others where Christian principle is not allowed to direct it. Such, I am ashamed to say, is that with which some have advocated the cause of negro slavery. It is necessary, forsooth, to the wealth of this country! No; if my country cannot prosper but at the expense of justice, humanity, and the happiness of mankind, let it be unprosperous! But this is not the case. Righteousness will be found to exalt a nation, and so to be true wisdom. The prosperity which we are directed to seek in behalf of our country involves no ill to any one, except to those who shall attempt its overthrow. Let those who fear not God, nor regard man, engage in schemes of aggrandizement, and let sordid parasites pray for their success. Our concern is to cultivate that patriotism which harmonizes with good-will to men. O my country, I will lament thy faults! Yet, with all your faults, I will seek your good; not only as a Briton, but as a Christian: "for my brethren and companions' sakes, I will say, Peace be within thee: because of the house of the Lord my God, I will seek thy good!"[4]

If we seek the good of our country, we shall certainly do nothing, and join in nothing, that tends to disturb its peace, or hinder its welfare. Whoever engages in plots and conspiracies to overturn its constitution, we shall not. Whoever deals in inflammatory speeches, or in any manner sows the seeds of discontent and disaffection, we shall not. Whoever labours to depreciate its governors, supreme or subordinate, in a manner tending to bring government itself into contempt, we shall not. Even in cases wherein we may be compelled to disapprove of measures, we shall either be silent, or express our disapprobation with respect and with regret. A dutiful son may see a fault in a father; but he will not take pleasure in exposing him. He that can employ his wit in degrading magistrates is not their friend, but their enemy; and he that is an enemy to magistrates is not far from being an enemy to magistracy, and, of course, to his country. A good man may be aggrieved; and, being so, may complain. Paul did so at Philippi. But the character of a complainer belongs only to those who walk after their own lusts.

If we seek the good of our country, we shall do everything in our power to promote its welfare. We shall not think it sufficient that we do it no harm, or that we stand still as neutrals, in its difficulties. If, indeed, our spirits be tainted with disaffection, we shall be apt to think we do great things by standing aloof from conspiracies, and refraining from inflammatory speeches; but this is no more than may be accomplished by the greatest traitor in the land, merely as a matter of prudence. It becomes Christians to bear positive good-will to their country, and to its government, considered as government, irrespective of the political party which may have the ascendency. We may have our preferences, and that without blame; but they ought never to prevent a cheerful obedience to the laws, a respectful demeanour towards those who frame and those who execute them, or a ready co-operation in every measure which the being or well-being of the nation may require. The civil power, what-

---

[4] Psalm 122:8.

ever political party is uppermost, while it maintains the great ends of government, ought, at all times, to be able to reckon upon religious people as its cordial friends; and if such we be, we shall be willing, in times of difficulty, to sacrifice private interest to public good; shall contribute of our substance without murmuring; and, in cases of imminent danger, shall be willing to expose even our lives in its defence.

Christian resistance to injustice is necessary
As the last of these particulars is a subject which deeply interests us at the present juncture, I shall be excused if I endeavour to establish the grounds on which I conceive its obligation to rest.

We know that the father of the faithful, who was only a sojourner in the land of Canaan, when his kinsman Lot with his family were taken captives by a body of plunderers, armed his trained servants, pursued the victors, and bravely recovered the spoil. It was on this occasion that Melchizedek blessed him, saying, "Blessed be Abraham of the most high God, possessor of heaven and earth: and blessed be the most high God, who hath delivered thine enemies into thine hand!"[5]

Perhaps it will be said, this was antecedent to the times of the New Testament; Jesus taught his disciples not to resist evil; and when Peter drew his sword, he ordered him to put it up again; saying, "All they that take the sword shall perish with the sword."[6]

You know, my brethren, I have always deprecated war, as one of the greatest calamities; but it does not follow, hence, that I must consider it in all cases unlawful.

Christianity, I allow, is a religion of peace; and whenever it universally prevails, in the spirit and power of it, wars will be unknown. But so will every other species of injustice; yet, while the world is as it is, some kind of resistance to injustice is necessary, though it may at some future time become unnecessary. If our Saviour's command that we resist not evil be taken literally and universally, it must have been wrong for Paul to have remonstrated against the magistrates at Philippi;[7] and he himself would not have reproved the person who smote him at the judgment-seat.[8]

---

[5] Genesis 14:19.
[6] Matthew 26:52.
[7] Acts 26.
[8] John 18:23.

Preaching Christ

I allow that the sword is the last weapon to which we should have recourse. As individuals, it may be lawful, by this instrument, to defend ourselves or our families against the attacks of an assassin; but, perhaps, this is the only case in which it is so; and even there, if it were possible to disarm and confine the party, it were much rather to be chosen than in that manner to take away his life. Christianity does not allow us, in any case, to retaliate from a principle of revenge. In ordinary injuries it teaches patience and forbearance. If an adversary "smite us on one cheek," we had better "turn to him the other also,"[9] than go about to avenge our own wrongs. The laws of honour, as acted upon in high life, are certainly in direct opposition to the laws of Christ; and various retaliating maxims, ordinarily practised among men, will no doubt be found among the works of the flesh.

And if, as nations, we were to act on Christian principles, we should never engage in war but for our own defence; nor for that, till every method of avoiding it had been tried in vain.

Once more, it is allowed that Christians, as such, are not permitted to have recourse to the sword, for the purpose of defending themselves against persecution for the gospel's sake. No weapon is admissible in this warfare but truth, whatever be the consequence. We may remonstrate, as Paul did at Philippi, and our Lord himself, when unjustly smitten; but it appears to me that this is all. When Peter drew his sword, it was with a desire to rescue his Master from the persecuting hands of his enemies, in the same spirit as when he opposed his going up to Jerusalem; in both which instances he was in the wrong: and the saying of our Saviour, that "all they that take the sword shall perish with the sword,"[10] has commonly been verified, in this sense of it.

I believe it will be found, that when Christians have resorted to the sword in order to resist persecution for the gospel's sake, as did the Albigenses, the Bohemians, the French protestants,[11] and some others,

---

[9] Matthew 5:39.
[10] Matthew 26:52.
[11] Fuller refers to the Albigensian (also called Cathars) Crusade, which was a twenty-year military action (1209–1229) in Southern France initiated by Pope Innocent III against the Albigenses. Northern France and Southern France were separate countries at the time and the North took Pope Innocent's call for a crusade against the heretics as an opportunity to brutally claim Southern France.

within the last six hundred years, the issue has commonly been, that they have perished by it; that is, they have been overcome by their enemies, and exterminated: whereas, in cases where their only weapons have been "the blood of the Lamb, and the word of their testimony, loving not their lives unto death,"[12] they have overcome. Like Israel in Egypt, the more they have been afflicted, the more they have increased.

But none of these things prove it unlawful to take up arms as members of civil society, when called upon to do so for the defence of our country. The ground on which our Saviour refused to let his servants fight for him, that he should not be delivered into the hands of the Jews, was, that his was a kingdom "not of this world;"[13] plainly intimating that if his kingdom had been of this world, a contrary line of conduct had been proper. Now this is what every other kingdom is; it is right, therefore, according to our Lord's reasoning, that the subjects of all civil states should, as such, when required, fight in defence of them.

Has not Christianity, I ask, in the most decided manner recognized civil government, by requiring Christians to be subject to it? Has it not expressly authorized the legal use of the sword? Christians are warned that the magistrate "beareth not the sword in vain;"[14] and that he is "the minister of God, a revenger, to execute wrath upon him that doeth evil."[15] But if it be right for the magistrate to bear the sword, and to use it upon evil-doers within the realm, it cannot be wrong to use it in repelling invaders from without; and if it be right on the part of the magistrate, it is right that the subject should assist him in it; for otherwise, his power would be merely nominal, and he would indeed "bear the sword in vain."

His reference to the French Protestants (Huguenots) points to what was known as the French Wars of Religion (1562-1598), one of the deadliest periods of religious wars in history primarily between French Protestants and Catholics.

He also refers to the Bohemians in the Thirty Years' War (1618-1648), a brutal conflict in central Europe. It began as a religious conflict between the Catholic and Protestant states of the Holy Roman empire. In 1618, Ferdinand II closed some Protestant churches in Bohemia sparking a Protestant revolt. Ferdinand responded by sending an army into Bohemia to crush the revolt. Ferdinand II essentially overturned the freedom that was granted by the Peace of Augsburg (1555) by attempting to force all citizens to adhere to Roman Catholicism.

[12] Revelation 12:11.
[13] John 18:36.
[14] Romans 13:4.
[15] Romans 13:4.

We have not been used, in things of a civil and moral nature, to consider one law as made for the religious part of a nation, and another for the irreligious. Whatever is the duty of one, allowing for different talents and situations in life, is the duty of all. If, therefore, it be not binding upon the former to unite in every necessary measure for the support of civil government, neither is it upon the latter; and if it be binding upon neither, it must follow that civil government itself ought not to be supported, and that the whole world should be left to become a prey to anarchy or despotism.

Further, if the use of arms were, of itself, and in all cases, inconsistent with Christianity, it were a sin to be a soldier; but nothing like this is held out to us in the New Testament. On the contrary, we there read of two believing centurions;[16] and neither of them was reproved on account of his office, or required to relinquish it. We also read of publicans and soldiers who came to John to be baptized, each asking, "What shall we do?" The answer to both proceeds on the same principle: they are warned against the abuses of their respective employments; but the employments themselves are tacitly allowed to be lawful. To the one he said, "Exact no more than that which is appointed you:" to the other, "Do violence to no man, neither accuse any falsely, and be content with your wages."[17] If either of these occupations had been in itself sinful, or inconsistent with that kingdom which it was John's grand object to announce, and into the faith of which his disciples were baptized, he ought, on this occasion, to have said so, or, at least, not to have said that which implies the contrary.

If it be objected that the sinfulness of war would not lie so much at the door of the centurions and soldiers as of the government by whose authority it was proclaimed and executed, I allow there is considerable force in this; but yet, if the thing itself were necessarily, and in all cases, sinful, every party voluntarily concerned in it must have been a partaker of the guilt, though it were in different degrees.

But granting, it may be said, that war is not, in itself, necessarily sinful; yet it becomes so by the injustice with which it is commonly undertaken and conducted. It is no part of my design to become the apologist

---

[16] Matthew 8:5–13; 27:54.
[17] Luke 3:14.

of injustice, on whatever scale it might be practised. But if wars be allowed to be generally undertaken and conducted without a regard to justice, it does not follow that they are always so; and still less that war itself is sinful. In ascertaining the justice or injustice of war, we have nothing to do with the motives of those who engage in it. The question is whether it be in itself unjust? If it appeared so to me, I should think it my duty to stand aloof from it as far as possible.

There is one thing, however, that requires to be noticed. Before we condemn any measure as unjust, we ought to be in possession of the means of forming a just judgment concerning it.

If a difference arise only between two families, or two individuals, though every person in the neighbourhood may be talking and giving his opinion upon it; yet it is easy to perceive that no one of them is competent to pronounce upon the justice or injustice of either side, till he has acquainted himself with all the circumstances of the case, by patiently hearing it on both sides. How much less, then, are we able to judge of the differences of nations, which are generally not a little complex, both in their origin and bearings; and of which we know but little, but through the channel of newspapers and vague reports! It is disgusting to hear people, whom no one would think of employing to decide upon a common difference between two neighbours, take upon them to pronounce, with the utmost freedom, upon the justice or injustice of national differences. Where those who are constitutionally appointed to judge in such matters have decided in favour of war, however painful it may be to my feelings, as a friend of mankind, I consider it my duty to submit, and to think well of their decision, till, by a careful and impartial examination of the grounds of the contest, I am compelled to think otherwise.

After all, there may be cases in which injustice may wear so prominent a feature, that every thinking and impartial mind shall be capable of perceiving it; and where it does so, the public sense of it will and ought to be expressed. In the present instance, however, there seems to be no ground of hesitation. In arming to resist a threatened invasion, we merely act on the defensive; and not to resist an enemy, whose ambition, under the pretense of liberating mankind, has carried desolation wherever he has gone, were to prove ourselves unworthy of the blessings we enjoy. Without taking upon me to decide on the original grounds of the difference, the question at issue with us is: is it right that any one nation should seek absolutely to ruin another, and that other not be warranted, and even obliged, to resist it? That such is the object of the enemy, at this time, cannot be reasonably doubted. If my country were engaged in an attempt to ruin France, as a nation, it would be a wicked undertaking; and if I were fully convinced of it, I should both hope and pray that they might be disappointed. Surely, then, I may be equally interested in behalf of my native land!

Pray
But there is another duty which we owe to our country; which is, that we pray to the Lord for it. It is supposed that religious people are a praying people. The godly Israelites, when carried into Babylon, were banished from temple-worship; but they still had access to their God. The devotional practice of Daniel was well known among the great men of that city, and proved the occasion of a conspiracy against his life.[18] King Darius knew so much of the character of the Jews as to request an interest in their prayers, in behalf of himself and his sons.[19] My brethren, your country claims an interest in yours; and I trust that, if no such claim were preferred, you would, of your own accord, remember it.

You are aware that all our dependence, as a nation, is upon God; and, therefore, should importune his assistance. After all the struggles for power, you know that in his sight all the inhabitants of the world are reputed as nothing: he does according to his will in the army of heaven, and among the inhabitants of the earth; and none can stay his hand, or say to him, "What doest thou?"[20] Indeed this has been acknowledged, and at times sensibly felt, by irreligious characters; but in general the great body of a nation, it is to be feared, think but little about it. Their dependence is upon an arm of flesh. It may be said, without uncharitableness, of many of our commanders, both by sea and land, as was said of Cyrus, "God hath girded them, though they have not known him."[21] But by how much you perceive a want of prayer and dependence on God in your countrymen, by so much more should you be concerned, as much as in you lies,

---

[18] Daniel 6:1–13.
[19] Ezra 6:10.
[20] Daniel 4:35.
[21] Isaiah 45:5.

to supply the defect. "The prayer of a righteous man availeth much."[22]

The guilt of the country
You are also aware, in some measure, of the load of guilt that lies upon your country; and should therefore supplicate mercy on its behalf. I acknowledge myself to have much greater fear from this quarter than from the boasting menaces of a vain man. If our iniquities provoke not the Lord to deliver us into his hand, his schemes and devices will come to nothing. When I think, among other things, of the detestable traffic before alluded to, in which we have taken so conspicuous a part, and have shed so much innocent blood, I tremble! When we have fasted and prayed, I have seemed to hear the voice of God, saying unto us, "Loose the bands of wickedness, undo the heavy burdens, let the oppressed go free, and break every yoke!"[23] Yet, peradventure, for his own name's sake, or from a regard to his own cause, which is here singularly protected, the Lord may hearken to our prayers, and save us from deserved ruin. We know that Sodom itself would have been spared if ten righteous men could have been found in her. I proceed to consider,

The motive by which these duties are enforced
"In the peace thereof shall ye have peace." The Lord has so wisely and mercifully interwoven the interests of mankind as to furnish motives to innumerable acts of justice and kindness. We cannot injure others, nor even refrain from doing them good, without injuring ourselves.

The interests of individuals and families are closely connected with those of a country. If the latter prosper, generally speaking, so do the former; and if the one be ruined, so must the other. It is impossible to describe, or to conceive beforehand, with any degree of accuracy, the miseries which the success of a foreign enemy, such as we have to deal with, must occasion to private families. To say nothing of the loss of property among the higher and middle classes of people (which must be severely felt, as plunder will, undoubtedly, be the grand stimulus of an invading army), who can calculate the loss of lives? Who can contemplate, without horror, the indecent excesses of a victorious, unprincipled, and brutal

---

[22] James 5:16.
[23] Isaiah 58:6.

soldiery? Let not the poorest man say, "I have nothing to lose." Yes, if men of opulence lose their property, you will lose your employment. You have also a cottage, and perhaps a wife and family, with whom, amidst all your hardships, you live in love; and would it be nothing to you to see your wife and daughters abused, and you yourself unable to protect them, or even to remonstrate, but at the hazard of being thrust through with the bayonet? If no other considerations will induce us to protect our country, and pray to the Lord for it, our own individual and domestic comfort might suffice.

To this may be added, our interests as Christians, no less than as men and as families, are interwoven with the well-being of our country. If Christians, while they are in the world, are, as has been already noticed, under various relative obligations, it is not without their receiving, in return, various relative advantages. What those advantages are we should know to our grief, were we once to lose them. So long have we enjoyed religious liberty in this country, that I fear we are become too insensible of its value. At present we worship God without interruption. What we might be permitted to do under a government which manifestly hates Christianity, and tolerates it even at home only as a matter of policy, we know not. This, however, is well known, that a large proportion of those unprincipled men, in our own country, who have been labouring to overturn its constitution, have a deep-rooted enmity to the religion of Jesus. May the Lord preserve us, and every part of the United Kingdom, from their machinations!

Some among us, to whatever extremities we may be reduced, will be incapable of bearing arms; but they may assist by their property, and in various other ways: even the hands of the aged poor, like those of Moses, may be lifted up in prayer; while their countrymen, and it may be their own children, are occupying the post of danger. I know it is the intention of several whom I now address freely to offer their services at this important period. Should you, dear young people, be called forth in the arduous contest, you will expect an interest in our prayers. Yes, and you will have it. Every one of us, every parent, wife, or Christian friend, if they can pray for anything, will importune the Lord of hosts to cover your heads in the day of battle!

Finally, it affords satisfaction to my mind to be persuaded that you will avail yourselves of the liberty granted to you of declining to learn your exercise on the Lord's day. Were you called to resist the landing of the enemy on that day, or any other work of necessity, you would not object to it; but, in other cases, I trust, you will "Render to Caesar the things that are Caesar's, and to God the things that are God's."[24]

---

[24] Matthew 22:21.

Instances, Evil, and Tendency of Delay, in the Concern of Religion[1]

[Preached at a Ministers' Meeting, held at Clipstone, April 27, 1791]

"Thus speaketh the Lord of hosts, saying, This people say, The time is not come, the time that the Lord's house should be built."
Haggai 1:2

When the children of Judah were delivered from their captivity, and allowed, by the proclamation of Cyrus, to return to their own land, one of the principal things which attracted their attention was the rebuilding of the house of God, which had been destroyed by the Babylonians. This was a work which Cyrus himself enjoined, and upon which the hearts of the people were fixed. It was not, however, to be accomplished at once; and as the worship of God was a matter of immediate and indispensable concern, they set up an altar, on which to offer sacrifices and offerings, till such time as the temple should be built.

In the second year after their return, the foundation of the Lord's house was laid; but opposition being made to it, by the adversaries of Judah and Benjamin, the work ceased all the days of Cyrus, until the reign of Darius, commonly distinguished by the name of Darius Hystaspes. During this period, which seems to have been about fourteen years, the people sunk into a spirit of indifference. At first they desisted from necessity; but afterwards, their attention being turned to the building and ornamenting of houses for themselves, they seemed very well contented that the house of the Lord should lie waste. For this their temper and conduct the land was smitten with barrenness; so that both the vintage and the harvest failed them. God also raised up Haggai and Zechariah to go and remonstrate against their supineness; and the efforts of these two prophets were the means of stirring up the people to resume the work.

---

[1] Fuller, "Instances, Evil, and Tendency of Delay, in the Concerns of Religion," *Complete Works*, 1:145–151.

The argument which the people used against building the house of God was that the time was not come.[2] It is possible they waited for a counter-order from the Persian court; if so, they might have waited long enough. A work of that nature ought to have been prosecuted of their own accord; at least they should have tried. It did not follow, because they were hindered once, that therefore they should never succeed. Or perhaps they meant to plead their present weakness and poverty. Something like this seems to be implied in the 4th verse, where they are reminded that they had strength enough to build and ornament houses for themselves. It looks as if they wished to build, and lay by fortunes for themselves and their families, and then, at some future time, they might contribute for the building of the house of God.

There is something of this procrastinating spirit that runs through a great part of our life, and is of great detriment to us in the work of God. We know of many things that should be done, and cannot in conscience directly oppose them; but still we find excuses for our inactivity. While we admit that many things should be done which are not done, we are apt to quiet ourselves with the thought that they need not be done just now: "The time is not come, the time that the Lord's house should be built."[3]

In discoursing to you upon the subject, brethren, I shall take notice of a few of the most remarkable cases in which this spirit is discovered; and then endeavour to show its evil nature and dangerous tendency.

The cases, or instances, in which it is discovered

A small degree of observation on mankind, and of reflection upon the workings of our own hearts, will furnish us with many of these; and convince us of its great influence on every description of men, in almost all their religious concerns.

Deceiving themselves
It is by this plea that a great part of mankind are constantly deceiving themselves in respect to a serious attention to the concerns of their souls. These are, doubtless, of the last importance; and there are times in which most men not only acknowledge this truth, but, in some sort, feel the

---

[2] Haggai 1:2.
[3] Haggai 1:2.

force of it. This is the case, especially, with those who have had a religious education, and have been used to attend upon the preaching of the gospel. They hear from the pulpit that men must be born again, must be converted, and become as little children, or never enter into the kingdom of God. Or the same things are impressed upon them by some threatening affliction or alarming providence. They feel themselves at those times very unhappy; and it is not unusual for them to resolve upon a sacrifice of their former sins, and a serious and close attention in future to the affairs of their souls. They think, while under these impressions, they will consider their ways, they will enter their closets, and shut to the door, and pray to the Lord that he would have mercy upon them; but, alas! no sooner do they retire from the house of God, or recover from their affliction, than the impression begins to subside, and then matters of this sort become less welcome to the mind. They must not be utterly rejected; but are let alone for the present. As conscience becomes less alarmed, and danger is viewed at a greater distance, the sinner, by degrees, recovers himself from his fright, and dismisses his religious concern, in some such manner as Felix did his reprove: "Go thy way for this time, when I have a convenient season I will call for thee."[4]

It is thus with the ardent youth; in the hour of serious reflection, he feels that religion is of importance; but his heart, still averse from what his conscience recommends, rises against the thought of sacrificing the prime of life to the gloomy duties of prayer and self-denial. He does not resolve never to attend to these things; but the time does not seem to be come. He hopes that the Almighty will excuse him a few years, at least, and impute his excesses to youthful folly and imbecility.

It is thus with the man of business; there are times in which he is obliged to retire from the hurry of life; and, at those times, thoughts of another life may arrest his attention. Conscience at those intervals may smite him for his living without prayer, without reflection, without God in all his thoughts; and what is his remedy? Does he lament his sin, and implore mercy through our Lord Jesus Christ? No, nor so much as promise to forsake it immediately; but this he promises, that when this busy time is over, and that favourite point is gained, and those intricate affairs are terminated, then it shall be otherwise.

---

[4] Acts 24:25.

It is thus with persons in single life: they will be better when they get settled in the world.

It is thus with the encumbered parent: she looks forward to the time when her family shall get off her hands.

It is thus with the drunkard and the debauchee: wearied in their own way, they intend to lead a new life as soon as they can but shake off their old connections. In short, it is thus with great numbers in all our towns, and villages, and congregations: they put off the great concern to another time, and think they may venture at least a little longer, till all is over with them, and a dying hour just awakens them, like the virgins in the parable, to bitter reflection on their own fatal folly.

Prevents us all from the cause of Christ
This plea not only affects the unconverted, but prevents us all from undertaking any great or good work for the cause of Christ, or the good of mankind. We see many things that should be done; but there are difficulties in the way, and we wait for the removal of these difficulties. We are very apt to indulge a kind of prudent caution (as we call it), which foresees and magnifies difficulties beyond what they really are. It is granted there may be such things in the way of an undertaking as may render it impracticable; and, in that case, it is our duty for the present to stand still; but it becomes us to beware lest we account that impracticable which only requires such a degree of exertion as we are not inclined to give it.

Perhaps the work requires expense; and covetousness says, "Wait a little longer, till I have gained so and so in trade, till I have rendered my circumstances respectable, and settled my children comfortably in the world." But is not this like ceiling our own houses, while the house of God lies waste?

Perhaps it requires concurrence; and we wait for everybody to be of a mind, which is never to be expected. He who through a dread of opposition and reproach desists from known duty is in danger of being found among the "fearful, the unbelieving, and the abominable."[5]

Had Luther and his contemporaries acted upon this principle, they had never gone about the glorious work of the Reformation. When he saw

---

[5] Revelation 21:8.

the abominations of popery, he might have said, "These things ought not to be; but what can I do? If the chief priests and rulers in different nations would but unite, something might be effected; but what can I do, an individual, and a poor man? I may render myself an object of persecution, or, which is worse, of universal contempt; and what good end will be answered by it?" Had Luther reasoned thus—had he fancied that, because princes and prelates were not the first to engage in the good work, therefore the time was not come to build the house of the Lord—the house of the Lord, for anything he had done, might have lain waste to this day.

Instead of waiting for the removal of difficulties, we ought, in many cases, to consider them as purposely laid in our way, in order to try the sincerity of our religion. He who had all power in heaven and earth could not only have sent forth his apostles into all the world, but have so ordered it that all the world should treat them with kindness, and aid them in their mission; but, instead of that, he told them to lay their accounts with persecution and the loss of all things. This was no doubt to try their sincerity; and the difficulties laid in our way are equally designed to try ours.

Let it be considered whether it is not owing to this principle that so few and so feeble efforts have been made for the propagation of the gospel in the world. When the Lord Jesus commissioned his apostles, he commanded them to go and teach "all nations," to preach the gospel to "every creature;"[6] and that notwithstanding the difficulties and oppositions that would lie in the way. The apostles executed their commission with assiduity and fidelity; but, since their days, we seem to sit down half contented that the greater part of the world should still remain in ignorance and idolatry. Some noble efforts have indeed been made; but they are small in number, when compared with the magnitude of the object. And why is it so? Are the souls of men of less value than heretofore? No. Is Christianity less true or less important than in former ages? This will not be pretended. Are there no opportunities for societies, or individuals, in Christian nations, to convey the gospel to the heathen? This cannot be pleaded so long as opportunities are found to trade with them, yea, and (what is a disgrace to the name of Christians) to buy them, and sell them, and treat them with worse than savage barbarity? We have opportunities

---

[6] Matthew 28:18-20; Mark 16:15-16.

in abundance the improvement of navigation, and the maritime and commercial turn of this country, furnish us with these; and it deserves to be considered whether this is not a circumstance that renders it a duty peculiarly binding on us.

The truth is, if I am not mistaken, we wait for we know not what; we seem to think "the time is not come, the time for the Spirit to be poured down from on high." We pray for the conversion and salvation of the world, and yet neglect the ordinary means by which those ends have been used to be accomplished. It pleased God, heretofore, by the foolishness of preaching, to save them that believed; and there is reason to think it will still please God to work by that distinguished means. Ought we not then at least to try by some means to convey more of the good news of salvation to the world around us than has hitherto been conveyed? The encouragement to the heathen is still in force,

> Whosoever shall call upon the name of the Lord shall be saved: but how shall they call on him in whom they have not believed? and how shall they believe in him of whom they have not heard? and how shall they hear without a preacher? and how shall they preach except they be sent?[7]

Let it be further considered, whether it is not owing to this principle that so few and so feeble efforts are made for the propagation of the gospel in places within our reach. There are many dark places in our own land—places where priests and people, it is to be feared, are alike destitute of true religion, "all looking to their own way, every one for his gain from his quarter."[8] Were every friend of Jesus Christ to avail himself of that liberty which the laws of his country allow him, and embrace every opportunity for the dissemination of evangelical principles, what effects might we hope to see! Were every true minister of the gospel to make a point of preaching as often as possible in the villages within his reach; and did those private Christians who are situated in such villages open their doors for preaching, and recommend the gospel by a holy and affectionate behaviour, might we not hope to see the wilderness become as a fruitful field? Surely, in these matters, we are too negligent. And when

---

[7] Romans 10:13–15.
[8] Isaiah 56:11.

we do preach to the unconverted, we do not feel as if we were to do any good. We are as if we knew not how to get at the hearts and consciences of people. We cast the net, without so much as expecting a draught. We are as those who cannot find their hands in the day of battle, who go forth not like men accustomed to conquest, but rather like those inured to defeat. Whence arises all this? Is it not owing, at least a considerable degree of it, to a notion we have that the time is not come for anything considerable to be effected?

Public acknowledgement of Christ
It is this plea that keeps many from a public profession of religion by a practical acknowledgment of Christ. Christ requires of his followers that they confess his name before men; that they be baptized, and commemorate his dying love in the ordinance of the supper. Yet there are many who consider themselves as Christians, and are considered so by others, who still live in the neglect of these ordinances. I speak not now of those who consider themselves as having been baptized in their infancy, but of such as admit the immersion of believers to be the only true baptism, and yet do not practise it, nor hold communion with any particular church of Christ. It is painful to think there should be a description of professed Christians who live in the neglect of Christ's commands. What can be the motives of such neglect? Probably they are various: there is one, however, that must have fallen under your observation; that is, the want of some powerful impression upon the mind, impelling them, as it were, to a compliance. Many persons wait for something of this sort; and because they go from year to year without it, conclude that the time is not come; or that it is not the mind of God that they should comply with those ordinances; at least, that they should comply with them at present. Impressions, it is allowed, are desirable, provided it be truth or duty that is impressed; otherwise they deserve no regard; but be they as desirable as they may, the want of them can never justify our living in the neglect of known duty. Nor are they at all adapted to show us what is duty, but merely to excite to the performance of that which may be proved to be duty without them. We might as well wait for impressions, and conclude, from the want of them, that the time is not come for the performance of other duties as those of baptism and the Lord's supper.

Some are kept from a public profession of Christ's name by mere mercenary motives. They have relations and friends that would be offended. The fear of being disinherited, or injured, in some sort, as to worldly circumstances, has made many a person keep his principles to himself, till such time as the party whose displeasure he fears shall be removed out of the way. This is wicked; as it amounts to a denial of Christ before men, and will, no doubt, expose the party, if he die without repentance for it, to be denied by Christ before his Father at the last day. "Lord," said one, "I will follow thee, but let me first go and bury my father," "Let me first go and bid them farewell who are at home," says another: "Jesus answered, 'Let the dead bury their dead, follow thou me. ... No man having put his hand to the plough, and looking back, is fit for the kingdom of God.'"[9]

Self-examination and self-denial
It is this plea that keeps us from a thorough self-examination and self-denial. The importance of being right in the sight of God, and our liability to err, even in the greatest of all concerns, render a close and frequent inquiry into our spiritual state absolutely necessary. It is a dangerous, as well as an uncomfortable life, to be always in suspense; not knowing what nor where we are, nor whither we are going. There are seasons, too, in which we feel the importance of such an inquiry, and think we will go about it, we will search and try our ways, and turn from our sins, and walk more closely with God. Such thoughts will occur when we hear matters urged home upon us from the pulpit, or when some affecting event draws off our attention from the present world, and causes us to reflect upon ourselves for our inordinate anxiety after it. We think of living otherwise than we have done; but when we come to put our thoughts into execution, we find a number of difficulties in the way, which too often deter us, at least for the present: "Here is an undertaking that must first be accomplished, before I can have time; here is also a troublesome affair that I must get through, before I can be composed; and then here are such temptations that I know not how to get over just now: if I wait a little longer, perhaps they may be removed." Alas! alas! thus we befool ourselves; thus we defer it to another time, till the impressions on our minds are effaced, and then we are less able to attend to those things than we

---

[9] Luke 9:61–62.

were at first. As one who puts off the examination of his accounts, and the retrenchment of his expenses, till, all on a sudden, he is involved in a bankruptcy; so do multitudes, in the religious world, neglect a close inspection into the concerns of their souls, till, at length, either a departure from some of the great principles of the gospel, or some foul and open fall, is the consequence.

Prepared for the Lord's coming
It is this principle that keeps us from preparedness for death, and thus being ready when our Lord shall come. There is nothing that Christ has more forcibly enjoined than this duty: "Be ye also ready, for at such an hour as ye think not the Son of man cometh,"[10] "What I say unto you I say unto all, 'Watch.'"[11] Why do we not immediately feel the force of these charges, and betake ourselves to habitual watchfulness, and prayer, and self-denial, and walking with God? Why are we not as men who wait for the coming of their Lord? Is it not from a secret thought that the time is not come? We know we must die, but we consider it as something at a distance; and thus, imagining that our Lord delays his coming, we delay to prepare to meet him, so that when he comes he finds us in confusion. Instead of our loins being girt, and our lights burning, we are engaged in a number of plans and pursuits, to the neglect of those things which, notwithstanding the necessary avocations of life, ought always to engross our supreme attention.

Let us next proceed to consider,

The evil nature and tendency of this procrastinating temper

I need not say much to prove to you that it is a sin. The conscience of every one of you will assist me in that part of the work. It is proper, however, in order that you may feel it the more forcibly, that you should consider wherein its evil nature consists.

It is contrary to the tenor of all God's commandments
All through the Scriptures we are required to attend to divine things immediately, and without delay:

---

[10] Matthew 24:44.
[11] Mark 13:37.

- "Work while it is called today; the night cometh when no man can work."[12]
- "Today, if ye will hear his voice, harden not your hearts." "While ye have light, believe in the light, that ye may be the children of light."[13]
- "Whatsoever thy hand findeth to do, do it with thy might; for there is no work, nor device, nor knowledge, nor wisdom, in the grave, whither thou goest."[14]

God not only requires us, in general, to do what we do quickly, but calls us to serve him particularly under those temptations or afflictions which we find placed in our way. The terms of discipleship are, "Deny thyself; take up thy cross, and follow me."[15] He does not call upon us to follow him barely when there are no troubles nor difficulties to encounter, nor allow us, when those difficulties occur, to wait a fairer opportunity; but to take our cross, as it were, upon our shoulders, and so follow him. It would be of use for us to consider every situation as a post in which God has placed us, and in which he calls upon us to serve and glorify him. If we are poor, we are required to glorify God by contentment; if afflicted, by patience; if bereaved, by submission; if persecuted, by firmness; if injured, by forgiveness; or if tempted, by denying ourselves for his sake. Nor can these duties be performed at other times; to put them off, therefore, to another opportunity, is the same thing, in effect, as refusing to comply with them at all.

Procrastination implies a lurking dislike
To put off things to another time implies a lurking dislike to the things themselves. We do not ordinarily do so, except in things wherein we have no delight. Whatever our hearts are set upon, we are for losing no time till it is accomplished. If the people of Judah had "had a mind to work," as is said of them on another occasion, they would not have pleaded that the time was not come. Sinful delay, therefore, arises from alienation of heart from God; than which nothing can be more offensive in his sight.

But, further, it is not only a sin, but a sin of dangerous tendency. This

---

[12] John 9:4.
[13] Hebrews 3:15; John 12:36.
[14] Ecclesiastes 9:10.
[15] Matthew 16:24; Mark 8:34; Luke 9:23.

is manifest by the effects it produces. Precious time is thereby murdered, and valuable opportunities lost, and lost beyond recall!

That there are opportunities possessed both by saints and sinners, is plain from the Scriptures. The former might do abundantly more for God than they do, and might enjoy much more of God and heaven than they actually enjoy; and no doubt it would be so, were it not for that idle, delaying temper, of which we have spoken. Like the Israelites, we are slothful to go up to possess the good land. Many are the opportunities, both of doing and enjoying good, that have already passed by. O what Christians might we have been before now, had we but availed ourselves of all those advantages which the gospel dispensation and the free exercise of our religion afford us!

Sinners also, as long as life lasts, have opportunity of escaping from the wrath to come. Hence they are exhorted to "seek the lord while he may be found,"[16] and to "call upon him while he is near."[17] Hence, also, there is a "door" represented as being, at present, "open;" which "the master of the house will," one day, "rise up and shut."[18] The "fountain" is described as being, at present, "open for sin and for uncleanness;" but there is a period approaching when it shall be said, "He that is filthy, let him be filthy still!"[19] It seems scarcely in the power of language to express the danger of delay in terms more forcible and impressive than those which are used in the above passages. Nor is there anything in the idea that clashes with the Scripture doctrine of decrees. All allow that men have opportunity, in natural things, to do what they do not, and to obtain what they obtain not; and if this can be made to consist with a universal providence, which "performeth the things that are appointed for us,"[20] why should not the other be allowed to consist with the purposes of him who does nothing without a plan, but "worketh all things after the counsel of his own will?"[21] A price is in the hands of those who have no heart to get wisdom.

O thoughtless sinner! trifle no longer with the murder of time, so short and uncertain in its duration; the morning of your existence; the

---

[16] Isaiah 55:6.
[17] Isaiah 55:6.
[18] Luke 13:25.
[19] Revelation 22:11.
[20] Job 23:14.
[21] Ephesians 1:11.

mould in which you receive an impression for eternity; the only period in which the Son of man has power to forgive sins! Should the remaining part of your life pass away in the same careless manner as that has which has already elapsed, what bitter reflection must follow! How cutting it must be to look back on all the means of salvation as gone forever; the harvest past, the summer ended, and you not saved![22]

Suppose a company, at the time of low water, should take an excursion upon the sands near the sea-shore: suppose yourself of the company: suppose that, on a presumption of the tide's not returning at present, you should all fall asleep: suppose all the company, except yourself, to awake out of their sleep, and, finding their danger, endeavour to awake you, and to persuade you to flee with them for your life; but you, like the sluggard, are for "a little more sleep, and a little more slumber:"[23] the consequence is, your companions escape, but you are left behind to perish in the waters, which, regardless of all your cries, rise and overwhelm you! What a situation would this be! How would you curse that love of sleep that made you refuse to be awaked—that delaying temper that wanted to indulge a little longer! But what is this situation compared with that of a lost soul? There will come a period when the bottom of the ocean would be deemed a refuge; when, to be crushed under falling rocks and mountains, instead of being viewed with terror as heretofore, will be earnestly desired. Yes, desired, but desired in vain. The sinner who has "neglected the great salvation" will not be able to "escape," nor hide himself "from the face of him that sitteth upon the throne,"[24] nor from "the wrath of the Lamb!"[25]

My dear hearers, consider your condition without delay. God says to you: Today, if ye will hear his voice, harden not your hearts. Today may be the only day you have to live. Go home, enter the closet, and shut to the door; confess your sins; implore mercy through our Lord Jesus Christ; "Kiss the Son, lest he be angry, and ye perish from the way, when his wrath is kindled but a little. Blessed are all they that put their trust in him!"[26]

---

[22] Jeremiah 8:20
[23] Proverbs 6:10; Proverbs 24:33.
[24] Revelation 6:16.
[25] Revelation 6:16.
[26] Psalm 2:12.

Conformity to the Death of Christ[1]

"Being made conformable unto his death" Philippians 3:10.

The death of Christ is a subject of so much importance in Christianity as to be essential to it. Without this, the sacrifices and prophecies of the Old Testament would be nearly void of meaning, and the other great facts recorded in the New Testament divested of importance. It is not so much a member of the body of Christian doctrine as the life-blood that runs through the whole of it. The doctrine of the cross is the Christian doctrine. In determining "not to know anything—save Jesus Christ, and him crucified," the apostle did not mean to contract his researches, or to confine his ministry to a monotonous repetition of a favourite point, to the neglect of other things; on the contrary, he shunned not to declare "the whole counsel of God."[2] The doctrine of "Christ, and him crucified,"[3] comprehended this: it contained a scope which, inspired as he was, surpassed his powers; and well it might, for angels could not comprehend it, but are described as merely desiring to look into it.[4] There is not an important truth, but what is presupposed by it, included in it, or arises out of it; nor any part of practical religion but what hangs upon it.

It was from this doctrine that the New Testament writers fetched their most powerful motives. Do they recommend humility? It is thus:

> Let this mind be in you which was also in Christ Jesus, who, being in the form of God, thought it not robbery to be equal with God; but made himself of no reputation, and took upon him the form of a servant, and was made in the likeness of men; and being found in fashion as a man, he humbled himself, and became obedient unto death, even the death of the cross.[5]

---

[1] Fuller, "Conformity to the Death of Christ," *Complete Works*, 1:310–316.
[2] Acts 20:27.
[3] 1 Corinthians 2:2.
[4] 1 Peter 1:12.
[5] Philippians 2:5–8.

Do they enforce an unreserved devotedness to God? It is thus: "You are not your own; for you are bought with a price; therefore glorify God in your body, and in your spirit, which are God's."[6] If they would provoke Christians to brotherly love, it is from the same consideration: "Herein is love, not that we loved God, but that he loved us, and sent his Son to be the propitiation for our sins. Beloved, if God so loved us, we ought also to love one another."[7] Do they urge a forgiving spirit? It is thus: "Be kind one to another, tender-hearted, forgiving one another, even as God for Christ's sake has forgiven you."[8] Do they recommend benevolence to the poor? It is from this: "For you know the grace of our Lord Jesus Christ, that, though he was rich, yet for your sakes he became poor, that ye through his poverty might be rich—thanks be to God for his unspeakable gift!"[9] Finally, the common duties of domestic life are enforced from this principle: "Husbands, love your wives, even as Christ also loved the church, and gave himself for it."[10]

It is an immediate relation to this great principle that both the ordinances of baptism and the supper appear to have been instituted. As many as were baptized, were baptized into Christ's death; and, in eating the bread and drinking the wine, they were directed to do it in remembrance of him. It was a wonderful instance of condescending love in the Lord Jesus to desire to be remembered by us. Had we requested in the language of the converted thief to be remembered by him, there had been nothing surprising in it; but it is of the nature of dying love to desire to live in the remembrance of those who are dear to us. It was not, however, on his own account, but on ours, that he left this dying request. He knew that to remember him would answer every case that could occur.

If afflicted, this would be our solace; if persecuted, the consideration of him that had endured such contradiction of sinners would prevent our being weary and faint in our minds; if guilty, this would point out the way of forgiveness; or if tempted to turn aside, this would bind us to his name and cause.

It was by a believing view of this great subject that the apostle, at the

---

[6] 1 Corinthians 6:19-20.
[7] 1 John 4:10-11.
[8] Ephesians 4:32.
[9] 2 Corinthians 8:9; 9:15.
[10] Ephesians 5:25.

first, counted all his former privileges and attainments loss; and though, in consequence of renouncing Judaism, he had exchanged all his earthly prospects for hunger, and thirst, and nakedness, and perils, and bitter persecutions, yet, after thirty years' experience, he does not repent, but, in a tone of heavenly triumph, adds,

> Yea, doubtless, and I count all things but loss for the excellency of the knowledge of Christ Jesus my Lord; for whom I have suffered the loss of all things, and do count them but dung, that I may win Christ, and be found in him, not having mine own righteousness, which is of the law, but that which is through the faith of Christ, the righteousness which is of God by faith![11]

A mind thus imbued with the sacred theme, we should think, must have known much of Christ already, and, compared with us, he must; yet, after all that he had thought, and preached, and written, he makes nothing of his attainments, but adopts the language of one that had, in a manner, everything to learn: "That I may know him, and the power of his resurrection, and the fellowship of his sufferings, being made conformable unto his death."[12]

The last of these vehement desires seems to be explanatory of some, if not all, that precede it. That is, he would know him, and the power of his resurrection, and the fellowship of sufferings, as "being made conformable unto his death."

The sentiment here conveyed appears to be that the death of Christ is a model to which Christians must aspire to be conformed. This sentiment we shall endeavour to illustrate and confirm.

There are other models beside the death of Christ but they are included in this. The law of God is that to which we must become conformed. If we be born from above, it is "written in our hearts." But one great end of Christ's death was to honour the divine law, not only in its precept, but its penalty, a conformity to the one must include a conformity to the other. The character of God also is represented as a model to which believers are conformed. The new man is created "after God, in righteousness and true holiness;"[13] but as in the death of Christ God was

---

[11] Philippians 3:8–9.
[12] Philippians 3:10.
[13] Ephesians 4:24.

glorified in the highest, a conformity to this must be a conformity to the divine character. The lives of holy men are also held up for our imitation; but as this is only in proportion as they are followers of Christ, a conformity to him includes all that is required of us respecting them.

We shall consider the death of Christ in four views: namely, in respect of the principles on which it proceeded—the motives by which it was induced—the spirit with which it was endured—and the ends which it accomplished. Under each of these views we shall find things to which we must be conformed.

The principles on which the death of Christ proceeded
In them we shall find a standard by which to form our principles, and shall be able to judge whether they be of God.

We deserved to die
The death of Christ presupposes that we deserved to die. A sense of this truth is at the foundation of all true religion; it requires, therefore, that we be made conformable to it. God, in the gift of his Son to die, judged us to have been worthy of death; Christ, in giving himself to die, evinced himself to be of the same mind; and such must be our mind, or we can have no interest in the glorious results. Until we see and feel that God is in the right, that we are in the wrong, and that if he had cast us off forever it had been no more than we deserved, we shall be strangers to repentance, and as incapable of believing in Christ for salvation as he that is whole is of appreciating the value of a physician.

The malignant nature of sin
The death of Christ presupposes that sin is exceedingly sinful. If it were a matter of small account, it may be presumed that the Father would not have made so much of it as to give his Son to be made a sacrifice to atone for it, and that the Son of God would not have laid down his life for that purpose. The curses of the law, and the judgments inflicted at different times on sinners, furnished strong proof of the malignant nature of sin; especially when the native goodness of God is taken into consideration, but the blood of the cross furnishes much stronger. It was a great thing for the Creator to destroy the work of his hands, and it is so represented: "The Lord said, I will destroy man, whom I have created, from the face

of the earth."[14] But to smite his beloved Son was greater. To be made conformable to this principle, we must not conceive of sin as the weakness, or frailty, of human nature, a mere imperfection which a good God must needs overlook. Neither must we give heed to those systems of religion which are founded upon these depreciating notions, which, however they may flatter us for the present, will, in the end, assuredly deceive us.

Our works are of no merit
The death of Christ presupposes that there was nothing, in all our doings or sufferings, that could furnish a ground of salvation, or a single consideration for which we might be forgiven. Had it been otherwise, Christ would not have died. Men have ever been busily employed in endeavours to propitiate the Deity; some by ceremonial observances, and some by moral; but instead of accomplishing the object, they have only made the case worse. Even those services which were of divine appointment became, in their hands, offensive; God was weary of their offerings. Christ is represented as taking the work out of their hands: "Sacrifice and offering you did not desire; my ears you have opened: burnt-offering and sin-offering you have not required. Then said I, lo, I come!"[15] They were, indeed, required as duties for the time, but not for the purpose of making atonement. Not tears, nor prayers, nor alms, nor any other of our doings, will avail as terms of acceptance with God. If we are conformed to the death of Christ, we shall know and feel this to be the case, and shall seek salvation by grace only, through the Mediator. If we are not conformed to the death of Christ in this respect, we have no reason to expect any interest in it.

A sacrifice of infinite value
The death of Christ presupposes that, for mercy to be exercised in a way consistent with the honour of God, it required to be through a sacrifice of infinite value. When the apostle declares that "it was not possible that the blood of bulls and of goats should take away sins,"[16] he plainly intimates that the inherent value of the sacrifice was of essential importance

---

[14] Genesis 6:7.
[15] Psalm 40:6-7.
[16] Hebrews 10:4.

as to its effect. If it were impossible for animal sacrifices to atone for sin, it must be on account of their insufficiency to demonstrate either the hatred of God to sin or his love to sinners; but the same reason would apply to the sacrifice of Christ, if he were merely a creature. Hence those who deny his divinity, with perfect consistency deny also his atonement. But, on the principles of his divinity, his sufferings were of infinite value; and to this the Scriptures ascribe their efficacy. A careful reader of the New Testament will perceive that, in exhibiting the value and efficacy of his death, it connects it with the inherent dignity of his person:

- "Who being the brightness of his glory, and the express image of his person, and upholding all things by the word of his power, when he had by himself purged our sins, sat down on the right hand of the Majesty on high."[17]
- "We have a great High Priest that is passed into the heavens, Jesus the Son of God."[18]
- "The blood of Jesus Christ, his Son, cleanseth us from all sin."[19]

The result is, that, to be made conformable to the death of Christ, we must think highly of it, and not reduce it to the death of a mere martyr. It is a serious thing to make light of the Saviour, and of the work of salvation:

> He that despised Moses' law died without mercy under two or three witnesses; of how much sorer punishment, suppose you, shall he be thought worthy, who has trodden underfoot the Son of God, and has counted the blood of the covenant, wherewith he was sanctified, an unholy (or common) thing, and has done despite to the Spirit of grace? For we know him that has said, "Vengeance belongs to me, I will recompense," says the Lord. And again, "the Lord shall judge his people." It is a fearful thing to fall into the hands of the living God![20]

Let us observe,

---

[17] Hebrews 1:3.
[18] Hebrews 4:14.
[19] 1 John 1:7.
[20] Hebrews 10:30–31.

David E. Prince

The motives by which the death of Christ was induced

In these we shall find a blessed example to imitate. They may all be summed up in love. Love to God and men; love, great, disinterested, and unparalleled.

There never was such an example of the "love of God" as that which is furnished by the obedience and death of Christ. It was his meat and drink to do the will of his Father. He did not know his nearest relations, but as doing his Father's will. When the bitter cup was presented to him, he said, "Now is my soul troubled; and what shall I say? Father, save me from this hour; but for this cause came I unto this hour. Father, glorify thy name."[21] What was this but exposing his breast, as we should say, to the sword of justice; consenting to be made a sacrifice, that God might be glorified in the salvation of sinners? It was love, working in a way of grief, that caused that affecting exclamation, "My God, my God, why hast thou forsaken me?"[22] He could endure the cross, and even despise the shame. He could bear to be betrayed, denied, and forsaken by his own disciples; but to be forsaken of God wounded him beyond anything. O to be made conformable to his death in these things; to love God, so as to account it our meat and drink to do his will; so as to reckon his friends our friends and his cause our cause; to be willing to do anything, or suffer any thing, for his name's sake; and to feel the withholding of his favour our severest loss!

As there never was such love to God as that which was manifested by Christ, so neither was there ever such love to men. "He loved us, and gave himself for us"[23]—loved us, and washed us from our sins in his own blood. The love of creatures is ordinarily founded on something lovely in the object, but Christ died for us while we were yet enemies. To be made conformable to his death in this is to bear good-will to men, to seek their present and everlasting welfare in every way that is within our power; and this notwithstanding the unloveliness of their character and conduct: "Love them that hate you, and pray for them that despitefully use you, and persecute you."[24]

---

[21] John 12:27-28.
[22] Matthew 27:46.
[23] Ephesians 5:2; Revelation 1:5.
[24] Matthew 5:44.

Preaching Christ

Unbelievers, who know no principle superior to self-love, have represented this precept of our Lord as unnatural and extravagant. Yet they themselves are daily partaking of his bounty, who causes his sun to rise on the evil and the good, and his rain to descend on the just and on the unjust. If they were the children of that Being whom they acknowledge, they would, in some degree, resemble him. Such was the example of Jesus, and such must be ours, if we be made conformable to him.

Let us observe,

The spirit with which Christ suffered and endured

In this we shall find a model for our spirit. The Lord Jesus was possessed of all the original passions of human nature; as love, joy, sorrow, grief, anger, indignation, etc. When reproached and injured, he felt it; his "enduring the cross, and despising the shame,"[25] was not owing to his being insensible to either, but to "the joy set before him."[26] The purity of his nature did not extinguish its passions, but rendered them subordinate to the will of his Father. With the greatest sensibility to reproach and injury, he was meek and lowly of heart. Under all the reproaches and false accusations that were preferred against him on his trial, he preserved a dignified silence; not a word was uttered tending to save his life: but, when questioned on the truth of his Messiahship, he, with equal dignity and firmness, avowed it, though he knew the avowal would cost him his life. Nor did the contradiction and abuse which he received from his executioners extinguish his compassion toward them: while they were nailing him to the cross he prayed, saying, "Father, forgive them: for they know not what they do."[27]

If we observe the spirit of the apostles, we shall find them to have made him their pattern: "of the world, and the off-scouring of all things, unto this day; being reviled, we bless; being persecuted, we suffer it; being defamed, we entreat: we are made as the filth."[28] There appears to have been a holy emulation in the apostle Paul to be a follower of his Lord, even to death. In all that befell him, he kept his eye on Christ:

---

[25] Hebrews 12:2.
[26] Hebrews 12:2.
[27] Luke 23:34.
[28] 1 Corinthians 4:12–13.

- "If we suffer, we shall also reign with him."[29]
- "We are troubled on every side, yet not distressed; perplexed, but not in despair; persecuted, but not forsaken; cast down, but not destroyed, always bearing about in the body the dying of the Lord Jesus, that the life also of Jesus might be made manifest in our body. For we which live are always delivered to death for Jesus' sake, that the life also of Jesus might be made manifest in our mortal flesh."[30]

Such was that conformity to the death of Christ, after which he panted with the most vehement desire. Nothing was further from his thoughts than partaking with him in the work of redemption; but so far as fellowship in his sufferings was admissible, it was the object of his most ardent desire. Oh to be thus made like him and like his faithful followers!

We proceed to observe,

The ends which the death of Christ accomplished
In them, though there is much which is peculiar to himself, yet there is also much in which we are made conformable to him.

We acquiesce in what Christ has done and suffered
Did he satisfy divine justice, and thereby open the way of salvation? Certainly, it is not for us to attempt anything like this; but, by believing in him, we acquiesce in what he has done and suffered, and so are made conformable to it. Nor is this confined to our first believing: the more we know of Christ, and the power of his resurrection, and the fellowship of his sufferings, the more we are, in this way, made conformable to his death. The death of Christ will give the impression to the very enjoyment of heaven. "The Lamb that was slain"[31] will be the theme of the song forever.

We wage war with sin
Was he "manifested to destroy the works of the devil?"[32] If we are made

---

[29] 2 Timothy 2:12.
[30] 2 Corinthians 4:8–10.
[31] Revelation 13:8.
[32] 1 John 3:8.

conformable to his death, we also shall wage war with them. If we live in sin, we are of the devil, and must needs be at variance with the death of Christ; sparing that which he was manifested in human nature to destroy. The finished work of Christ upon the cross did not supersede the necessity of our being active in overcoming evil. We must set our feet upon the necks of these spiritual enemies, taking a part in their destruction. Neither did it supersede the necessity of our active perseverance in the use of all means by which we may disengage our souls from the entanglements of sin, praying and struggling from under its dominion, perfecting holiness in the fear of God. It is thus that we have to "work out our own salvation with fear and trembling,"[33] which, instead of superseding the death of Christ, is being made conformable to it. From his having died for sin, we are exhorted to die to it, and to live to God. We cannot enter into the end of Christ's death, which was to make an end of sin, unless we become dead to sin; nor into his resurrection, without rising with him into newness of life!

In waging war with sin, it is necessary to begin with ourselves, but not to end there. If we are made conformable to the death of Christ, we shall be adverse to sin wherever we find it; avoiding all participation in it through complaisance or worldly interest, and uniting to promote sobriety, righteousness, and godliness in its place.

We seek the salvation of sinners
Finally, Christ died "to save sinners;" and if we are made conformable to his death, we also shall seek their salvation. Some of the first thoughts which occur to a believer's mind, on having found rest for his own soul, respect the salvation of his kindred and acquaintance; and the direction given to one who had obtained mercy gives countenance to such thoughts and desires: "Go home to your friends, and tell them how great things the Lord has done for you, and has had compassion on you."[34]

It is not for ministers only to take an interest in the salvation of men; the army of the Lamb is composed of the whole body of Christians. Every disciple of Jesus should consider himself as a missionary. All, indeed, are not apostles, nor evangelists, nor preachers; but all must be engaged in

---

[33] Philippians 2:12.
[34] Mark 5:19.

serving the Lord: some by preaching, some by contributing of their substance, and all by prayer and recommending the Saviour by a holy conversation.

The death of Christ stands connected, in the divine promise, with the salvation of sinners. This is "the travail of his soul," which he was to see, and be satisfied; the "joy set before him," in view of which he endured the cross, and despised the shame. To be made conformable to his death, therefore, we must combine that which God has combined with it. It is a high honour conferred on us to be instruments in thus saving our fellow sinners, and in thus crowning our Redeemer; nor will it be less advantageous to us, since he has said, "To him that overcomes will I grant to sit with me in my throne, even as I also overcame, and am set down with my Father in his throne."[35]

---

[35] Revelation 3:21.

3
Preparing Sermons to Preach Christ

Andrew Fuller was first and foremost a pastor and a preacher. His activities as a theologian, apologist, itinerant evangelist, missions advocate, and administrator were all derivatives of his primary calling as a shepherd of the word of Christ in a local church. Keith S. Grant rightly contends that for Andrew Fuller,

> evangelical renewal did not take place alongside the local church, but especially in congregational ecclesiology, there was a transformation within the existing pastoral office, as it became in the words of a Kettering deacon and diarist, "very affecting and evangelical."[1]

The faithful ministry and passion of a local church pastor in the small English market town of Kettering, a town with a population of about 3,500 people, had global gospel impact.

By 1781, through reading John Bunyan, John Owen, David Brainerd, Jonathan Edwards, and through countless conversations with friends Robert Hall (1728-1791), John Ryland Jr. (1753-1825), and John Sutcliff (1752-1814), and most importantly, an intense study of the Scriptures, Fuller's conscience would not allow him to continue on the same course of his previous ministry labors. He became convinced that his preaching ministry was defective in that it said far less than Scripture regarding exhortations for all hearers to repent and believe in Christ. Nothing would so define Fuller's ministry and preaching passion as his seminal work, *The Gospel of Christ Worthy of All Acceptation*. Michael Haykin refers to *The Gospel Worthy* as the foundational document for a missionary spirituality.[2] Haykin also asserts, "With regard to Fuller's own ministry, the

---

[1] Keith S. Grant, *Andrew Fuller and the Evangelical Renewal of Pastoral Theology* (Milton Keynes: Paternoster, 2013), 2-3.

[2] Michael Haykin ed., *The Armies of the Lamb: The Spirituality of Andrew Fuller* (Dundas: Joshua Press, 2001), 29.

book was a key factor in determining the shape of that ministry in the years to come."[3]

He had come to believe that it was a dangerous error to teach, as he previously had, and as was common in his sphere of ministry, that only sinners who were distressed about their spiritual condition had the right or warrant to believe on Christ. Fuller became convinced that genuine faith is centered on Christ. Rather than placing an inordinate focus on the self, to see if signs were evident to provide warrant for faith, Fuller became entrenched in the idea that the Scripture mandates the free offer of salvation to sinners without distinction. To put it simply, Fuller believed that it is the duty of all to put their faith in Christ, and it is the duty of pastors to preach the gospel to all without distinction. *The Gospel Worthy* was a manifesto for that kind of promiscuous gospel preaching, which would in turn produce missionary Christians. As Fuller avers, "The true churches of Jesus Christ travail in birth for the salvation of men. They are the armies of the Lamb, the grand object of whose existence is to extend the Redeemer's kingdom."[4] He adds, "Every disciple of Jesus should consider himself as a missionary."[5]

Sermons that equip the army of the Lamb

Fuller was concerned with the process of preparing sermons because he believed preaching was an act of spiritual war. To young ministers, Fuller said, "It is a work to which you may expect great opposition—Satan will dispute every inch of ground with you, and his opposition will be varied."[6] He believed the gospel mission of the church mandated willing sacrifice and suffering. He wrote, "The very existence of Christian churches is in subserviency to the preaching of the gospel; or they would not have been described as 'golden candlesticks,' the use of which is to impart light to those around them."[7] He continued,

> The primitive churches were not mere assemblies of men who agreed to meet together once or twice a week, and to subscribe for

---

[3] Michael Haykin, "Introduction," in *The Works of Andrew Fuller* (Carlisle: The Banner of Truth Trust, 2007), ii.
[4] Fuller, "The Promise of the Spirit," *Complete Works*, 3:359.
[5] Fuller, "Conformity to the Death of Christ," *Complete Works*, 1:315.
[6] Fuller, "The Christian Ministry a Great Work," *Complete Works*, 1:514.
[7] Fuller, "The Pastor's Address," *Complete Works*, 3:345.

the support of an accomplished man who should on those occasions deliver lectures on religion. They were men gathered out of the world by the preaching of the cross, and formed into society for the promotion of Christ's kingdom in their own souls and in the world around them. It was not the concern of the ministers or elders only; the body of the people were interested in all that was done, and, according to their several abilities and stations, took part in it. Neither were they assemblies of heady, high-minded, contentious people, meeting together to argue on points of doctrine or discipline, and converting the worship of God into scenes of strife. They spoke the truth; but it was in love: they observed discipline; but, like an army of chosen men, it was that they might attack the kingdom of Satan to greater advantage. Happy were it for our churches if we could come to a closer imitation of this model![8]

Fuller believed that not only was gospel preaching vital, but that the manner of preaching should provide evidence that the preacher knows that he is engaging in spiritual battle, and that eternity hangs in the balance. In his diary on February 5, 1781, Fuller expressed his understanding of the weight of the preaching task,

A pulpit seems an awful place!—An opportunity for addressing a company of immortals on their eternal interests—Oh how important! We preach for eternity. We in a sense are set for the rising and falling of many in Israel. And our own rise or fall is equally therein involved.[9]

In an ordination charge, Fuller exhorted, "You may preach even the gospel dryly. It must be preached faithfully, firmly, earnestly, affectionately. The apostle so spoke that many believed. Manner is a means of conveying truth. A cold manner disgraces important truth."[10] Fuller warns about the danger of preaching an "unfelt gospel,"[11]

When we are thinking or preaching, we need to *burn*, as well as shine. When we study, we may rack our brains, and form plans;

---

[8] Fuller, "The Pastor's Address," *Complete Works*, 3:346.
[9] Fuller, "Memoirs," *Complete Works*, 1:25.
[10] Fuller, "Affectionate Concern of a Minister," *Complete Works*, 1:510.
[11] Fuller, "Ministers Should Be Concerned Not to Be Despised," *Complete Works*, 1:489.

Preparing sermons

but unless "our hearts burn within us," all will be mere skeleton—our thoughts mere bones; whatever be their number, they will all be dry—very dry; and if we do not feel what we say, our preaching will be poor dead work. Affected zeal will not do. A gilded fire may shine, but it will not warm. We may smite with the hand, and stamp with the foot, and throw ourselves into violent agitations; but if we feel not, it is not likely the people will—unless, indeed, it be a feeling of disgust.[12]

Expository preaching and the biblical context

Fuller was committed to expository preaching that was doctrinal, practical, and Christ-centered. He was also committed to extemporaneous preaching utilizing scant notes. Thus, the only full sermon manuscripts we have of Fuller are those that were prepared for publication. Biographer J.W. Morris says of Fuller's commitment to biblical exposition, "had his life been continued, he would, in all probability, have completed his exposition of the sacred volume."[13] He explains his commitment to preach the whole counsel of God,

> Be concerned to have treasures, and to bring them forth. I would advise that one service of every Sabbath consist of a well-digested exposition, that your hearers may become Bible Christians. Be concerned to understand and to teach the doctrine of Christianity—"the truth as it is in Jesus."[14]

After preaching for twenty-two years at the Baptist Church in Kettering, Fuller wrote in the dedicatory preface to his *Expository Discourses on the Book of Genesis*, "I acknowledge that, as I have proceeded, the work of exposition has become more and more interesting to my heart."[15] He explained the benefit to both the preacher and the congregation of a steady diet of expository sermons,

> I have found it not a little useful, both to myself and to the people, to appropriate one part of every Lord's day to the exposition of a

---

[12] Fuller, "Knowledge and Love Essential to the Ministry," *Complete Works*, 1:480.

[13] J.W. Morris, *Memoirs of the life and writings of the Rev. Andrew Fuller, late pastor of the Baptist church at Kettering, and first secretary to the Baptist Missionary Society* (Boston: Lincoln and Edmands, 1830), 72.

[14] Fuller, "Ministers and Churches Exhorted," *Complete Works*, 1:544.

[15] Fuller, "Expository Discourses on the Book of Genesis," *Complete Works*, 3:1.

chapter, or part of a chapter, in the sacred writings. In this way, during the last eighteen years, I have gone over the greater part of the Old Testament, and some books in the New. It is advantageous to a minister to feel himself necessitated, as it were, to understand every part of Scripture, in order to explain it to the people. It is also advantageous to a people that what they hear should come directly from the word of God, and that they should be led to see the scope and connexion of the sacred writers.[16]

Fuller's language about seeing the scope and connection of the text is important to understanding his method. He was committed to understanding each passage of Scripture in its immediate context but also within the larger biblical Christ-centered canonical context. Fuller, referring to this contextual understanding stated, "The great thing necessary for expounding the Scriptures is to enter into their true meaning."[17] He often uses "true meaning" or "true system" language to signify his commitment that no particular text or truth is rightly understood when it is abstracted from either the biblical storyline or redemptive history because to do so would inevitably lead to a false meaning. Fuller warns,

> I shall attempt to show the importance of a true system; and to prove that truth itself, by being displaced from those connections which it occupies in the Scriptures, may be perverted, and prove injurious to those that hold it. No system can be supposed to be wholly erroneous; but if a considerable part of it be false, the whole will be vitiated, and that which is true will be divested of its salutary influence. "If you be circumcised," said the apostle to the Galatians, "Christ shall profit you nothing."[18] As one truth, thoroughly imbibed, will lead to a hundred more, so will one error. False doctrine will eat as doth a gangrene,[19] which, though it may seem to be confined to one part of the body, infects the whole mass, and, if not extracted, must issue in death.[20]

Fuller goes on in his letter "Importance of a True System," to argue that when true ideas are incorporated into a false system, what we might

---

[16] Fuller, "Letter I, Expounding the Scriptures," *Complete Works*, 1:712.
[17] Fuller, "Letter I, Expounding the Scriptures," *Complete Works*, 1:712.
[18] Galatians 5:2.
[19] 2 Timothy 2:17.
[20] Fuller, "The Importance of a True System," *Complete Works*, 1:685.

call a worldview, the result is delusion, because no particular scriptural truth is meant to be understood apart from its larger scriptural connections. He illustrates this point with reference to Israel,

> The Jews, in the time of our Saviour, professed the same creed, in the main, as their forefathers; they reckoned themselves to believe Moses; but, holding with Moses to the exclusion of Christ, their faith was rendered void. "If ye believed Moses," said our Lord, "ye would believe me; for he wrote of me."[21] Thus it is with us: if we hold the law of Moses to the exclusion of Christ, or any otherwise than as subservient to the gospel, or Christ and the gospel to the exclusion of the law of Moses, neither the one nor the other will profit us.[22]

Fuller adds,

> God's election of the posterity of Abraham was of sovereign favour, and not on account of any excellence in them, natural or moral; in which view it was humbling, and no doubt had a good effect on the godly Israelites. But the Jews in our Saviour's time turned this their national election into another kind of doctrine, full of flattery towards themselves, and of the most intolerable contempt and malignity towards others. And thus the doctrine of "eternal and personal election viewed in a similar light becomes a source of pride, bitterness, sloth, and presumption. Conceive of the love of God as capricious fondness—imagine, because it had no inducement from the goodness of the creature, that therefore it was without reason, only so it was and so it must be—view it, not as a means by which God would assert the sovereignty of his grace, but as an end to which everything must become subservient—conceive of yourself as a darling of heaven, a favourite of providence, for whom divine interpositions next to miracles are continually occurring—and, instead of being humbled before God as a poor sinner, you will feel like a person who in a dream or a reverie imagines himself a king, takes state to himself, and treats every one about him with distant contempt.[23]

---

[21] John 5:46.
[22] Fuller, "The Importance of a True System," *Complete Works*, 1:68.
[23] Fuller, "The Importance of a True System," *Complete Works*, 1:687.

Fuller is critical of approaches to expository preaching that lose the larger biblical scope, connections, and canonical meaning of the text in favor of monotonous, myopic textual concerns and proof texting. He explains, "The scope of the sacred writers is of greater importance in understanding the Scriptures than the most critical examination of terms, or the most laborious comparison of the use of them in different places."[24] The preacher is to call hearers to apply their lives to the testimony of the story of Scripture and not merely isolate and abstract truths in an individualized way. He cautions,

> We may read them, and talk about them, again and again, without imparting any light concerning them. If the hearer, when you have done, understand no more of that part of Scripture than he did before, your labour is lost. Yet this is commonly the case with those attempts at expounding which consist of little else than comparing parallel passages, or, by the help of a concordance, tracing the use of the same word in other places, going from text to text till both the preacher and the people are wearied and lost. This is troubling the Scriptures rather than expounding them. If I were to open a chest of oranges among my friends, and, in order to ascertain their quality, were to hold up one, and lay it down; then hold up another, and say, This is like the last; then a third, a fourth, a fifth, and so on, till I came to the bottom of the chest, saying of each, It is like the other; of what account would it be? The company would doubtless be weary, and had much rather have tasted two or three of them.[25]

The expositor, according to Fuller, needs to be so familiar with the biblical testimony in the pursuit of "the true meaning of the Scriptures" that they "drink into the spirit of the writers." He clarifies this statement by explaining he is not suggesting a mystical direct revelatory inspiration apart from the Scriptures, but rather "a spiritual frame of mind," or what is described as "unction from the Holy One," by which "he can understand more of the Scriptures in an hour than he can at other times, with the utmost application, in a week."[26] Fuller's commitment to the absolute sufficiency of the Scripture is demonstrated in a letter he wrote to a

---

[24] Fuller, "Letter I, Expounding the Scriptures," *Complete Works*, 1:713.
[25] Fuller, "Letter I, Expounding the Scriptures," *Complete Works*, 1:712–713.
[26] Fuller, "Letter I, Expounding the Scriptures," *Complete Works*, 1:713.

church member in which he declared, "we ought not look for any new revelation of the mind of God, but to rest satisfied with what has been revealed already, in his word."[27]

In an article for *Evangelical Magazine* titled "Thoughts on the Manner which Divine Truth is Communicated in the Holy Scriptures," Fuller noted that God did not reveal himself to us in an abstract and hyper-systematized fashion, but rather in the context of particular examples in redemptive history. He writes,

> It is a fact which must have struck every attentive reader, that God has not communicated his mind to us by giving us a set of principles, arranged in the form of a scheme; or that we have no such creed as formally includes all the things necessary to be believed in either the Old or New Testament. On the contrary, we see divine truth introduced rather incidentally than systematically. It is scattered from one end to the other, through all the historical, devotional, prophetic, and epistolary writings.[28]

As mentioned in chapter 1, Fuller's description of biblical truth as being introduced "incidentally," points to the fact the Scriptural revelation is progressive and rooted in history. In other words, the Bible provides a narrative framework of historical interaction with image bearers, which makes it important to know how biblical texts fit together. Understanding what Fuller often calls the "connections" of Scripture is vital for effectively calling sermon hearers to apply themselves to biblical truth—having the story of the hearer's lives transformed by the gospel story of the Bible. He writes,

> The conduct of God in this matter resembles that of a wise physician, who, in prescribing for a child, directs that its medicines be mixed up with its necessary food.
> Moreover, Scripture doctrines being introduced in some practical connection, we learn them in that connection. The occasions

---

[27] Fuller, as quoted in John Ryland, *The Work of Faith, the Labor of Love and the Patience of Hope Illustrated in the Life and Death of the Rev. Andrew Fuller* (London: Button and Son, 1818), 376.

[28] Fuller, "Thoughts on the Manner which Divine Truth Is Communicated," *Complete Works*, 3:537.

and ends of truth being associated in our minds with the truth itself, the great design of God in giving us a revelation, which is to sanctify our spirits and fit us for every good word and work, is more effectually answered. To one that has learned truth from the Scriptures, and in whom it dwells richly, in all wisdom and spiritual understanding, it is scarcely possible to think of a doctrine but in connection with its correspondent duties, or of a duty without the principles by which it is enforced.[29]

According to Fuller, preachers would do well to understand that the way God has chosen to reveal himself in Scripture reflects his wisdom and allows hearers to be exposed to the whole mind of God. God's design in imbedding his self-revelation in biblical redemptive history helps to safeguard from picking and choosing certain doctrinal categories and elevating them out of proper biblical proportion. Thus, as the Bible is preached on its own terms, listeners gradually gain a better understanding and commitment to biblical doctrine and principles without necessarily recognizing them as such.

Preparation and dependence in preaching
Fuller was described as approaching his pastoral labors with "constitutional ardour."[30] According to a letter Fuller's wife wrote to Ryland upon his death, when she warned him against wearing himself out in his pastoral and mission's efforts and suggested that he needed recreation, he replied, "Oh no: all my recreation is a change of work." She continued, "If I expressed an apprehension that he would soon wear himself out, he would reply, 'I cannot be worn out in a better cause. We must work while it is day;' or, 'Whatever thy hand findeth to do, do it with all thy might.'"[31]

Upon his death, his wife Ann said, "I am fully persuaded that my dear husband fell a sacrifice to his unremitting application to the concerns of the mission, but I dare not murmur. The Lord has done as it pleased him; and I know that whatever he does is right."[32] In *The Baptist Heritage*,

---

[29] Fuller, "Thoughts on the Manner Which Divine Truth Is Communicated," *Complete Works*, 3:540.
[30] Fuller, "Memoirs," *Complete Works*, 1:34.
[31] Fuller, "Memoirs," *Complete Works*, 1:110.
[32] Fuller, "Memoirs," *Complete Works*, 1:110.

Preparing sermons

Leon McBeth described Fuller as a diligent, focused, hard-working pastor,

> A man of incredible energy, Fuller slept little, worked tirelessly, and took little thought for rest or ease. While some majored on the devotional aspects of religion, Fuller's strength turned to the intellectual and practical aspects of faith. While engaged in his study and writing, he was reluctant to be disturbed by casual visitors. When such appeared, Fuller would block the door with his massive frame, deal with them as quickly as possible, sometimes by glancing at and pointing to a plaque on the wall reading, "He who steals my purse steals my money; he who steals my time steals my life."[33]

Fuller's advice to pastors on preparation for the pulpit combined a commitment to hard, diligent, exegetical work, and an utter dependence on the supernatural grace of God. In a letter on sermon preparation, Fuller wrote, "Though we must think for ourselves, we must not depend on ourselves, but, as little children, learn at the feet of the Saviour."[34] Fuller warned about using divine favor as an excuse for inadequate preparation, "It is a shameful abuse of the doctrine of divine influence to allege it as a reason for neglecting diligent study for the pulpit."[35] In Fuller's biography of Samuel Pearce, he includes a letter from Pearce to a young minister explaining his personal approach to sermon preparation as a model for other ministers to follow,

> Could I choose my frames, I would say respecting industry in preparation for public work, as is frequently said respecting Christian obedience—I would apply as close as though I expected no help from the Lord, whilst I would depend upon the Lord for assistance as though I had never made any preparation at all.[36]

---

[33] H. Leon McBeth, *The Baptist Heritage: Four Centuries of Baptist Witness* (Nashville: Broadman Press, 1987), 182.
[34] Fuller, "Letter II, Sermons—Subject-Matter of Them," *Complete Works*, 1:714.
[35] Fuller, "Habitual Devotedness to the Ministry," *Complete Works*, 1:506.
[36] Samuel Pearce as quoted in Fuller, "To a young Minister, Mr. Cave, of Leicester, on preparation for the pulpit," *Complete Works*, 3:442; See also Andrew Fuller, *The Life of Samuel Pearce* (Peterborough: H&E Publishing, 2020), 154.

According to Fuller, it is only after the preacher becomes personally conversant with a portion of Scripture, by prayerfully reading and pondering the Scriptural text as a Christian, and not simply as a preacher or student, that the he should consult biblical commentaries. He writes,

> When I have read a psalm or chapter, which I mean to expound, and have endeavoured to understand it, I have commonly thought it right to consult the best expositors I could obtain, trying and comparing my ideas with theirs. Hereby I have generally obtained some interesting thought which had not occurred to me, and sometimes have seen reason to retract what before appeared to me to be the meaning. But to go first to expositors is to preclude the exercise of your own judgment; and, after all, that which is furnished by the labours of another, though equally good in itself, will be far less interesting to us than that which is the result of our own application.[37]

In "Reading the Scriptures," Fuller explains why the preacher should not turn to commentaries too soon for help in sermon preparation,

> I do not mean to depreciate the labours of those who have commented on the sacred writings; but we may read expositors, and consult critics, while the "spirit and life" of the word utterly escape us. A tender, humble, holy frame is perhaps of more importance to our entering into the mind of the Holy Spirit than all other means united. It is thus that, by "an unction from the Holy One, we know all things." In reading by myself, I have also felt the advantage of being able to pause, and think, as well as pray; and to inquire how far the subject is any way applicable to my case, and conduct in life.
> In the course of a morning's exercise it may be supposed that some things will appear hard to be understood; and I may feel myself, after all my application, unable to resolve them. Here, then, let me avail myself of commentators and expositors. If I read them instead of reading the Scriptures, I may indeed derive some knowledge; but my mind will not be stored with the best riches; nor will the word "dwell richly in me in all wisdom and spiritual understanding." If, on the other hand, I read the Scriptures, and

---

[37] Fuller, "Letter II, Sermons—Subject-Matter of Them," *Complete Works*, 1:714.

exercise my own mind on their meaning, only using the helps with which I am furnished when I particularly need them, such knowledge will avail me more than any other; for, having felt and laboured at the difficulty myself, what I obtain from others towards the solution of it becomes more interesting and abiding than if I had read it without any such previous efforts. And as to my own thoughts, though they may not be superior nor equal to those of others, in themselves considered, yet, if they be just, their having been the result of pleasing toil renders them of superior value to me. A small portion obtained by our own labour is sweeter than a large inheritance bequeathed by our predecessors. Knowledge thus obtained will not only be always accumulating, but of special use in times of trial; not like the cumbrous armour which does not fit us, but like the sling and the stone, which, though less brilliant, will be more efficacious.[38]

Biographer J.W. Morris notes, "The composition of a sermon seldom cost Mr. Fuller much trouble; owing to his constant habits of thinking, it was generally the easiest part of all his labours."[39] He added, "His mind retained a verdant freshness, capable of new productions; and his daily converse with the Scriptures rendered it an agreeable task, to combine the varieties of thought which they suggested."[40] Further Morris contends, "he was all intent on searching out its riches, sounding its depth, comparing it with the analogy of faith, pointing out its application, and deducing consequences, seldom obvious to the hearer, but meeting his judgment in all their force, and carrying conviction to the heart."[41] The point is not that Fuller was slack in sermon preparation but rather that his mind was always engaged in thinking about the gospel in every aspect of life in such a way that sermon preparation was, in a sense, perpetually occurring.

Fuller also believed that part of the preparation to preach effectively included a study of the people to whom you preach as well as a study of the scriptural text. He believed the preacher must be aware of the way his listeners viewed the world and the ways in which they struggle so he

---

[38] Fuller, "Reading the Scriptures," *Complete Works*, 3:788-789.

[39] J.W. Morris, *Memoirs of the Life of the Rev. Andrew Fuller, Late Pastor of the Baptist Church at Kettering, and the First Secretary to the Baptist Missionary Society* (Boston: Lincoln and Edmands, 1830), 70.

[40] Morris, *Memoirs of the Life of the Rev. Andrew Fuller*, 71.

[41] Morris, *Memoirs of the Life of the Rev. Andrew Fuller*, 72.

could effectively press and apply the gospel at the point of their greatest need. By "experimental preaching," Fuller means preaching that is pointed and applicable in a way that it penetrates the affections of the heart. Frustrated with his own failings in this area Fuller confessed in his diary on July 29, 1780,

> Surely, I do not study the cases of the people enough in my preaching. I find by conversation today, with one seemingly in dying circumstances, that but little of my preaching has been suited to her case. Visiting the sick, and conversing sometimes even with the unconverted part of my hearers about their souls, and especially with the godly, would have a tendency to make my preaching more experimental.[42]

He believed that the faithful proclamation of the truth demanded that scriptural truth be applied to the consciences and "the cases of the people." Doing so meant that preparation to preach included studying the congregants as well as the Scripture. He explains, "We must trace the workings of a depraved heart, in order to detect its shiftings and subterfuges—the doubts and difficulties of a desponding heart, in order to remove them, and to point out the way of life—and the general operations of a gracious heart, in order to distinguish between genuine and spurious religion, lest, while we comfort the real Christian, we should soothe the hypocrite."[43]

Plain, urgent, Christian speech—sermon delivery and notes

Fuller urged the preacher not to think of himself as a formally trained and polished orator performing for his listeners, but rather as a "herald, whose object is to publish, or proclaim good tidings."[44] His preaching style was direct, simple, and urgent. Morris explains in a lengthy and blunt description of Fuller's sermon delivery,

> As a preacher he soon became popular, without any of the ordinary means of popularity. He had none of that easy elocution, none of the graceful fluency, which melts upon the ear, and captivates the

---

[42] Fuller, "Memoirs," *Complete Works*, 1:23.
[43] Fuller, "Ministers Fellow Laborers with God," *Complete Works*, 1:492.
[44] Fuller, "Sermon—Subject-Matter of Them," *Complete Works*, 1:717.

Preparing sermons

attention of an auditor. His enunciation was laborious and slow; his voice strong and heavy; occasionally plaintive, and capable of an agreeable modulation. He had none of that eloquence which consists in a felicitous selection of terms, or in the harmonious construction of periods; he had a boldness in his manner, a masculine delivery, and great force of expression. His style was often deformed by colloquialisms and coarse provincials; but in the roughest of his compositions, "the bones of a giant might be seen."

In entering the pulpit he studied very little decorum, and often hastened out of it with the appearance of precipitation; but while there he seldom failed to acquit himself with honor and success. His attitude, too, was sufficiently negligent. Not aware of his awkwardness, in the course of his delivery he would insensibly place one hand upon his breast, or behind him, and gradually twist off button from his coat, which some of his domestics had the frequent occasion to replace. The habit was in process of time much corrected, and many other protuberances were smoothed away by the improvement of his taste, and the collisions of society; but certainly in these respects he was not the model of an orator.

His presence in the pulpit was imposing, grave, and manly; tending to inspire awe, rather than conciliate esteem.[45]

Morris' assertion that Fuller "was not the model of an orator" is interesting in light of the fact Fuller directly stated "In preaching the gospel, we must not imitate the orator whose attention is taken up with his performance, but rather the herald."[46] Elsewhere Fuller said in an ordination sermon, "I abhor the spirit that shall send for an orator, merely for the purpose of gathering a respectable congregation."[47] Fuller advises preachers:

Avoid all affectation in your manner. Do not affect the man of learning by useless criticisms, many do this, only to display their knowledge. Nor yet the orator, by high-sounding words, or airs, or gestures. Useful learning and an impressive delivery should by no

---

[45] Morris, *Memoirs of the Life of the Rev. Andrew Fuller*, 68–69.
[46] Fuller, "Letter II, Sermons—Subject-Matter of Them," *Complete Works*, 1:716.
[47] Fuller, "The Work and Encouragements of a Christian Minister," *Complete Works*, 1:499.

means be slighted; but they must not be affected, or men will be sure to despise you.[48]

According to Paul Brewster, John Ryland, another Fuller friend and biographer "implied that Morris was less than charitable at some points in his memoirs," noting that Fuller and Morris had a personal rift over Morris's bankruptcy.[49] Nevertheless, I do not think Fuller would have objected to Morris's critiques because they were all regarding things that in Fuller's appraisal were of secondary importance in sermon delivery. Fuller affirms the words of his friend Samuel Pearce who urged a young minister,

> Divest yourself of all fear. If you should break the rules of grammar, or put in or leave out a word, and recollect at the end of the sentence the impropriety, unless it makes nonsense, or bad divinity, never try to mend it, but let it pass.[50]

Fuller taught that plain, passionate speech, and simplicity of style were necessary components for effective Christ-centered expository sermons. According to Fuller, "The form or manner in which a sermon is composed and delivered is of some importance, inasmuch as it influences the attention, and renders the matter delivered more or less easy of being comprehended and retained."[51] He warned, "There are many sermons that cannot fairly be charged with untruth, which yet have a tendency to lead off the mind from the simplicity of the gospel."[52] Fuller explains his commitment to sermonic plainness of speech,

> In general, I do not think a minister of Jesus Christ should aim at fine composition for the pulpit. We ought to use sound speech, and good sense; but if we aspire after great elegance of expression, or become very exact in the formation of our periods, though we may

---

[48] Fuller, "Ministers Appointed to Root out Evil, and to Cultivate Good," *Complete Works*, 1:489.

[49] Paul Brewster, *Andrew Fuller: Model Pastor-Theologian* (Nashville: Broadman and Holman Academic, 2010), 114.

[50] Samuel Pearce as quoted in Fuller, "To a young Minister, Mr. Cave, of Leicester, on preparation for the pulpit," *Complete Works*, 3:443.

[51] Fuller, "Letter 3: The Composition of a sermon," *Complete Works*, 1:717.

[52] Fuller, "The Qualifications and Encouragement of a Faithful Minister," *Complete Works*, 1:140.

amuse and please the ears of a few, we shall not profit the many, and consequently shall not answer the great end of our ministry. Illiterate hearers may be very poor judges of preaching; yet the effect which it produces upon them is the best criterion of its real excellence.[53]

Fuller did not envision preaching as reading the results of one's exegesis but rather he was committed to preparing sermons with orality in mind because the sermon is what is said and not what is written down by the preacher. Below is a list where I have enumerated some of Fuller's advice from "Letter IV, The Composition of a Sermon."

1. Do not overload your memory with words.
2. Write down a few leading things for the sake of arrangement and assistance of memory; but not a great deal. Memory must not be overburdened.
3. Never carry what you write into the pulpit.
4. Avoid vulgar expressions: do not affect finical [unnecessarily elaborate] ones, nor words out of common use.
5. As to division and arrangement, it barely respects the assortment of your materials. You must endeavour to understand and feel your subject, or the manner in which you divide it will signify but little.
6. But if both these may be taken for granted, then I should say much depends, as to your being heard with pleasure and profit, on a proper discussion and management of the subject. At all events avoid a multiplying of heads and particulars. A few well-chosen thoughts, matured, proved, and improved, are abundantly more acceptable than when the whole is chopped, as it were, into mincemeat.[54]

---

[53] Fuller, "Letter 3: The Composition of a Sermon," *Complete Works*, 1:717.
[54] Fuller, "Letter 4: The Composition of a Sermon," *Complete Works*, 1:724.

Fuller offers this blunt assertion, "To preach the gospel as we ought to preach it requires, not the subtlety of the metaphysician, but the simplicity of the Christian."[55] He explains his commitment to urgently prepare and deliver gospel sermons in plain Christian speech, and to do so with eternity in view,

> In preparing for the pulpit, it would be well to reflect in some such manner as this: I am expected to preach, it may be to some hundreds of people, some of whom may come several miles to hear; and what have I to say to them? Is it for me to sit here studying a text merely to find something thing to say to fill up the hour? I may do this without imparting any useful instruction, without commending myself to any man's conscience, and without winning, or even aiming to win, one soul to Christ. It is possible there may be in the audience a poor miserable creature, labouring under the load of a guilty conscience. If he departs without being told how to obtain rest for his soul, what may be the consequence? Or, it may be, some stranger may be there who has never heard the way of salvation in his life. If he should depart without hearing it now, and should die before another opportunity occurs, how shall I meet him at the bar of God? Possibly some one of my constant hearers may die in the following week; and is there nothing I should wish to say to him before his departure? It may be that I myself may die before another Lord's Day: this may be the last time that I shall ascend the pulpit; and have I no important testimony to leave with the people of my care?[56]

Unity of design

As we have already noted, Fuller believed the preacher needs to approach the text personally, as a Christian, with faith and prayer, because he needs a spiritual frame of mind to rightly understand the Scriptures. His approach demands patient and thoughtful meditation on the Scripture and its central message—Jesus Christ. Fuller urged that after the preacher had recruited his leading truths and thoughts from his study of the text, he must then "arrange them in order, or to give each thought

---

[55] Fuller, "The Nature of the Gospel," *Complete Works*, 1:496.
[56] Fuller, "Sermons—the Subject Matter of Them," *Complete Works*, 1:715–716.

Preparing sermons

that place in your discourse which it will occupy to the greatest advantage."[57] Fuller approves of his friend Samuel Pearce's advice to a young minister, "First, endeavour to think in a train. Let one idea depend upon another in your discourses, as one link does upon another in a chain."[58] Fuller explains the problem of sermons that are not marked by a unity of design,

> Many sermons are a mob of ideas; they contain very good sentiments, but they have no object in view; so that the hearer is continually answering the preacher, "Very true, very true; but what then? What is it you are aiming at? What is this to the purpose?" A preacher, then, if he would interest a judicious hearer, must have an object at which he aims, and must never lose sight of it throughout his discourse. This is what writers on these subjects call a unity of design; and this is a matter of far greater importance than studying well-turned periods or forming pretty expressions. It is this that nails the attention of an audience. One thing at once is a maxim in common life, by which the greatest men have made the greatest proficiency. Shun, therefore, a multitude of divisions and subdivisions. He who aims to say everything in a single discourse, in effect says nothing. Avoid making a head or particular of every thought. Unity of design may be preserved consistently with various methods of division; but the thing itself is indispensable to good preaching.[59]

Fuller further enumerates his reasons for advocating that sermons have a clear unity of design and connectedness,

1. The human mind is so formed as to delight in unity.[60]
2. It has been said, and I think justly, that evidence should constitute the body or substance of every doctrinal discourse.[61]

---

[57] Fuller, "Letter 3—The Composition of a Sermon," *Complete Works*, 1:719.
[58] Samuel Pearce as quoted in Fuller, "To a young Minister, Mr. Cave, of Leicester, on preparation for the pulpit," *Complete Works*, 3:443.
[59] Fuller, "Letter 3—The Composition of a Sermon," *Complete Works*, 1:719.
[60] Fuller, "Letter 3—The Composition of a Sermon," *Complete Works*, 1:719.
[61] Fuller, "Letter 3—The Composition of a Sermon," *Complete Works*, 1:720.

3. It is greatly assisting to memory, both with respect to the preacher and the hearer. Memory is exercised by the relation of one thing to another.[62]
4. I cannot so well satisfy my conscience unless I have some interesting truth to communicate, or some important duty to enforce.[63]

He illustrates the power of sermonic unity of design with a couple of helpful and vivid illustrations:

> Where this is not the case, the preacher gives himself no opportunity of advancing evidence; consequently his sermon, if it may be so called, will be without body, without substance, and will contain nothing that shall leave any strong impression upon a thinking mind. In opening a battery against a wall, you would not throw your balls at random, first at one place and then at another, but direct your whole force against a particular spot. In the one case your labour would be thrown away; in the other you are likely to make an effectual impression.[64]

> Were you to attempt to remember seven different objects which bore no manner of relation to each other, such as water, time, wisdom, fruit, contentment, fowls, and revenues, you would find it almost impossible; but take seven objects which, though different in nature, yet possess some point of unity, which associates them in the mind, and the work is easy. Thus, sun, moon, stars, earth, air, fire, and water, are readily remembered, being so many principal parts of the one creation.[65]

Bold, heart preaching, applied to the mind and heart

According to Fuller, sermons need to possess a unity of design because faithful sermons are always on a gospel errand to which the preacher is calling all of his listeners to respond. The purpose of the sermon is never merely information but is always gospel transformation. Fuller's sermon delivery was described as bold, courageous, authoritative, urgent, and

---

[62] Fuller, "Letter 3—The Composition of a Sermon," *Complete Works*, 1:720.
[63] Fuller, "Letter 3—The Composition of a Sermon," *Complete Works*, 1:720.
[64] Fuller, "Letter 3—The Composition of a Sermon," *Complete Works*, 1:720.
[65] Fuller, "Letter 3—The Composition of a Sermon," *Complete Works*, 1:720.

manly. Fuller was committed to being a persistent, courageous gospel agitator in the pulpit and he encouraged this kind of dangerous heart preaching in others in other ministers as well,

> You must not calculate consequences as they respect this life. If you would preach the gospel as you ought to preach it, the approbation of God must be your main object. What if you were to lose your friends and diminish your income; nay, what if you lose your liberty, or even your life—what would this all be, compared with the loss of the favour and friendship of God? Woe unto us, if we shun to declare any part of the counsel of God! He that is afraid or ashamed to preach the whole of the gospel, in all its implications and bearings, let him stand aside; he is utterly unworthy of being a soldier of Jesus Christ. Sometimes, if you would speak the whole truth, you may be reproached as unsound and heterodox. But you must not yield to popular clamour. If you have truth on your side, stand firm against all opposition.[66]

Fuller continues,

> The gospel is a message full of importance, and therefore you must be in earnest. If your message respected the health of your hearers, or their temporal interest, or their reputation, it would be thought important. But what are these compared with the salvation of their souls! Salvation by Jesus Christ is God's last remedy—his ultimatum with a lost world (Mark 16:16; Acts 4:12). There remaineth no other sacrifice for sins. Then do not trifle on such subjects as these, lest you lose your own soul. What can be thought of you if you employ your time in making pretty speeches, and turning elegant periods, instead of endeavouring to "save yourself and them that hear you!" What if, instead of beseeching sinners to be reconciled to God, you should crack jokes before them, to excite a laugh![67]

Fuller believed that "there are two main objects to be attained in the work of the Christian ministry—enlightening the minds and affecting the

---

[66] Fuller, "The Nature of the Gospel," *Complete Works*, 1:495.
[67] Fuller, "The Nature of the Gospel," *Complete Works*, 1:495.

hearts of the people."[68] He understood the heart and the mind are inseparable constituent parts of a life surrendered to the glory of God in Christ. Fuller quotes and affirms Jonathan Edwards' *Treatise on the Affections* about the nature of spiritual knowledge,

> And therefore that kind of understanding or knowledge which is the proper foundation of true religion must be the knowledge of the loveliness of divine things. For, doubtless, that knowledge which is the proper foundation of love is the knowledge of loveliness. ... Spiritual understanding primarily consists in this sense, or taste, of the moral beauty of divine things; so that no knowledge can be called spiritual any further than it arises from this, and has this in it. But, secondarily, it includes all that discerning and knowledge of things of religion which depends upon and flows from such a sense.[69]

For Fuller, faithful sermons are Christ-centered biblical expositions which strive to help hearers understand with their mind, and feel with their affections, the truth of the gospel. The preacher must not preach an unfelt gospel and he must not be satisfied with his listeners assenting to an unfelt gospel. In an ordination sermon, Fuller charged the pastor regarding his congregation, "You could never expect to do them good, unless you were interested in their affections."[70] Unapologetically, Fuller preached to move the feelings and affections of his hearers, but he was burdened to do so with scriptural, gospel truth, and not apart from it. The goal of preaching was not moralism or emotionalism but true virtue, the obedience of faith motivated by the gospel—clear and felt.

The Fuller readings to follow were chosen in an attempt to gather in one location his writings that focus specifically on sermon preparation. In "Reading the Scriptures," Fuller briefly explains his commitment to the priority of personally reading and meditating on the Scripture. Then there are a series of letters from Fuller called "Thoughts on Preaching"

---

[68] Fuller, "Spiritual Knowledge and Love Necessary for the Ministry," *Complete Works*, 1:479.

[69] Fuller, "The Connexion Between Knowledge and Disposition," *Complete Works*, 2:603-604. See Chris Chun, *The Legacy of Jonathan Edwards in the Theology of Andrew Fuller* (Leiden: Brill, 2012) for an excellent treatment on Andrew Fuller's theological indebtedness to Jonathan Edwards.

[70] Fuller, "The Work and Encouragements of the Christian Minister," *Complete Works*, 1:497.

written to help young preachers: "Letter I, Expounding the Scriptures," "Letter II, Sermons—Subject-Matter of Them," "Letter III, The Composition of a Sermon," "Letter IV, The Composition of a Sermon." "The Abuse of Allegory in Preaching" was written for *Evangelical Magazine* and focuses on preachers who do not take the biblical text seriously by using the text merely as a springboard for their own fanciful thoughts. Finally, "The Nature and Importance of Walking by Faith" was preached in 1784 at the Northamptonshire Baptist Association is the most complete and lengthy Fuller sermon transcription and provides the reader a window into his style and pulpit approach.

Reading the Scriptures[1]

I do not wish the following remarks to supersede any other answer which may enter more fully into the subject. All I have to offer will be a few hints from my own experience.

Appoint set times for reading Scripture

In the first place, I have found it good to appoint set times for reading the Scriptures; and none have been so profitable as part of the season appropriated to private devotion on rising in the morning. The mind at this time is reinvigorated and unencumbered. To read a part of the Scriptures, previous to prayer, I have found to be very useful. It tends to collect the thoughts, to spiritualize the affections, and to furnish us with sentiments wherewith to plead at a throne of grace. And as reading assists prayer, so prayer assists reading. At these seasons we shall be less in danger of falling into idle speculations, and of perverting Scripture in support of hypotheses. A spiritual frame of mind, as Mr. Pearce[2] somewhere observes, is as a good light in viewing a painting; it will not a little facilitate the understanding of the Scriptures. I do not mean to depreciate the labours of those who have commented on the sacred writings; but we may read expositors, and consult critics, while the "spirit and life" of the word utterly escape us. A tender, humble, holy frame is perhaps of more importance to our entering into the mind of the Holy Spirit than all other means united. It is thus that, by "an unction from the Holy One, we know all things."[3]

In reading by myself, I have also felt the advantage of being able to pause, and think, as well as pray; and to inquire how far the subject is any way applicable to my case, and conduct in life.

Commentaries only after Scripture reading

In the course of a morning's exercise it may be supposed that some things

---

[1] Fuller, "Reading the Scriptures," *Complete Works*, 3:788–789.
[2] Samuel Pearce (1766–1799).
[3] 1 John 2:20.

will appear hard to be understood; and I may feel myself, after all my application, unable to resolve them. Here, then, let me avail myself of commentators and expositors. If I read them instead of reading the Scriptures, I may indeed derive some knowledge; but my mind will not be stored with the best riches; nor will the word "dwell richly in me in all wisdom and spiritual understanding."[4] If, on the other hand, I read the Scriptures, and exercise my own mind on their meaning, only using the helps with which I am furnished when I particularly need them, such knowledge will avail me more than any other; for, having felt and laboured at the difficulty myself, what I obtain from others towards the solution of it becomes more interesting and abiding than if I had read it without any such previous efforts. And as to my own thoughts, though they may not be superior nor equal to those of others, in themselves considered, yet, if they be just, their having been the result of pleasing toil renders them of superior value to me. A small portion obtained by our own labour is sweeter than a large inheritance bequeathed by our predecessors. Knowledge thus obtained will not only be always accumulating, but of special use in times of trial; not like the cumbrous armour which does not fit us, but like the sling and the stone, which, though less brilliant, will be more efficacious.

Commit to write down your thoughts

I may add, it were well for those who can find leisure to commit to writing the most interesting thoughts which occur at these seasons. It is thus that they will be fixed in the memory, and the revision of them may serve to rekindle some of the best sensations in our life.

---

[4] Colossians 3:16

Thoughts on Preaching in Letters to a Young Minister

Letter 1: Expounding the Scriptures[1]

My Dear Brother:

As you have expressed a wish for a few of my thoughts on your principal work as a Christian minister, I will endeavour to comply with your request, persuaded that what I write will be read with candour and seriousness.

The work in which you are engaged is of great importance. To declare the whole counsel of God in such a way as to save yourself and them that hear you—or, if they are not saved, to be pure from their blood—is no small matter. The character of the preaching in an age contributes, more than most other things, to give a character to the Christians of that age. A great and solemn trust, therefore, is reposed in us, of which we must shortly give an account.

The work of a Christian minister, as it respects the pulpit, may be distinguished into two general branches; namely, expounding the Scriptures, and discoursing on divine subjects. In this letter I shall offer a few remarks on the former.

An expository approach

I have found it not a little useful, both to myself and to the people, to appropriate one part of every Lord's Day to the exposition of a chapter, or part of a chapter, in the sacred writings. In this way, during the last eighteen years, I have gone over the greater part of the Old Testament, and some books in the New. It is advantageous to a minister to feel himself necessitated, as it were, to understand every part of Scripture, in order to explain it to the people. It is also advantageous to a people that what they hear should come directly from the word of God, and that they should be led to see the scope and connection of the sacred writers. For

---

[1] Fuller, "Letter 1—Expounding the Scriptures," *Complete Works*, 1:712–714.

want of this, a great number of Scripture passages are misunderstood and misapplied. In going over a book, I have frequently been struck with surprise in meeting with texts which, as they had always occurred to me, I had understood in a sense utterly foreign from what manifestly appeared to be their meaning when viewed in connection with the context.

The great thing necessary for expounding the Scriptures is to enter into their true meaning. We may read them, and talk about them, again and again, without imparting any light concerning them. If the hearer, when you have done, understand no more of that part of Scripture than he did before, your labour is lost. Yet this is commonly the case with those attempts at expounding which consist of little else than comparing parallel passages, or, by the help of a Concordance, tracing the use of the same word in other places, going from text to text till both the preacher and the people are wearied and lost. This is troubling the Scriptures rather than expounding them. If I were to open a chest of oranges among my friends, and, in order to ascertain their quality, were to hold up one, and lay it down; then hold up another, and say, "This is like the last;" then a third, a fourth, a fifth, and so on, till I came to the bottom of the chest, saying of each, "It is like the other;" of what account would it be? The company would doubtless be weary, and had much rather have tasted two or three of them.

A biblical-theological approach
The scope of the sacred writers is of greater importance in understanding the Scriptures than the most critical examination of terms, or the most laborious comparison of the use of them in different places. For want of attending to this, not only particular passages, but whole chapters, are frequently misunderstood. The reasonings of both Christ and his apostles frequently proceed, not upon what is true in fact, but merely in the estimation of the parties addressed; that is to say, they reason with them on their own principles. It was not true that Simon the Pharisee was a little sinner, nor a forgiven sinner, nor that he loved Christ a little, but he thought thus of himself, and upon these principles Christ reasoned with him. It was not true that the Pharisees were just men, and needed no repentance, but such were their thoughts of themselves, and Christ suggested that therefore they had no need of him; for that he came "not to

call the righteous, but sinners to repentance."[2] Finally, It was not true that the Pharisees who murmured at Christ's receiving publicans and sinners had never, like the ninety-nine sheep in the wilderness, gone astray; nor that, like the elder son, they had served God, and never at any time transgressed his commandment; nor that all which God had was theirs: but such were their own views, and Christ reasons with them accordingly. It is as if he had said, be it so that you are righteous and happy; yet why should you murmur at the return of these poor sinners? Now, to mistake the principle on which such reasonings proceed, is to lose all the benefit of them, and to fall into many errors.

A spiritual frame of mind
Moreover, to enter into the true meaning of the Scriptures, it is absolutely necessary that we drink into the spirit of the writers. This is the greatest of all accomplishments. I do not mean that you are to expect a spirit of extraordinary inspiration; but that of power, and of love, and of a sound mind. It is impossible to enter into the sentiments of any great writer without a kindred mind. Who but a Pope, or a Cowper, could have translated Homer? and who can explain the oracles of God, but he who, in a measure, drinks into the same spirit? Every Christian knows by experience that, in a spiritual frame of mind, he can understand more of the Scriptures in an hour than he can at other times, with the utmost application, in a week. It is by an unction from the Holy One that we know all things.

I may add, there are some things which, when known, wonderfully facilitate the knowledge of other things. It is thus that a view of the glory of the divine character and government opens the door to the whole mystery of redemption. It is thus also that a lively faith in the sufferings of Christ, and the glory arising out of them, is a key which unlocks a large part of the sacred oracles. While the disciples remained ignorant of his death, they knew but little of the Scriptures; but, having learned the design of this great event, a flood of light poured in upon them, and the Old Testament became plain and deeply interesting.

A humble sense of our own ignorance, and of our entire dependence upon God, has also a great influence on our coming at the true meaning

---

[2] Luke 5:32.

of his word. There are few things which tend more to blind the mind than a conceit of our own powers. Hence we perceive the justness of such language as the following: "Proud, knowing nothing;"[3] "He that thinketh he knoweth anything, knoweth nothing as he ought to know;"[4] "If any man will be wise, let him first become a fool, that he may be wise."[5]

Read Scripture as a Christian

To understand the Scriptures in such a manner as profitably to expound them, it is necessary to be conversant with them in private; and to mix, not only faith, but the prayer of faith, with what we read. There is a great difference between reading the Scriptures as a student, in order to find something to say to the people, and reading them as a Christian, with a view to get good from them to one's own soul. That which is gained in the latter of these ways is, beyond all comparison, of the greatest use, both to ourselves and others. That which we communicate will freeze upon our lips, unless we have first applied it to ourselves; or, to use the language of Scripture, "tasted, felt, and handled the word of life."[6]

Use commentaries after you have your own thoughts

When I have read a psalm or chapter, which I mean to expound, and have endeavoured to understand it, I have commonly thought it right to consult the best expositors I could obtain, trying and comparing my ideas with theirs. Hereby I have generally obtained some interesting thought which had not occurred to me, and sometimes have seen reason to retract what before appeared to me to be the meaning. But to go first to expositors is to preclude the exercise of your own judgment; and, after all, that which is furnished by the labours of another, though equally good in itself, will be far less interesting to us than that which is the result of our own application.

Write down expository notes

I will only add that I have found it not a little useful to keep a book in which I write down all my expository notes, which, though illegible to

---

[3] 1 Timothy 6:4.
[4] 1 Corinthians 8:2.
[5] 1 Corinthians 3:18.
[6] 1 John 1:1.

others, yet answer two purposes to myself: first, by looking them over before I go into the pulpit, I have a clear understanding of every sentence; and, secondly, I can have recourse to them on future occasions.

Letter 2: Sermons—the Subject-Matter of Them[7]

Though expounding the Scriptures be an important part of the public work of a minister, yet it is not the whole of it. There is a great variety of subjects, both in doctrinal and practical religion, which require to be illustrated, established, and improved; which cannot be done in an exposition. Discourses of this kind are properly called sermons.

You request me to give you my thoughts on this part of your work somewhat more particularly. I will endeavour to do so, by considering what must be the matter and the manner of preaching, if we wish to do good to the souls of men.

Unless the subject-matter of your preaching be truly evangelical, you had better be anything than a minister. When the apostle speaks of a necessity being laid upon him to preach the gospel, he might mean that he was not at liberty to relinquish his work in favour of ease, or honour, or any other worldly object; but he was not bound to preach merely, but to preach that doctrine which had been delivered unto him. The same may be said of us; woe unto us if we preach not the gospel!

It may seem to be a very easy thing, with the Bible in our hands, to learn the truth, clear of all impure mixtures, and to make it the subject of our ministry. But it is not so. We talk much of thinking and judging for ourselves; but who can justly pretend to be free from the influences which surround him, especially in early life? We are insensibly, and almost irresistibly, assimilated by the books we read, and the company with which we associate; and the principles current in our age and connections will ordinarily influence our minds. Nor is the danger solely from without: we are "slow of heart"[8] to believe in a doctrine so holy and divine, and prone to deviate at every point. If, therefore, we were wholly to think for ourselves, that were no security for our keeping to the mind of Christ.

---

[7] Fuller, "Sermons—The Subject-Matter of Them," *Complete Works*, 1:714–717.
[8] Luke 24:25.

Preparing sermons

I mention these things, not to deter you from either reading or thinking for yourself; but rather to inculcate the necessity of prayer for divine guidance, and a close adherence to the Scriptures. Though we must think for ourselves, we must not depend upon ourselves, but, as little children, learn at the feet of our Saviour.

If you look over the New Testament, you will find the subject-matter of your preaching briefly yet fully expressed in such language as the following:

- "Preach the word."[9]
- "Preach the gospel."[10]
- "Preach the gospel to every creature."[11]
- "Thus it is written, and thus it behoved Christ to suffer, and to rise from the dead the third day, and that repentance and remission of sins should be preached in his name, among all nations, beginning at Jerusalem."[12]
- "I declare unto you the gospel which I preached unto you, which also ye have received, and wherein ye stand, if ye keep in memory what I preached unto you, unless ye have believed in vain. For I delivered unto you, first of all, that which I also received, how that Christ died for our sins according to the Scriptures; and that he was buried, and that he rose again on the third day according to the Scriptures."[13]
- "We preach Christ crucified."[14]
- "I am determined to know nothing among you but Jesus Christ and him crucified."[15]
- "This is the record, that God hath given unto us eternal life, and this life is in his Son."[16]
- "We are ambassadors for Christ, as though God did beseech men

---

[9] 2 Timothy 4:2
[10] Mark 16:15; Luke 4:18; Acts 16:10; Romans 1:15; 10:15; 15:20; 1 Corinthians 1:17; 9:14, 16, 18; 10:16.
[11] Mark 16:15
[12] Luke 24:46–47.
[13] 1 Corinthians 15:1–4.
[14] 1 Corinthians 1:23.
[15] 1 Corinthians 2:2.
[16] 1 John 5:11.

by us, we pray them in Christ's stead, saying, Be ye reconciled unto God."
- "For he hath made him to be sin for us who knew no sin, that we might be made the righteousness of God in him."[17]
- "I have kept back nothing that was profitable unto you, but have showed you, and have taught you publicly, and from house to house, testifying both to the Jews, and also to the Greeks, repentance toward God, and faith toward our Lord Jesus Christ."[18]

Such, my brother, is the concurrent language of the New Testament. Every one of the foregoing passages contains an epitome of the gospel ministry. You will not expect me to expatiate upon their various connections. I may, however, notice three or four particulars, which follow from them.

Every sermon must be on a gospel errand

First, in every sermon we should have an errand; and one of such importance that if it be received or complied with it will issue in eternal salvation. I say nothing of those preachers who profess to go into the pulpit without an errand, and to depend upon the Holy Spirit to furnish them with one at the time. I write not for them, but for such as make a point of thinking before they attempt to preach. Even of these I have heard some who, in studying their texts, have appeared to me to have no other object in view than to find something to say, in order to fill up the time. This, however, is not preaching, but merely talking about good things. Such ministers, though they think of something beforehand, yet appear to me to resemble Ahimaaz,[19] who ran without tidings. I have also heard many an ingenious discourse, in which I could not but admire the talents of the preacher; but his only object appeared to be to correct the grosser vices, and to form the manners of his audience, so as to render them useful members of civil society. Such ministers have an errand; but not of such importance as to save those who receive it, which sufficiently proves that it is not the gospel.

In preparing for the pulpit, it would be well to reflect in some such

---
[17] 2 Corinthians 5:20–21.
[18] Acts 20:20–21.
[19] 2 Samuel 18:22.

manner as this: I am expected to preach, it may be to some hundreds of people, some of whom may come several miles to hear; and what have I to say to them? Is it for me to sit here studying a text merely to find something thing to say to fill up the hour? I may do this without imparting any useful instruction, without commending myself to any man's conscience, and without winning, or even aiming to win, one soul to Christ. It is possible there may be in the audience a poor miserable creature, labouring under the load of a guilty conscience. If he depart without being told how to obtain rest for his soul, what may be the consequence? Or, it may be, some stranger may be there who has never heard the way of salvation in his life. If he should depart without hearing it now, and should die before another opportunity occurs, how shall I meet him at the bar of God? Possibly some one of my constant hearers may die in the following week; and is there nothing I should wish to say to him before his departure? It may be that I myself may die before another Lord's Day: this may be the last time that I shall ascend the pulpit; and have I no important testimony to leave with the people of my care?

Every sermon must preach Christ
Secondly, every sermon should contain a portion of the doctrine of salvation by the death of Christ. If there be any meaning in the foregoing passages, this is emphatically called the gospel. A sermon, therefore, in which this doctrine has not a place, and I might add, a prominent place, cannot be a gospel sermon. It may be ingenious, it may be eloquent; but a want of the doctrine of the cross is a defect which no pulpit excellence can supply.

Far be it from me to encourage that fastidious humour manifested by some hearers, who object to a sermon unless the cross of Christ be the immediate and direct topic of discourse. There is a rich variety in the sacred writings, and so there ought to be in our ministrations. There are various important truths supposed by this great doctrine, and these require to be illustrated and established. There are various branches pertaining to it, which require to be distinctly considered; various consequences arising from it, which require to be pointed out; various duties corresponding with it, which require to be inculcated; and various evils inimical to it, which may require to be exposed. All I mean to say is, that as there is a relation between these subjects and the doctrine of the cross, if we would introduce them in a truly evangelical manner, it requires to be in that relation. I may establish the moral character and government of God; the holiness, justice, goodness, and perpetual obligation of the law; the evil of sin; and the exposedness of the sinner to endless punishment; but if I have any other end in view than, by convincing him of his lost condition, to make him feel the need of a Saviour, I cannot be said to have preached the gospel; nor is my reasoning, however forcible, likely to produce any good effect. I may be very pointed in pressing the practical parts of religion, and in reproving the sins of the times; but if I enforce the one, or inveigh against the other, on any other than evangelical principles, I, in so doing, preach not the gospel. All scriptural preaching is practical; but when practice is enforced in opposition to doctrine, or even to the neglect of it, it becomes anti-scriptural. The apostolic precept runs thus: "Preach the word; be instant in season, and out of season; reprove, rebuke, exhort, with all long-suffering and doctrine."[20]

We are gospel heralds, not performers

Thirdly, in preaching the gospel, we must not imitate the orator, whose attention is taken up with his performance, but rather the herald, whose object is to publish, or proclaim, good tidings. There is in the one an earnestness, a fulness of heart, a mind so interested in the subject as to be inattentive to other things, which is not in the other. "We believe, and therefore speak."[21] The emphatical meaning of the terms κηρυσσω, εὐαγγελιζω, to preach, and preach the gospel, is noticeable in the account given of the ministry of John the Baptist. "The law and the prophets were until John; since that time the kingdom of God is preached, and every man presseth into it."[22] Moses and the prophets spoke of things at a distance; but John did more than prophesy: his was "the voice of one that cried;" he announced the fulfilment of what had been foretold, proclaiming the Messiah as being among them, and his kingdom as at hand. He opened the door of salvation, and great numbers pressed in!

Preach reconciliation with earnest gospel invitations

Fourthly, though the doctrine of reconciliation by the blood of Christ

---

[20] 2 Timothy 4:2.
[21] 2 Corinthians 4:13.
[22] Luke 16:16.

Preparing sermons

forms the ground-work of the gospel embassy, yet it belongs to the work of the ministry, not merely to declare that truth, but to accompany it with earnest calls, and pressing invitations, to sinners to receive it, together with the most solemn warnings and threatenings to unbelievers who shall continue to reject it.

The preaching of both John and Christ is, indeed, distinguished from the calls to repentance and faith which they addressed to their hearers, as being the ground on which they rested; but the latter were no less essential to their work than the former. John came "preaching in the wilderness of Judea, and saying, repent ye,"[23] &c. After John was put in prison, Jesus came into Galilee, "preaching the gospel of the kingdom of God, and saying, The time is fulfilled, and the kingdom of God is at hand—repent ye, and believe the gospel."[24] And thus the apostle explains the ministry of reconciliation as comprehending not only a declaration of the doctrine, but the persuading of men, "beseeching" them to be "reconciled to God" (2 Cor. 5:18–20).

There is nothing in all this which clashes with the most entire dependence on the influence of the Holy Spirit to give success to our ministry. Though we invite men, yet it is not on their pliability that we must rest our hopes, but on the power and promise of God. These are a part of the weapons of our warfare; but it is through God that they become mighty to the pulling down of strong holds.

Letter 3: The Composition of a Sermon[25]

You have requested my thoughts on the composition of a sermon. There are several publications on this subject well worthy of your notice. If what I may offer have any peculiar claim to your attention, it will be on account of its familiarity.

The form or manner in which a sermon is composed and delivered is of some importance, inasmuch as it influences the attention, and renders the matter delivered more or less easy of being comprehended and retained.

---

[23] Matthew 3:1–2.
[24] Mark 1:14–15.
[25] Fuller, "Letter 3—The Composition of a Sermon," *Complete Works*, 1:717–723.

David E. Prince

Spiritual things are spiritually discerned

In general, I do not think a minister of Jesus Christ should aim at fine composition for the pulpit. We ought to use sound speech, and good sense; but if we aspire after great elegance of expression, or become very exact in the formation of our periods, though we may amuse and please the ears of a few, we shall not profit the many, and consequently shall not answer the great end of our ministry. Illiterate hearers may be very poor judges of preaching; yet the effect which it produces upon them is the best criterion of its real excellence.

A considerable part of the ministerial gift consists in fruitfulness of invention, but that which greatly aids in the composition and delivery of a sermon is spirituality of mind. Without this we shall get no good ourselves, and be likely to do but little good to others. The first thing, therefore before we sit down to study, should be to draw near to God in prayer. Spiritual things are spiritually discerned.

When a passage of Scripture is fixed on as the ground of a sermon, it is necessary to read it in connection with the context, and endeavour by your own judgment to gain a clear idea of its genuine meaning. Having formed your own judgment, I would then advise you to consult expositors, who may throw additional light upon it, or give a different sense to it; and if the sense which they give appear to have evidence in its favour, you must relinquish your own. Be satisfied, at all events, that you have the mind of the Holy Spirit before you proceed.

Understanding the force of key terms

In the next place, having determined on the meaning of the text, it is necessary to examine the force of each word or term of importance in it. This may be done by examining the use of the same terms in other places of Scripture by the help of a concordance; but here a good judgment of your own is required, that you may select a few out of the many parallel texts which really illustrate that on which you have fixed. Some of the worst sermons are made out of a concordance, being a mere collection of similar sounds, which, instead of throwing light upon the subject, only throw it into confusion.

The force of words or terms of importance may also be examined to great advantage by a judicious use of contrast. Place all the important terms of your text, one at a time, in contrast with other things, or examine to what ideas they stand opposed. For example, let your text be Psalm 145:16, "Thou openest thy hand, and satisfiest the desire of every living thing." Begin with the term "openest": "Thou openest thy hand." What an idea does this convey of the paternal goodness of the great Father of his creation! How opposite to the conduct of many of his creatures one to another, whose hands and hearts are shut! What an idea also does it convey of the ease with which the wants of the whole creation are supplied? Let me pause a moment and think of their wants. What a quantity of vegetable and animal food is daily consumed in one town! What a quantity in a large city like London! What a quantity in a nation; in the whole world! But men do not compose a hundredth part of "every living thing!" Oh what innumerable wants throughout all animate nature; in the earth, in the air, in the waters! Whence comes their supply? "Thou openest thy hand," and all are satisfied. And can all these wants be supplied by only the opening of his hand? What then must sin be, and salvation from it? That is a work of wonderful expense. God opens his hand, and satisfies all creation, but he must purchase the church with his blood![26] God is all-sufficient as to power in the one case as well as in the other; but there are things relative to his moral conduct which he cannot do: he cannot deny himself. Here lies the great difficulty of salvation. In what a variety of ways are our wants supplied! The earth is fruitful, the air is full of life, the clouds empty themselves upon the earth, the sun pours forth its genial rays; but the operation of all these second causes is only the opening of his hand! Nay, further: look we to instruments as well as means? Parents feed us in our childhood, and supply our youthful wants; ways are opened for our future subsistence; connections are formed, which prove sources of comfort. Friends are kind in seasons of extremity. Supplies are presented from quarters that we never expected. What are all these but the opening of his hand? If his hand were shut, what a world would this be! The heavens brass, the earth iron; famine, pestilence, and death must follow (See Psalm 104:27–29).

Next take up the pronoun "thou." You will infer from this: If thou openest thy hand, should I shut mine against my poor brother? This important sentiment will properly occupy the place of improvement towards the close of the discourse.

---

[26] Acts 20:28; Ephesians 1:7; 1 Peter 1:18–19.

Consider next the term "hand." There is a difference between the hand and the heart. God opens his hand, in the way of providence, towards his worst enemies. He gave Nebuchadnezzar all the kingdoms of the earth. But he opens his heart in the gospel of his Son. This is the better portion of the two. While we are thankful for the one, let us not rest satisfied in it. It is merely a hand portion. Rather let us pray with Jabez to be blessed indeed; and that we might have a Joseph's portion—not only the precious things of the earth and the fulness thereof, but "the goodwill of him that dwelt in the bush!"[27]

Proceed: "Thou satisfiest the desire," &c. God, I see, does not give grudgingly. It seems to be a characteristic of the divine nature, both in the natural and moral world, to raise desires, not with a view to disappoint, but to satisfy them. O what a consoling thought is this! If there be any desires in us which are not satisfied, it is through their being self-created ones, which is our own fault; or through artificial scarcity arising from men's luxury, which is the fault of our species. God raises no desires as our Creator but he gives us enough to satisfy them; and none as our Redeemer and Sanctifier but what shall be actually satisfied. Oh the wonderful munificence of God! "How great is his goodness, and how great is his beauty!"[28]

Unity of design

Now, having examined the force of every term of importance, by contrasting it with the opposite idea or ideas, you will find yourself in possession of a number of interesting thoughts, which you may consider as so many recruits, and, having noted them down as they occurred, your next business is to arrange them in order, or to give each thought that place in your discourse which it will occupy to the greatest advantage. Many sermons are a mob of ideas; they contain very good sentiments, but they have no object in view; so that the hearer is continually answering the preacher, "Very true, very true;" but what then? What is it you are aiming at? What is this to the purpose? A preacher, then, if he would interest a judicious hearer, must have an object at which he aims, and must never lose sight of it throughout his discourse. This is what writers

---

[27] Deuteronomy 33:16.
[28] Zechariah 9:17.

on these subjects call a unity of design; and this is a matter of far greater importance than studying well-turned periods, or forming pretty expressions. It is this that nails the attention of an audience. One thing at once is a maxim in common life, by which the greatest men have made the greatest proficiency. Shun, therefore, a multitude of divisions and subdivisions. He who aims to say everything in a single discourse, in effect says nothing. Avoid making a head or particular of every thought. Unity of design may be preserved consistently with various methods of division; but the thing itself is indispensable to good preaching.

The following reasons have induced me to hold this opinion:

1. The human mind is so formed as to delight in unity. To divide the attention is to weaken, if not destroy it. President [Jonathan] Edward's sermons, though in some respects not proper for imitation, yet, in this, are worthy of notice. They all hold up someone great leading truth; and that truth is the spirit of his text, and serves for the title of his sermon. Look over the table of contents to his *Thirty-three Sermons*, and you will find the title of each sermon throw an amazing light upon the text. The sentiment expressed in the title, he calls the doctrine of the text; and all he says is to illustrate, establish, or improve it. It might be of use, if, in the composition of sermons, we were to oblige ourselves to give titles to them. Many of what are called sermons would be found to require three or four titles to answer to their contents; which at once proves that, properly speaking, they are not sermons.

2. It has been said, and I think justly, that evidence should constitute the body or substance of every doctrinal discourse. Evidence may be drawn from various sources; as Scripture testimony, example, the reason of things, &c.; but evidence always implies a leading truth to be proved. Where this is not the case, the preacher gives himself no opportunity of advancing evidence; consequently his sermon, if it may be so called, will be without body, without substance, and will contain nothing that shall leave any strong impression upon a thinking mind. In opening a battery against a wall, you would not throw your balls at random, first at one place and then at another, but direct your whole force against a particular spot. In the one case your labour would be thrown away; in the other you are likely to make an effectual impression.

3. It is greatly assisting to memory, both with respect to the preacher

and the hearer. Memory is exercised by the relation of one thing to another. Were you to attempt to remember seven different objects which bore no manner of relation to each other, such as water, time, wisdom, fruit, contentment, fowls, and revenues, you would find it almost impossible; but take seven objects which, though different in nature, yet possess some point of unity, which associates them in the mind, and the work is easy. Thus, sun, moon, stars, earth, air, fire, and water, are readily remembered, being so many principal parts of the one creation.

4. I cannot so well satisfy my conscience unless I have some interesting truth to communicate, or some important duty to enforce. When I have been thinking of the approach of the Lord's Day, the questions have occurred to my mind, what message have I to deliver to the people of my charge? What important doctrine to establish? What sin to expose? What duty to inculcate? What case to meet? What acknowledged truth to improve? The method frequently used seems to afford an answer to none of these questions; but it is rather saying, none at all, only I have a text of Scripture, on the different parts of which I may say something that will fill up the time.

Divisions are either topical, textual, or compound. The first, or topical method, is to collect all your remarks upon a text, and reduce them to a point, like so many rays of light in a focus. In other words, ask yourself, "What important truth is it that the text contains, and which I feel impressed upon my own mind, and wish to impress upon that of the congregation?" And make this the topic of discourse.

After going over the passage before mentioned, as above, you could be at no loss to determine that the leading sentiment would be—the bounty of providence. This is what the old divines called the doctrine of the text; and when they printed their discourses, this was the title of them.

But, you may ask, what am I to do with this doctrine when I have found it? Am I to make no divisions, or subdivisions? Of what is my discourse to be composed? Yes, there must be divisions, and perhaps subdivisions; but let them not be so many distinct subjects, which have no relation to each other, but so many parts of a whole. When I have a subject before me, I sometimes ask myself three questions: What is it? On what evidence does it rest? And what does it concern me, or any of the people, if it be true? The division of many subjects will therefore be, 1. Explain

Preparing sermons

the doctrine, 2. Establish it, 3. Improve it.

Let us try the above subject on this plan, and see whether we cannot find a place, under one or other of these heads, for all the foregoing thoughts, which occurred spontaneously on looking over the terms; and perhaps, as we go along, others no less interesting may occur.

Introduction

However men have been in the dark respecting God, it has not been for want of evidence. He is not far from every one of us; for in him we live, and move, and have our being. Creation is full of God.

There is something in this passage wonderfully sublime. It expresses a great truth in the most simple language. It represents the great Creator as the Father of his creation, encompassed round by an innumerable family, whose eyes all wait on him for daily food; while he, with paternal goodness, opens his bounteous hand, and satisfies their various wants.

The subject which invites our attention is—the bounty of providence. In discoursing on it, I shall offer some remarks by way of explanation—notice the evidence on which it rests—and then improve the subject.

Explanation

Offer some remarks upon the subject by way of explanation. There is much discontent among men. Many objections may arise in the mind to this doctrine, and but few feel themselves duly impressed with its reality. In order to obviate such objections, I would observe,

1. The desires which God satisfies are to be restricted to those of his own creating. Men have a number of artificial, self-created, and sinful desires. ... These he does not engage to satisfy; but merely those which are purely natural.

2. Though God satisfies the desire of every living thing, yet not all in the same way, but of every creature according to its nature and circumstances. Many of the creatures, like the lily, neither toil nor spin, but receive the bounties of providence ready prepared to their hand; but this is not the case with all. It is not thus with man; for though we are forbidden to be inordinately careful, yet we must commonly labour for what we have. It is a part of the load laid upon us, that by the sweat of the brow we shall eat bread. Nor do I know whether there be more of judgment than of mercy in this sentence. Idleness is certainly a soil on which sin grows

to its greatest perfection. Considering what man is, it is a mercy that we have employment. It is among the rich who have nothing to do, and the very poor who will do but little, that wickedness is most prevalent.

3. The text expresses what God does ordinarily, not universally, or in all cases. There are cases of famine; seasons in which God as it were shuts his hand, on account of the sins of men; and if he shuts his hand, the heavens become brass, and the earth iron, and millions perish for want of bread. There are also cases more common than famine; great numbers of mankind labour under the hardships of poverty, pine away, and are stricken through, for want of the fruits of the field. But this is one of those evils under which the world groans, owing to the sin of man. If there were no waste or intemperance among one part of mankind, there would be a sufficiency, and more than a sufficiency, for all.

Evidences

We proceed to notice a few of the evidences by which this important truth is supported. There are some subjects which are difficult to prove, not from a scarcity, but from a profusion of evidence. Where this is the case, the difficulty lies in selection: I shall content myself with offering three things to your consideration.

1. The supplies we constantly receive cannot be ascribed to our own labour as their first cause. The whole of human labour is but a kind of manufactory of the materials with which God is pleased to furnish us. We make nothing. We only change the forms of different productions, to suit our convenience. We are as really, though not as sensibly, dependent on God as Israel in the wilderness, who were fed with manna from heaven. To this may be added, when we have laboured to the utmost, it amounts to nothing without a divine blessing upon it. All, therefore, that we possess proceeds from the opening of his hand.

2. A consideration of the number and magnitude of the wants of creatures will convince us that nothing short of the all-sufficiency of God can supply them. What a quantity of vegetable and animal food is required by a single town, for only one day! More for a city, more for a nation, more still for a world, and that for a succession of ages! And what are men, when compared with the whole animate creation? All nature teems with life. The earth, the air, the sea, each swarms with being. Whence can all these be continually supplied, but by him that made them? "Thou

openest thy hand, and satisfiest the desire of every living thing."

3. If we consider the various ways and means by which our supplies reach us, we shall be convinced of the truth in question. God does not satisfy our desires immediately, so much as through the medium of second causes; and though we may be too insensible of that hand which puts all in motion, yet it is no less engaged than if we were supplied by miracle. A concatenation, or chain of causes, is apparent in the works of God. Our food is prepared by a complicated but beautiful machinery. The heavens are made to hear the earth, the earth to hear the corn, the wine, and the oil, and the corn, the wine, and the oil to hear the people. What is that tendency of various parts of the creation to satisfy the desires of other parts, but the operation of his hand, who is concerned to uphold and render happy the creatures that he hath made? The earth abounds in fertility, and the air with salubrity [healthfulness]; the clouds pour forth their waters on the earth, and the sun its genial rays. Fire and hail, snow, and winds, and seas contribute to our welfare. We inhale life with every breath we breathe. The elements are employed for our sustenance and happiness.

Look we to instruments as well as means? Tender parents have supplied us during our childhood and youth; ways have been opened for our future subsistence; endearing connections have been formed, which have proved a source of much enjoyment: in seasons of difficulty friends have kindly aided us; supplies have arisen from quarters that we never expected: what are these but the openings of his hand?

Improve the subject
There is no divine truth but is of some account, and this will be found not a little fruitful.

1. If such be the bounty of divine providence, under what obligations do we lie. Yet what actual returns have we made for all this goodness? All the return that God requires is a grateful heart: "Thou shalt love the Lord thy God with all thy heart."[29] But, alas, are there not many of you who are this day his enemies? The idea is shocking, that such a God should have an enemy, yet so it is. The worst thing that was said of one of the worst of men was, "He hath eaten at my table, and hath lifted up his heel

---
[29] Deuteronomy 6:5; Matthew 22:37.

against me!"[30] God has been feeding a generation of vipers; which, under the frost of childhood or adversity, seemed to claim his pity; but which, under the sunshine of maturer years and prosperous circumstances, do not fail to hiss and spit there venom in his face! These things must all come into account. All God's goodness, and all our abuses of it, will be brought to light at the last day.

2. From this view of the divine beneficence, what encouragment is there to trust in the Lord under all our wants and difficulties. With what ease can he supply our wants! In how many ways, unknown to us, and unexpected by us, can he give a favourable turn to our affairs. "Trust in the Lord, and do good: so shalt thou dwell in the land, and verily thou shalt be fed;"[31] "Young lions do lack, and suffer hunger; but they that seek the Lord shall not want any good thing."[32]

3. If such be the bounty of providence, what is that of grace? If this be the opening of his hand, that is the opening of his heart. If he satisfies natural desires, much more those that are spiritual (See verse 19). That which is only done generally in the one case is done universally in the other. Not one soul shall perish through famine, or any kind of want, whose desires terminate on Christ.

While therefore we cherish gratitude for temporal mercies, let us not rest satisfied in them. God gave Nebuchadnezzar all the kingdoms of the earth. See how light he makes of worldly good, to bestow it on the basest of men; to throw it away, as it were, on his worst enemies. Do not be content with Nebuchadnezzar's portion; but rather covet, with Jabez, to be blessed indeed. Worldly good, though a blessing in itself, is capable of being turned by sin into a curse. Covet the crowning point of Joseph's portion; not only the precious things of the earth, and the fulness thereof; but "the good-will of him that dwelt in the bush!"[33]

4. If God be thus good, what must sin be, that can induce him to load this world with such a degree of misery!

5. If God can with such ease supply all creation, what a blessing must redemption be. For the one he has only to open his hand, and the work is done; the other must be accomplished by the purchase of his blood! God

---

[30] Psalm 41:9.
[31] Psalm 37:3.
[32] Psalm 34:10.
[33] Deuteronomy 33:16.

was sufficient for the latter, as well as for the former, as to power; but there are things relative to his moral conduct which he cannot do—he cannot deny himself. Here lies the great difficulty of salvation.

6. What a motive is here to be kind to the poor and needy! If we be children of God, we must imitate him: "Thou shalt open thy hand wide unto thy brother, to thy poor, and to thy needy in thy land."[34]

This may serve as an example of the topical method of preaching; and where it can be accomplished, it is very interesting. But there are some texts which cannot be easily reduced to a single topic; and indeed it is better not to be confined to one method, but to indulge variety. Whatever method may be pursued consistent with a unity of design is very allowable. This object may be attained in what is called the textual method of division, on which I shall next proceed to offer a few observations.[35]

Letter 4: The Composition of a Sermon (Continued)[36]

To explain

Endeavour to understand a subject before you speak of it. Do not overload your memory with words. Write down a few leading things for the sake of arrangement and assistance of memory; but not a great deal. Memory must not be overburdened. Never carry what you write into the pulpit. Avoid vulgar expressions: do not affect finical ones, nor words out of common use. As to division and arrangement, it barely respects the assortment of your materials. You must endeavour to understand and feel your subject, or the manner in which you divide it will signify but little. But if both these may be taken for granted, then I should say much depends, as to your being heard with pleasure and profit, on a proper discussion and management of the subject. At all events avoid a multiplying of heads and particulars. A few well-chosen thoughts, matured, proved, and improved, are abundantly more acceptable than when the whole is chopped, as it were, into mincemeat. It is very common to divide in a textual way, i.e., to propose to discourse first upon one part or branch of

---

[34] Deuteronomy 15:11.
[35] [N.B. Mr. Fuller appears not to have fulfilled his intention of proceeding with the subject, the foregoing letters being all that can be found of the series. The letter which follows was addressed to another of Mr. Fuller's friends].
[36] Fuller, "Letter 4—The Composition of a Sermon," *Complete Works*, 1:724–726.

it, secondly, upon another, &c. As, for example:

"In thy light we shall see light" Psalm 36:9.

First, inquire what is meant by that light which is ascribed to God, "Thy light;" secondly, what is that light which we see in God's light; thirdly, what is included in seeing this light. I cannot say I approve of this method. It is not, properly speaking, a sermon. A sermon is a discourse on some divine subject, or a train of interesting thoughts on some sacred theme. The above process, I think, should be brought into the introduction and explication of the text, and should be done in about five minutes. Then, having made the text plain by explaining the difficult parts of it, I should state the leading truth taught in the text as the subject or theme of the discourse. For example:

"In thy light we shall see light" Psalm 36:9.

There is a great boast of light in the world, and there is some ground for it in natural things; but, as of old the world by wisdom knew not God, so of late. If ever we know God, it must be through the medium of his word. This I take to be the meaning of the passage I have read. The term light in the last clause means the true knowledge of God; and, in the first, the true medium of attaining it, viz. divine revelation. The sum seems to amount to this: the word of God is the grand medium by which we can attain a true and saving knowledge of God. What the sun and stars are to the regions of matter, that revelation is to the mental region (Gen. 1:13, 17).

To establish
Let us try to illustrate this important truth by a few observations.

1. The knowledge of God was objectively manifested by the light of nature, but through man's depravity rendered inoperative (Rom. 1:28). It is the revelation of the law of the Lord that converts the soul (Ps. 19:1-11).

2. The true knowledge of God was obtained under the patriarchal or Mosaic dispensation by great numbers, but it was through the medium of revelation. As revelation increased, the knowledge of God increased with

it; prophecies, promises, and precepts; types, and shadows. In this light they saw light, though not so clearly as in after-days.

3. The true knowledge of God has obtained still more ground under the gospel dispensation; but it is still through the medium of revelation. Whenever the latter has gone among the Gentiles, the former has gone along with it; and as revelation is more perfect, God has the more honoured it.

4. The light of the gospel dispensation is not yet perfect (Isa. 30:26), but whatever degree of brilliancy arises, it will be through this medium. We must not think we have exhausted Scripture knowledge. We know but little of it yet. A thousand promises and prophecies will appear in a glory, of which we have now but faint ideas. Let us now—

To improve it

1. Be thankful for the light of revelation. Regard not the *ignis fatuus* which wanders about under the name of reason in modern productions (2 Pet. 1:19).

2. Walk in it particularly in finding your way to eternal life; for settling disputed principles, and regulating your lives.

3. There are many things of which you may entertain no doubt, concerning which there may be no manner of dispute; yet make a point of seeing them in God's light. Many content themselves with seeing them in the light in which great and good men have placed them; but, though angels, they are not the true light: they all view things partially. If what they say be true, yet, if we receive it merely on their representation, our faith will stand in the wisdom of men, and not in the power of God (1 Cor. 2:9). That knowledge or faith which has not God's word for its ground will not stand the day of trial.

4. Endeavour to spread it in your connections and in the world at large, &c.

I do not pretend to say that sermons should be formed after this or any other mode. Every subject, in some degree, requires a mode of discussion for itself. There are, however, some general observations, that will ordinarily apply to most subjects. In doctrinal subjects, in which some great truth is taught, your business is to find out that truth, and state it in the introduction. If clearly stated, search for the evidences, and make it one head of the discourse to establish it. If it be a truth to be illustrated, set it before the hearers in various points of light; and as no divine truth is merely speculative, but some way or other concerns the hearers, the latter part of the subject should consist in improvement. 1. To explain, 2. To establish, 3. To improve it.

What? why? what then?
But in all cases the division must be governed by the materials you have to divide. It would be absurd to explain a subject that was already as plain as you could make it, or in which there appeared no difficulties or liability to misunderstand. There are three questions I have often put to myself in thinking on a subject: what? why? what then? In other words—what am I going to teach? why? or on what ground do I advance it as a truth? and what does it concern any or all of my hearers if it be true?

On practical subjects there is seldom much room for you to prove and improve. Not the former, since there is no truth to be established; not the latter, because the whole sermon is an address upon those things of which no improvement is made. I have generally found that exhortations include matter for a twofold division, and have very commonly proposed, first, to inquire into the meaning and extent of the exhortation; secondly, to enforce it. Under the former there is room to expatiate upon every idea or branch of the duty. In the latter, to introduce any motive that serves either for that or other texts.

If a text be partly doctrinal and partly practical, the practical part may often be introduced first. I think the doctrinal part will come as a motive to enforce it.

The Abuse of Allegory in Preaching[1]

[The subject of the following paper,
which originally appeared in the *Evangelical Magazine*]

After what several able writers have produced of late years upon this practice, particularly the late Dr. Stennett[2] on the parable of the sower,[3] it might have been expected that this evil would at least have been considerably diminished. But the misfortune is, those who are most addicted to this way of preaching seem in general to have very little inclination to read. Whether they deem it unlawful, as involving them in the sin charged upon the prophets, of stealing everyone from his neighbour—or whether they be so enamoured of their own thoughts as to set all others at defiance—I cannot decide; but certain it is, that many preach as if they had never read or thought upon the subject.

Very little observation will convince us that the preachers with whom this practice mostly prevails are of the lower sort with respect to seriousness and good sense, however high they may affect to soar in their notions. Of such characters I have but little hope. But as some godly men are, I believe, too much infected with this disease, if the editor will indulge me with two or three pages in the magazine, I will expostulate with one of them on the causes and consequences of his conduct.

A warning about turning all Scripture into allegory

Let me entreat you then, my friend, to consider, in the first place, whether, when you turn plain historical facts into allegory, you treat the word of God with becoming reverence. Can you seriously think the Scriptures to be a book of riddles and conundrums, and that a Christian minister is properly employed in giving scope to his fancy, in order to discover their solution? I have been asked the meaning of certain passages of Scripture; and when I have answered according to what appeared to

---

[1] Fuller, "The Abuse of Allegory in Preaching," *Complete Works*, 3:442–443.
[2] Samuel Stennett (1727-1795).
[3] Matthew 13:1-23; Mark 4:1-20; Luke 8:4-15.

be the scope of the sacred writer, it has been said, "Yes, that may be the literal meaning; but what is the spiritual meaning of it?" as though every part of Scripture had a spiritual, that is, a hidden or allegorical meaning, besides its obvious one. That some parts of Scripture are allegorical—that some prophecies have a double reference—and that the principle suggested by many a passage may be applied to other things besides what is immediately intended—there is no doubt; but this is very different from the practice to which I allude. All Scripture is profitable in some way. Some for doctrine, some for reproof, some for correction, and some for instruction in righteousness; but all is not to be turned into allegory. If we must play, let it be with things of less consequence than the word of the eternal God!

Beware of vanity

Secondly, consider whether the motive that stimulates you to such a manner of treating the sacred oracles be any other than vanity. If you preached to a people possessed of anything like good sense, they would consider it as perverting the whole word of God and whipping it into froth. Instead of applauding you, they would be unable to endure it. But if your people be ignorant, such things will please them; and they may gaze, and admire, and smile, and say one to another, it may be in your hearing too, "Well, what a man! Who would have thought that he would have found so much gospel in that text? Ah, very true: who indeed?" But what would the apostle Paul say? "Are ye not carnal?"[4] Is it for a man of God to "court a grin when he should woo a soul?"[5] For shame! desist from such folly or lay aside the Christian ministry. You are commanded to "feed the church of God, which he hath purchased with his own

---

[4] 1 Corinthians 3:3
[5] William Cowper, "The Timepiece" in *The Task* (London: John Sharpe, 1817), 47. The full stanza reads,

"He that negotiates between God and man,
As God's ambassador, the grand concerns
Of judgment and of mercy, should beware
Of lightness in his speech. 'Tis pitiful
To court a grin when you should woo a soul:
To break a jest when pity should inspire
Pathetic exhortation; and address
The skittish fancies with facetious tales
When sent with God's commission to the heart."

blood;"[6] but it is not everything pleasing to a people that feeds them in the sense of the apostle. He did not mean to direct the Ephesian elders to feed men's fancies,[7] and still less their prejudices; but their spiritual desires: and this is accomplished only by administering to them the words of truth and soberness. If your preaching be such as God approves, and if you study to show yourself approved of him, it will lead the people to admire your Saviour rather than you, and render him the topic of their conversation.

Mistaking spiritualizing for spirituality
Thirdly, consider whether both you and your people be not in danger of mistaking this spiritualizing passion for spirituality of mind and a being led into "the deep things of God."[8] There are few objects at a greater distance than the effervescence of a vain imagination and that holy and humble spirit by which spiritual things are discerned, yet the one is often mistaken for the other. The preacher dreams of deep discoveries, and the people wonder to hear them; but what says the Scriptures? "The prophet that hath only a dream must tell his dream, but he that hath God's word, let him speak it faithfully; for what is the chaff to the wheat."[9]

Finally, consider the consequences which must follow from this practice. If an unbeliever come into your assembly, and find you arraying Christianity in this fancy dress, is it likely he should be convinced of all — and, the secrets of his heart being made manifest, fall down and worship God, and report that God is among you, and that of a truth? If he hears you treat of the historical parts of Scripture as meaning something very different from what they appear to mean, will he not say you are mad, and be furnished with a handle for representing religion itself as void of truth and good sense? Or if he hears you interpret the miracles, which Christ wrought in proof of his Messiahship, of that change which is now wrought in the minds of sinners by the Spirit of God, will he not say that you yourselves appear to consider the whole as a string of fables, and are employed in finding out the morals of them?

But perhaps you are seldom attended by men of this description. Be

---

[6] Acts 20:28.
[7] Acts 20:17–38.
[8] 1 Corinthians 2:10.
[9] Jeremiah 23:28.

it so, what, think you, must be the effect of such preaching on professing Christians, either nominal or real? The former will either fall asleep under it, as something which does not concern them; or, if they attend to you, and understand your interpretations, they will think they are quite in the secret, and set themselves down for deep Christians; when, in truth, they know nothing yet as they ought to know. And as to real Christians, their souls will either pine under your ministry, or, by contracting a false taste, will thirst after the froth of human fancy, to the neglect of the sincere milk of the word; and instead of growing in grace, and in the knowledge of our Lord Jesus Christ, will make no progress in either.

It is an easy thing for a man of a luxuriant imagination, unencumbered by judgment, to make anything he pleases of the Scriptures, as well as any other book; but in so doing he must destroy their simplicity, and of course their efficacy; which in fact is reducing them to nothing. If they be not applied to their appropriate uses, they are perverted; and a perverted good proves the greatest of evils. Thus it is that characters abound who are full of Scripture language, while yet they are awfully destitute of Scripture knowledge, or Scriptural religion.

The Nature and Importance of Walking by Faith[1]

[Preached at Nottingham, before the Northamptonshire Association, June 2, 1784]

"We walk by faith, not by sight." 2 Corinthians 5:7.

Much is said concerning faith in the holy Scriptures, especially in the New Testament; and great stress is laid upon it, especially by the author of the Epistle to the Hebrews. This, I apprehend, is not very difficult to be accounted for. Ever since the fall of man, we have been entirely dependent on the mercy of God through a Mediator. We all lie at his discretion, and are beholden to his mere sovereign grace for all the happiness we enjoy. We have nothing on which we can rely for the possession or continuance of any good, but the word and will of God. The only life, therefore, proper for a fallen creature in our world, is a life of faith—to be constantly sensible of our dependence upon God, continually going to him, and receiving all from him, for the life that now is and that which is to come.

Believers, and they only, are brought to be of a spirit suitable to such a kind of life. The hearts of all others are too full of pride and self-sufficiency; but these are contented to be pensioners on the bounty of another, can willingly commit their all into Christ's hands, and venture their present and everlasting concerns upon his word. "The just shall live by faith."[2]

Self-renunciation, and confidence in another, are ideas which seem ever to accompany that of faith. The apostle speaks of being justified by faith;[3] that is, not by our own righteousness, but by the righteousness of another: of living by faith;[4] that is, not by our own earnings, so to speak,

---

[1] Fuller, "The Nature and Importance of Walking by Faith," *Complete Works*, 1:117-134.
[2] Romans 1:17; Galatians 3:11; Hebrews 10:38.
[3] Galatians 2:16; Romans 5:1; 3:28.
[4] Romans 1:17; Galatians 3:11; Hebrews 10:38.

but by the generosity of another: of standing by faith;[5] that is, not upon our own legs, as we should say, but upon those of another: and here, of walking by faith; which is as much as if he had said, "We walk, not trusting our own eyes, but the eyes of another. We are blind, and cannot guide ourselves. We must therefore rely upon God for direction and instruction." This, my brethren, is the life we must live, while in this world, and this the manner in which we must walk in our progress toward the heavenly state. Great is the wisdom and goodness of God in so ordering it; great glory hereby redounds to him, and great good accrues to us.

All I shall attempt will be to explain the nature, and show the importance, of the Christian's walk by faith. Both are necessary. The one, that we may form just ideas of what we have to do; and the other, that we may feel our hearts excited to do it. O may the same Spirit who indited the sacred passage breathe upon us, that these ends may be accomplished!

The nature of walking by faith

Let us inquire what is intended by the sacred writer, when he says, "We walk by faith, not by sight." Faith and sight, it is easy to see, here stand opposed; as, indeed, they do in many other parts of Scripture; especially in that remarkable definition of faith wherein the apostle to the Hebrews calls it "the evidence of things not seen."[6] But what kind of sight it is opposed to may deserve our attentive inquiry.

And here, before I proceed any further, in order to make the way clear, I will advert to a notion which has been too generally received, but which appears to me unscriptural and pernicious; what I refer to is, that faith is to be considered as opposed to spiritual sight, or spiritual discernment. It is true I never heard of any person, either in preaching, writing, or conversation, who said so in express words; but expressions are often used which convey the same idea. When the terms faith and sense are used, it is common with many to understand, by the latter, sensible communion with God. So it is common to hear a life of faith opposed to a life of frames and feelings. Those times in which we have the most spiritual discernment of God's glory, sensible communion with him, and feel our

---

[5] 1 Corinthians 16:13
[6] Hebrews 11:1.

love most ardently drawn out to him, are thought to have the least of the exercise of faith. It is common to say there is no need for faith then; at those times we live by sense; but that when all our graces seem dead, and we can see no evidence from which to draw the favourable conclusion, then is the time to walk by faith. The meaning is, then is the time to believe all is well, and so rest easy, whether we have evidence that it is so or not.

Thus we have often heard several passages of Scripture applied, or rather miserably misapplied; for instance, that in the last chapter of Habakkuk:

> Although the fig tree shall not blossom, neither shall fruit be in the vines, the labour of the olive shall fail, and the fields shall yield no meat, the flock shall be cut off from the fold, and no herd in the stalls; yet will I rejoice in the Lord, I will joy in the God of my salvation.[7]

As if by the fig-tree not blossoming were meant the Christian graces not being in exercise; and that then was the time to walk by faith, to rejoice in the God of our salvation. That passage also concerning Abraham, "who, against hope, believed in hope,"[8] has been understood as if to be strong in faith, giving glory to God, like Abraham, was to maintain an unshaken persuasion of the goodness of our state, whether we have evidence or no evidence.

So also that passage in the fiftieth of Isaiah has been frequently brought for this purpose: "Who is among you that feareth the Lord, that obeyeth the voice of his servant, that walketh in darkness, and hath no light? let him trust in the name of the Lord, and stay upon his God."[9] As though a state of darkness there meant a state of mind wherein a person could discern no evidence whatever of his being a good man; and as though such were there encouraged to make themselves easy, and leave the matter with God, not doubting the goodness of their state. Our Lord's rebuke to Thomas has been understood in the same manner: "Because thou hast seen me, thou hast believed; blessed are they that have

---

[7] Habakkuk 3:17–18.
[8] Romans 4:18.
[9] Isaiah 50:10.

Preparing sermons

not seen, and yet have believed."[10] As if a blessing should rest upon those who, destitute of all discernible evidence of their Christianity, nevertheless believe it with an unshaken confidence. If this is to walk by faith, then faith must stand opposed to spiritual sight or spiritual discernment.

I doubt not but there is such a thing as to live upon frames, which ought to be guarded against. If I imagine, for instance, that God changes as I change—that he admires me at one time, and not another—of that his great love, whence all my hope of salvation springs, rises and falls according to the state of my mind; this is, doubtless, to dishonour God, as it strikes at the immutability of his love. So if I derive my chief consolation from reflecting upon what I am, instead of reflecting upon what Christ is, this is to dishonour Christ, and may very properly stand opposed to living by faith. But this is not the common idea of living upon frames. It has been usual with many to account that man to live upon frames, who, when he is stupid, and dark, and carnal, cannot be confident about the safety of his state; and him to live by faith who can maintain his confidence in the worst of frames. Allow me, brethren, to offer three or four plain reasons against this notion of the subject.

1. Faith is the only means of spiritual discernment and communion with God, and therefore cannot be opposed to them. Our best frames are those in which faith is most in exercise; and our worst when it is the least. Faith is the eye of the mind. It is that by which we realize invisible and spiritual objects, and so have fellowship with God. Yes, it is by this grace that we "behold the glory of the Lord,"[11] and are changed into the same image from glory to glory, by the "Spirit of the Lord."[12]

2. If faith is opposed to spiritual discernment and communion with God, then it must work alone. It must never act in conjunction with any of those graces wherein we feel our hearts go out to God; for this would be to confound faith and sense together. But this is contrary to fact. When we have most faith in exercise, we have most love, most hope, most joy, and so of all the graces. All sweetly act in harmony. Thus the Scriptures represent it as ever accompanied by other graces; especially by love, purity, and lowliness of heart. It is expressly said to "work by love;"[13] and,

---

[10] John 20:29.
[11] 2 Corinthians 3:18.
[12] 2 Corinthians 3:18.
[13] Galatians 5:6.

it should seem, never works without it. It is also said to "purify the heart."[14] The exercise of faith, therefore, and the exercise of holiness, can never be separated. Equally true is it that it is ever attended with "lowliness of heart."[15] There are two instances of faith recorded which our Lord particularly commended, saying, he had not seen such great faith, no, not in Israel. The one was the case of the woman of Canaan, and the other that of the Roman centurion; and both these were attended with great humility. The one was contented to be treated as a dog,[16] and the other thought himself unworthy that Christ should come under his roof.[17] A confidence unaccompanied with these, if it may be called faith at all, seems nearly to resemble what the apostle James called "faith without works,"[18] which he pronounced to be "dead, being alone."[19]

3. If faith is to be understood in this sense, then it not only works without other graces, but contrary to them. The Scriptures encourage a spirit of self-examination and godly jealousy. These are modest and upright graces, and constitute much of the beauty of Christianity. "Examine yourselves, whether ye be in the faith,[20]" say the inspired writers; "try your own selves!"[21] "Let us fear, lest, a promise being left us of entering into his rest, any of us should seem to come short of it;"[22] "Let us pass the time of our sojourning here in fear."[23] But always to be confident of the safety of our state, let the work of sanctification go on as it may, is not only unfriendly to such a spirit, but subversive of it. Hence it is common, with some, to call every degree of godly jealousy by the name of unbelief, and to impute it to the enemy; yea, to shun it, and cry out against it, as if it were itself a devil! This is not the most favourable symptom of an honest heart. Surely a heart truly upright would not wish to receive comfort itself, but upon solid evidence; and where it was taught to call such a fear by the name of unbelief I know not; I think I may say, it never came from the word of God. If the veracity of God were called in

---

[14] James 4:8.
[15] Matthew 11:29.
[16] Matthew 15:27.
[17] Matthew 8:8.
[18] James 2:14.
[19] James 2:17.
[20] 2 Corinthians 13:5.
[21] 2 Corinthians 13:5.
[22] Hebrew 1:4.
[23] 1 Peter 1:17.

question, no doubt it would be unbelief; but the question, at those times, with a sincere mind, is not whether God will prove faithful in saving those that trust in him, but whether he be indeed the subject of that trust. His doubts do not respect God, but himself. Love and fear are the two great springs and guardians of right action. When love is in exercise, we do not stand in need of fear to stimulate or guide us; but when we are not constrained by the former, it is well to be restrained by the latter.

4. Faith, in that case, must be unsupported by evidence. God's word affords us no warrant to conclude ourselves interested in his promises, and so in a state of safety, unless we bear the characters to which the promises are made. We have no right, for instance, to apply to ourselves that promise: "Fear thou not, for I am with thee: be not dismayed, for I am thy God: I will strengthen thee, yea, I will help thee, yea, I will uphold thee with the right hand of my righteousness,"[24] unless we bear the character of the party there addressed. This is expressed in the foregoing verse, "But thou, Israel, art my servant."[25] If, from the real desire of our hearts, we yield not ourselves servants to God, no impression of this passage upon our minds can warrant us to conclude that God is indeed our God, or that we shall be strengthened, helped, or upholden by him. So also no man has any right to conclude himself interested in that promise, "I have loved thee with an everlasting love, therefore with loving-kindness have I drawn thee,"[26] unless he be so drawn from the love of sin, self, and the world, as to love God better than any of them. But if we are to hold fast the confidence of our safety, whatever be the condition of our mind or the evils in our conduct, then we are, in that instance, to believe without evidence. If the work of sanctification be the only Scriptural evidence of our interest in Christ, then, in proportion to that work increasing or declining, our evidence must be strong or weak. When we degenerate into carnality and indifference, it must of course, diminish. To say, then, that those are the times in which we exercise most faith, is the same thing as to say we exercise most faith when we have least evidence; and, consequently, it must be a kind of faith, if it be faith at all, that is unsupported by evidence.

There are but two cases, that I recollect, in the whole system of true

---

[24] Isaiah 41:10.
[25] Isaiah 41:8.
[26] Jeremiah 31:3.

Christian experience, which so much as seem to resemble this notion; and these are, in fact, essentially different from it.

Well-grounded persuasion
One is that of the most eminent Christians having a general and well-grounded persuasion of their interest in Christ, even at those times wherein they may not experience such evident and sensible exercises of grace as they do at other times. But then, it is to be observed, grace has more ways than one of being in exercise. The grace of love, for instance sometimes is exercised in the most tender and affectionate feelings of the heart towards Christ, longing to be with him, and to enjoy him in the world to come. At other times, it works more in a way of serving him, and promoting his interest in the present world. This latter may not so sensibly strike the person himself as being an exercise of love, but perhaps other people may consider it superior evidence.

The industrious peasant, sitting in his evening chair, sees his children gathering round him, and courting his affections by a hundred little winning ways. He looks, and smiles, and loves. The next day he returns to his labour, and cheerfully bears the burden of the day, in order to provide for these his little ones, and promote their interest. During his day's labour, he may not feel his love operate in such sensible emotions as he did the evening before. Nay, he may be so attentive to other things as not immediately to have them in his thoughts. What then? he loves his children, indeed he gives proof of it, by cheerfully enduring the toils of labour, and willingly denying himself of many a comfort, that they might share their part; and were he to hear of their being injured or afflicted, he would quickly feel the returns of glowing affection, in as strong, and perhaps stronger, emotions than ever.

Thus the believer may have real love to God in exercise, exciting him to a cheerful and habitual discharge of duty, and a careful watch against evil, and yet feel little, or none of that desirable tenderness of heart which, at other times, he experiences. He has grace in exercise, only it does not work in the same way as it does at some other times; and he in general enjoys a conscious satisfaction that the more he knows of God, his holy law, and glorious gospel, the more he loves them. During this, he may have an abiding satisfaction that things are right with him. But this is a very different thing from a person, at all events, maintaining the safety of his state; yea, and reckoning himself, in so doing, to be strong in faith, giving glory to God, while carnality governs his spirit, and folly debases his conversation.

Immediate application to the Lord
The other case is when, on a failure of evidence from a reflection on *past* experiences, the believer has recourse to an immediate application to the Lord Jesus Christ, casting himself directly on his mercy, and relying on his word; seeing he has said, "Him that cometh to me, I will in no wise cast out." This case no doubt often occurs. The believer, through the prevalence of carnality, with some other causes, too often finds his evidences for glory so obscured, that past experiences will afford but small consolation. At such a time, his mind is either easy and carnally disposed (in that case, a few painful fears will do him no harm), or else his heart is depressed with perplexity and gloom, in which case nothing is better than immediately to go to Christ as a poor sinner for salvation. This is the shortest, and it is commonly the surest way. It is not best in such a state of mind to stand disputing whether we have believed or not; be that as it may, the door of mercy is still open, and the Redeemer still says, "Him that cometh to me I will in no wise cast out."[27] It is best, therefore, to make a fresh venture of our souls upon him; that if we have never before trusted in him, we may now.

This is no more than he has a warrant at any time to do, let things be as they may with him; for though internal qualifications are necessary to our concluding ourselves interested in Christ, yet it is not so in respect of application to him. The perplexed soul need not stay, before he ventures, to inquire whether he be fit to come to Christ. It is not required that he should prove his saintship before he applies for mercy, though it is before he claims an interest in gospel blessings. All that is necessary here is that he be sensible of his being a vile and lost sinner; and that is not to be considered as a qualification, giving him a right to come, but as a state of mind essential to the act itself of coming.

Many a Christian has found sweet rest to his soul by such a direct application to Christ; and surely it would be much better for Christians

---

[27] John 6:37.

who go almost all their life in painful perplexity, lest they should be mistaken at last, if, instead of perpetually poring on past experiences, they were to practise more in this way. This would furnish them with present evidence, which is much the best, and what God best approves; for he loves to have us continue to exercise our graces, and not barely to remember that we have exercised them some time or other heretofore. This in some sort may be called walking by faith, and not by sight; and, in this case, faith may in some sense be opposed to spiritual sight. It is opposed to that discernment which we sometimes have of being true Christians, from a review of past experiences. But then this is ever attended with present spiritual discernment of Christ's excellence, and a longing desire after interest in him; and herein essentially differs from what we have been opposing. Confidence in the one case is nothing else but carnal security, tending to make men easy without God. Confidence in the other is an actual venture of the soul afresh on the Lord Jesus, encouraged by his gracious testimony. The subject of the one considers himself as an established saint; the other as a poor lost sinner, and deals with Christ for salvation just as he did when he first applied to him. To the one we say, "Be not high-minded, but fear;" to the other, "Fear not, thou shalt not be ashamed; none ever trusted in him, and was confounded."

In what sense then do we walk by faith, and not by sight? I answer in general: walking by faith is a going forward in the ways of godliness, as influenced, not by sensible, but by invisible objects—objects of reality which we have no evidence but the testimony of God. But perhaps faith may be considered as opposed to sight more particularly in three senses; namely, to corporal sight, to the discoveries of mere reason, and to ultimate vision.

Walk by faith, not by sight
To walk by faith is opposed to walking by corporal sight. In this sense we shall find it plentifully used in the eleventh chapter to the Hebrews, concerning Abel, Enoch, Noah, Abraham, and others. Thus Abel, by faith, offered a more excellent offering than Cain.[28] God had said in effect, once for all, that he would never speak nor be spoken to in a way of friendship by any of the human race, but through a mediator. This was intimated

---

[28] Hebrews 11:4.

Preparing sermons

partly by man's being debarred from all access to the tree of life, partly by the promise of the woman's Seed,[29] and partly by the institution of sacrifices. Cain overlooked all these, and approached God without an expiatory sacrifice; as if there had been no breach between them, and so no need of an atonement. This was an instance of daring unbelief. Abel, on the contrary, took God at his word, perceived the evil of sin and the awful breach made by it, dared not to bring an offering without a victim for atonement, had respect to the promised Messiah, and thus, by faith in the unseen Lamb, offered a more excellent offering than Cain.

Thus also it is said of Noah, "By faith he, being warned of God of things not seen as yet, moved with fear, prepared an ark to the saving of his house; by the which he condemned the world."[30] No doubt the world was ready to despise Noah, while building his ark, as an enthusiast whose faculties were probably deranged, who put himself to a deal of trouble, and wanted to put other people to as much, merely through a notion that ran in his head that the world should be drowned. Why, was there anything in the world that looked like it, or seemed to portend such an event? Nothing at all. All things seemed to continue as they were from the creation. What then could induce Noah to do as he did? Nothing but the testimony of God, which he credited, and acted accordingly.

So also it is said of Abraham, when called to go into another country, "by faith he obeyed, and went out, not knowing whither he went." A pretty errand it would seem to his friends and neighbours! It is possible that some of these, observing him preparing for a journey, might inquire whither he was going:

[Abraham:] "Going? I am going to a land which the Lord is to show me."

[Inquierer:] "And have you ever seen this land?"

[Abraham:] "No. I neither know the country, nor a step of the way to it."

[Inquierer:] "A fine tale, indeed! but, seriously, what in the world can move you to such an undertaking?"

[Abraham:] "I rely upon the testimony of God. He hath said, 'Get thee out of thy country, and from thy kindred, unto a land that I will show

---

[29] Genesis 3:15.
[30] Hebrews 11:7.

thee.' I take him at his word, and act accordingly."

These were cases in point for the apostle to quote. The Hebrews seemed hardly contented with an unseen high priest, an invisible religion. They had been used to priests and sacrifices that they could hear, and see, and handle with their bodily senses. Like their fathers by Moses, therefore, they were ready to say of Jesus, "We know not where he is gone; come, let us make us a captain, and return to Judaism." "Judaism!" says the apostle, "me thinks true Judaism would condemn you. All your forefathers acted upon a principle which you seem about to abandon. They walked by faith, not by sight. They lived, they died, in the faith, even in the faith of that very Messiah of whom you make so light."

In this sense, it is easy to see, faith and sight are to be taken in our Lord's rebuke to Thomas, when he says, "Blessed are they that have not seen, and yet have believed."[31] It is as if he had said, "You think you have acted very prudently; but what must the Christian world do in after-ages, if they act upon your principle? Christianity in the whole of it will depend upon testimony; whoever receives it after your death, yea, in your lifetime, besides yourselves, must receive it upon your testimony. Blessed are they that shall cordially so receive it; and blessed had you been, Thomas, to have set them the example, by believing the testimony of your brethren."

Faith, not mere reason
Faith may be considered as opposed to the discoveries of mere reason unassisted by revelation. In this sense it seems to be used in reference to Sarah. "Through faith she received strength to conceive seed, and was delivered of a child when she was past age, because she judged him faithful who had promised."[32] How Sarah should have a son was not only indiscernible by the corporal eye, but by an eye of reason; since it must be, if at all, entirely beside the common course of nature. She had nothing to rely upon in this case but the promise of God.

We do not suppose faith and right reason to be opposites—that be far from us. On the contrary, nothing is more evident than that Christianity is entirely a rational system, and it is its glory that it is so. We should

---

[31] John 20:29.
[32] Hebrews 11:11.

never have been required to give a reason for the hope that is in us, if there had been no reason to be given. But though nothing in revelation be contrary to right reason, yet there are many things which our reason could never have found out, had they not been made known by the supreme intelligence. The plan of redemption by Jesus Christ, in particular, contains a set of truths which the eye had never seen, nor the ear heard, nor had they entered the heart of man to conceive, had not God revealed them to us by his Spirit. For all the pleasure that we enjoy, brethren, in contemplating these glorious truths, we are wholly indebted to the testimony of God. Indeed, so far are they from being discoverable by mere reason, that every blessing contains in it abundantly more than men or angels could have asked or thought! It staggers our reason to receive it, even now it is told us. At every pause we must stand and wonder, saying, "Is this the manner of man, O Lord!"[33]

Not only was our reason incapable of finding out many truths before they were revealed; but even now they are revealed, they contain things above our comprehension. It is one thing to say that Scripture is contrary to right reason, and another thing to say it may exhibit truths too great for our reason to grasp.[34] God must have told us nothing about his own

---

[33] 2 Samuel 7:19

[34] May not the great disputes which have taken place concerning faith and reason, as if the one were opposite to the other, have arisen, in a great degree, from using the term reason without defining it? The word reason, like the word understanding, has two senses. 1. It signifies the fitness of things. So the apostles used it, when they said, "It is not reason that we should leave the word of God, and serve tables;" that is, it is not fit or proper. 2. It signifies our power or capacity of reasoning. So it is said of Nebuchadnezzar that his reason returned to him; that is, his power or capacity of reasoning. Now it is easy to see that these are two essentially different ideas: the one is perfect and immutable, remaining always the same; the other is shattered and broken by sin, and liable to a thousand variations through blindness and prejudice. No divine truth can disagree with the former; but it may be both above and contrary to the latter.

If people were to talk, in matters of science and philosophy, as some have affected to talk in religion, they would be treated as fools, and deemed unworthy of attention. A philosopher, for instance, tells an unlettered countryman that it is generally thought that the earth turns round, everyday, upon its own axis, and not the sun round the earth. The countryman replies, "I don't believe it." "Very likely," says the philosopher; "but why not?" "It is contrary to my reason." "Contrary to your reason? that may be, but I hope you do not think that everything contrary to your reason is contrary to right reason!" Were men of the greatest understanding but to consider that there is a far greater disproportion between some truths respecting the existence of a God and their capacities than between any truths of human science and the capacity of the most ignorant rustic, they would be ashamed to disbelieve a truth because it is not according to their reason.

existence and infinite perfections, if he had told us nothing but what we could fully comprehend. In this case, it becomes us to know our littleness, and to bow our understandings to the supreme intelligence. It is the most rational thing in the world so to do. If God has said anything, we ought to rest assured that so it is. In these cases, we ought to trust his eyes, so to speak, rather than our own, and be content to walk by faith, not by sight.

Faith, not ultimate vision
Faith may be considered as opposed to ultimate vision. The saints in glory are described as "seeing Christ as he is,"[35] as "knowing even as they are known," and as being citizens of a city where there shall be "no night,"[36] and where they shall need "no candle, neither light of the sun, nor light of the moon, for the Lord God shall be the light thereof."[37] Our knowledge of things there will be immediate and intuitive, and not, as it is here, through the medium of the word and ordinances. The sacred Scriptures are to us (with reverence be it spoken) like a letter from a distant friend; but when we come face to face, ink and paper shall be needed no more. However, for the present, it is otherwise. We are yet in the body; and while such, as the apostle observes in the verse preceding the text, "we are absent from the Lord,"[38] and must be glad of these helps. Let us make much of this letter, and be thankful that we can walk by it through this world, as by a "light in a dark place,"[39] till we come to a better, where we shall no more walk by faith, but by sight.

Thus far I have dwelt chiefly upon the terms, but, that we may obtain a more comprehensive view of the thing itself (namely, of a Christian's walking by faith), let us take a view of a few of those circumstances and situations through which he has to pass during the present life. It is in

---

It is right, and stands commended in Scripture, to apply our hearts to understanding; but it is wrong, and stands condemned in Scripture, by the same pen, and in the same page, to lean to our own understanding. So, I apprehend, it is right to adhere to right reason, and to use all means to find out what it is; but it is wrong and presumptuous to set up our reason as a standard competent to decide what is truth, and what is error; for that is the same thing as supposing that our ideas of fitness and unfitness always accord with the real fitness of things.

[35] 1 Corinthians 13:12.
[36] Revelation 21:25.
[37] Revelation 21:23.
[38] 2 Corinthians 5:6.
[39] 2 Peter 1:19.

these that faith, as well as every other grace, is exercised. Allow me, then, to request your attention, brethren, to four or five observations on the subject.

Observations on walking by faith
Dark seasons
There are many dark seasons in God's providential dealings with us, in which we can see no way of escape, nor find any source of comfort, but the testimony of God. God's friends are not distinguished in this world by an exemption from trying providences; he views that, methinks, as too trifling a badge of distinction. They shall be known by what is far more noble and advantageous; namely, by patience, obedience, submission, and divine support under them. Moreover, as we profess to be friends of God, and to trust the salvation of our souls with all our concerns in his hands, he sees it proper to prove the sincerity of our professions, and the stability of our hearts. He brings us into such circumstances, therefore, as shall try us, whether we will confide in him or not.

Christ has told his followers, once for all, that "all power in heaven and earth is in his hands;"[40] that he is "Head over all things to the church;"[41] that he "will surely do them good;"[42] that however things may seem, "all things shall work together for good to them that love God, to them who are the called according to his purpose;"[43] that as to temporal things, let them but "trust in the Lord, and do good, and they shall dwell in the land, and verily they shall be fed;"[44] and as to eternal things, if they have a few light afflictions, they shall last but for a "moment,"[45] and shall "work for them a far more exceeding and eternal weight of glory."[46] These promises seem easy to be believed, when things are smooth and pleasing; and it is very natural for us, in a day of prosperity, to talk of these things, and try and comfort those with them who are labouring in adversity. But the greatest trial is when it comes home to ourselves. Then it is well if we fall not under the reproof of Eliphaz: "Thy

---

[40] Matthew 28:18.
[41] Ephesians 1:22.
[42] Genesis 32:12.
[43] Romans 8:28.
[44] Psalm 37:3.
[45] 2 Corinthians 4:17.
[46] 2 Corinthians 4:17.

words have upholden him that was falling, and thou hast strengthened the feeble knees: but now it is come upon thee, and thou faintest; it toucheth thee, and thou art troubled."[47] Then, if ever, is the time for us to walk by faith, and not by sight.

We create to ourselves darlings, and place much of our happiness in their enjoyment. God not unfrequently takes these first away, as being most his rivals. If one child is more beloved than all the rest, if he must be clothed with a coat of many colours, the coat must quickly be returned without the owner.[48] Yes, the period must soon arrive when it shall be said, "Joseph is not!" These, with a few more strokes of the kind, will try Jacob's faith to the uttermost, and he will find it hard work to reconcile promises with providences. "Thou saidst, I will surely do thee good;"[49] but "all these things are against me."[50] Ah, he fails! He fails, like Asaph in a similar condition, who could not see how God could be "good to Israel," when "waters of a full cup were wrung out to them."[51] The Shunammitish woman will set us a better example than either the patriarch or the prophet. "Is it well?" said Elisha's servant, when her child lay dead in her house. She replied, "It is well."[52] This was, in effect, saying, "Whether I can see it or not, I know he does all things well." This is believing when we cannot see, taking God at his word, against all the rebellion of sense and feeling. This is what Jacob should have done, but oh that Jacob had failed alone! If to resemble him, in this instance, would constitute us Israelites, we should most of us be Israelites indeed!

We are often very thrifty in devising plans for futurity, and apt to promise ourselves great degrees of happiness, when they are accomplished. Here it is common for God to throw confusion upon our schemes, and cause things to run in a different channel from what we expected. Job, while in prosperity, sat like a bird in her well-feathered nest and thought within himself, "I shall live to enjoy numerous years of uninterrupted prosperity, to see children's children, and then go down to the grave in peace;" or, as he himself afterwards, in the bitter hour of reflection, expressed it, "I said, 'I shall die in my nest, I shall multiply

---

[47] Job 4:4–5.
[48] Genesis 37:32.
[49] Genesis 32:12.
[50] Genesis 42:36.
[51] Psalm 73:10.
[52] 2 Kings 4:23.

Preparing sermons

my days as the sand!'" Well, so he did at last; but there was a melancholy chasm in his life which he never expected. Such there are, more or less, in all our lives; and, in such situations, it is well if we do not think hard of our best friend. Some have been ready to ask, "Is this love? Is this his doing who has said, 'I will surely do thee good?'" Yes, and you shall see it in the end, as Asaph did; who, after he had been to God's sanctuary, and saw things as they were, went home, it seems, and penned the seventy-third Psalm, beginning it all in ecstasy, saying, "Truly God is good to Israel!"[53] Christians, how criminal, how cruel, that he that never failed us at any time should be so mistrusted as he is. It should seem to suggest as if he were such a God that we cannot trust him out of sight!

How amiable is that spirit, how happy is that heart, that, in every situation, places unbounded confidence in Jehovah's word! Such may be hedged up on every side, and encompassed, like Israel at the Red Sea, with seemingly insurmountable difficulties; yet, even here, they will follow Israel's example, they will cry unto God, and rely upon his mercy. If means can be used, they will use them. If not, they will "stand still and see the salvation of the Lord."[54] "Speak unto the children of Israel," said the Lord, "that they go forward."[55] Go forward! they might have replied; what, leap at once into the jaws of destruction! But nothing of this. At first, indeed, their faith seemed to fail them, but they soon recovered themselves. "Speak unto the children of Israel," said the Lord, "that they go forward." They went a way that was made in the sea, and a path in the mighty waters. Well may it be said, "by faith Israel passed through the Red Sea. Minds thus disposed might defy the united sources of worldly sorrow to render them unhappy. Let poverty stare them in the face, let pinching want stretch over them her miserable sceptre, they have been known, even here, by faith, to break forth into songs of praise." Thus sang good Habakkuk (and this evidently appears to be his situation, and not a state of spiritual declension), "Although the fig tree shall not blossom, neither shall fruit be in the vines, the labour of the olive shall fail, and the fields shall yield no meat, the flock shall be cut off from the fold, and no herd in the stalls; yet will I rejoice in the Lord, I will joy in

---

[53] Psalm 73:1.
[54] Exodus 14:13.
[55] Exodus 14:15.

the God of my salvation."[56] Thus also sang the church, even in her captivity, when her country was laid waste, Jerusalem razed to the ground, and the temple burnt to ashes: "The Lord is my portion, saith my soul, therefore will I hope in him!"[57]

One with Christ by faith
In all our approaches to and fellowship with Christ, it is by faith in the account that God has given of him in his word. Christ's excellence, undertaking, and benefits are the joy, and even the life, of our souls, if we are true Christians. But what evidence have we of all or any of these? Yea, what evidence have we that there is, or ever was, such a person as Jesus Christ? or if there was, that he was the Messiah, the Son of God? We neither saw him alive, nor die, rise again, nor ascend to heaven. We never saw the miracles he wrought, nor heard the voice from the excellent glory, saying, "This is my beloved Son, hear ye him."[58] We speak of his personal excellences, divine and human; of his love, zeal, righteousness, meekness, patience, &c.; but what know we of them? We rejoice in his being constituted our Surety, to obey the law and endure the curse in our stead; but how know we that so indeed it is? We glory in the imputation of his righteousness, and exult in the hope of being found in him, and being forever with him, faultless before his throne, to serve him day and night in his temple; but on what do we rely for all this? If our expectations are but just, truly they are noble; but if groundless, extravagant. Are they, then, well-founded? Yes, the testimony of God is the rock whereon they rest. He has told us by the mouth of his servants, the inspired writers, all that is necessary for as to know, of the character, conduct, and errand of his Son; of every office he sustained, and every end for which he came into the world. To all this he has added that "whosoever believeth on him shall not perish, but have everlasting life."[59] So they have preached, and so we have believed. We have, through grace, ventured our everlasting all in his hands. Nor is it in the hands of we know not whom: "we know whom we have trusted, and are persuaded that he is able to keep

---

[56] Habakkuk 3:17-18.
[57] Lamentations 3:24.
[58] Mark 9:7; Luke 9:35.
[59] John 3:16.

Preparing sermons

that which we have committed to him against that day."[60] For though none of these things are visible to our mortal eye, yet, having evidence that God has said them, we are satisfied. We would as soon trust God's word as our own eyes. Thus we walk, like Moses, "as seeing him who is invisible;"[61] and thus answer to that description, "Whom having not seen ye love, in whom, though now ye see him not, yet believing, ye rejoice with joy unspeakable, and full of glory."[62]

In all our applications to Christ, we have to rely merely upon the testimony of God. Here is a poor, self-condemned sinner, who comes pressing through the crowd of discouraging apprehensions, that he may, so to speak, touch the hem of the Redeemer's garment and be made whole. As he approaches, one set of thoughts suggests, "How can such a monster hope for mercy? Is it not doubtful whether there be efficacy enough in the blood of Christ itself to pardon such heinous crimes?—I know my crimes are heinous beyond expression," replies the burdened soul, "and I should doubtless give up my case as desperate, but that I have heard of him that 'he is able to save to the uttermost all that come unto God by him.'[63] I will go, therefore; who can tell?"—As he goes, other objections assail him, questioning whether Christ can find in his heart to accept of such a one? "I should think not, indeed," rejoins the poor man; "but he has said, 'Him that cometh to me I will in nowise cast out.' I know, were I to consult nothing but my feelings, and only to fix my eyes on the enormity of my sin, I should utterly despair; but encouraged by his word, I will go forward. I will walk by faith, not by sight: O, I hear him say, 'come unto me, all ye that labour, and are heavy laden and ye shall find rest unto your souls!'[64] This, this is what I want! Depart from me, all ye that vex my soul: I will go in the strength of the Lord God!"

Self-denial
We have to give up many present enjoyments, for Christ's sake, wherein we have no visible prospect of recompense, none of any kind but what arises from the promise of God. Self-denial is one of the initial laws of

---

[60] 2 Timothy 1:12.
[61] Hebrews 11:27.
[62] 1 Peter 1:8.
[63] Hebrews 7:25.
[64] Matthew 11:28.

Christ's kingdom. Far from enticing people into his service by promises of wealth, ease, and honour, he set out with this public declaration, "Whosoever will be my disciple must deny himself, take up his cross, and follow me."[65] But who would enter upon these terms? Who would give up houses, lands, friends, and reputation, and expose himself to hardships, persecution, and death, for nothing? Yet many followed him, and that to the day of their death; yea, and upon these very terms too: "they left all, and followed him."[66] What then induced them? Did not they act irrationally? Prophets, apostles, and martyrs! What do you mean? Have you no regard for yourselves? What! Are you destitute of the feelings of men?—No such thing; we "have respect unto the recompense of reward."[67]—Reward! what can that be? Nothing surely below the sun, unless it were everything the reverse of what is agreeable to human nature!—True; but our Lord has declared, "Whosoever shall forsake houses, or brethren, or sisters, or father, or mother, or wife, or children, or lands, for my name's sake, shall receive a hundredfold and inherit everlasting life."[68] We rely upon this, and this supports us.

God's friends, in all ages, have forsaken sensible for invisible enjoyments. Encouraged by considerations like these, Ruth forsook her father and her mother, and the land of her nativity, and came to a people whom she knew not. It was this that determined her to go forward, when, as Naomi told her, there were no earthly prospects before her. It was this that made her resolve not to go back with Orpah, but to cast in her lot with the friends of the God of Israel. "The Lord recompense thy work," said Boaz to her afterwards, "and a full reward be given thee of the Lord God of Israel, under whose wings thou art come to trust!"[69]

The same things influenced Moses, it seems, to refuse a crown. It has been thought that, in virtue of his adoption, he might have been king of Egypt; but that throne not only, like other thrones, exposed him that sat thereon to numberless snares, but probably was inaccessible to any but those who would continue the system of idolatry and oppression. In that case Moses, in order to become king of Egypt, must have sacrificed a

---

[65] Matthew 16:24; Luke 9:23; Mark 8:34.
[66] Luke 5:11.
[67] Hebrews 11:26.
[68] Matthew 19:29.
[69] Ruth 2:12.

Preparing sermons

good conscience, despised a crown of glory that fades not away, and united in persecuting his own and the Lord's people. Moses seems fully to have weighed this matter. The result was, he "refused to be called the son of Pharaoh's daughter, choosing rather to suffer affliction with the people of God than to enjoy the pleasures of sin for a season; esteeming even the reproach of Christ greater riches than the treasures in Egypt."[70] He, therefore, freely leaves the life of a courtier; avows himself the friend of the poor despised captives; and dares to retire into Midian, to lead the life of an obscure shepherd. I say, he dared to retire; for it required a greater degree of courage thus to deny himself, than to stand in the forefront of a battle, or to face the mouth of a cannon! But "by faith he forsook Egypt, and went and lived a stranger in a strange land; for he endured as seeing him who is invisible;" yes, "he had respect unto the recompense of reward."[71]

In short, through this, the holy tribes of martyrs, in all ages, loved not their lives unto the death. By faith in invisible realities, as the apostle to the Hebrews largely proves, they bore all manner of cruelties, not accepting deliverance itself upon dishonourable conditions; suffered all kinds of deaths with unremitting fortitude, and, in some sort, like their glorious Leader, triumphed over principalities and powers when they fell.

Indeed, every man in the world may be said to walk either by faith or by sight. There is not only a giving up sensible for invisible enjoyments, by actually parting with them, but by not setting our hearts upon them, as our chief good. This may be done where there is no call actually to give them up, and is done by all real Christians in the world. Men whose chief good consists in the profits, pleasures, or honours of this life live by sight; they derive their life from objects before their eyes, having neither patience nor inclination to wait for a portion in the world to come. But good men, as well the rich as the poor, derive their life from above, and so live by faith; their "life is hid with Christ in God."[72]

Perhaps here, as much as anywhere, is required the peculiar exercise of faith. For one actually divested of earthly good to look upward, and set his heart on things above, is faith; but for one still possessed of this—one on whom Providence smiles, prospering him in all he sets his hand to,

---

[70] Hebrews 11:24–26.
[71] Hebrews 11:26–27.
[72] Colossians 3:3.

blessing him with wife and children, houses and lands, in abundance—for him to exercise such a degree of indifference to all these as to derive his chief happiness from invisible realities, this is faith indeed! This seems to have been exemplified in Abraham, and other patriarchs. Of him it is said, "By faith he sojourned in the land of promise, as in a strange country."[73] How is this? We do not wonder that when he and Sarah went into Egypt, on account of a famine, he should consider himself a sojourner there; but how is it that he should do so in Canaan, the land of promise, his own estate, as it were? The next verse informs us; "for he looked for a city which hath foundations, whose builder and maker is God."[74] So Jacob, when before Pharaoh, called his whole life a pilgrimage, though the far greater part of it was spent in the Land of Promise; and "they that say such things," adds the apostle, "declare plainly that they seek a country."[75] Though God had given them the good land, they would not make it their chief good. They could not be contented with this Canaan, but longed for another. Noble souls! bid them lift up their eyes eastward, and westward, and northward, and southward, and tell them all they can see is their own; still they will not live by sight, but by faith; "they will desire a better country, that is, a heavenly."

Faith in the promise of God
There are many low and distressing seasons to which the church of God is subject, in which there is little or no visible ground of encouragement, scarcely any but what arises from the promise of God. The whole church of God, as individuals, has, in all ages, had its day of adversity set over against the day of prosperity. Israel, after their deliverance from Egypt and settlement in Canaan, enjoyed pretty much prosperity, especially in the days of David and Solomon. But afterwards, by a series of provocations, they procured to themselves the Babylonish captivity. At that melancholy period, those amongst them that feared the Lord must be supposed to be all in darkness. Jerusalem laid waste, the temple burnt with fire, Judah carried captive. Ah, what becomes of God's interest in the world! The "foundations" of his visible kingdom seemed to be "laid in the holy mountains" round about Jerusalem. If these are destroyed, what

---

[73] Hebrews 11:9.
[74] Hebrews 11:10.
[75] Hebrews 11:14.

can the righteous do? They had long sighed and cried for the idolatrous abominations of their countrymen, and prayed and hoped that mercy might be lengthened out; but now all seems over. For their idolatry, they must go, and have enough of idolaters: they that feared the Lord must also go with them. By the rivers of Babylon they must go, and sit down. Those that had been used to sound the high praises of God in Zion must now hang their harps upon the willows, as having no use for them! Nor is this the worst. They must be taunted, and their God derided, by their insulting lords: "Come," said they, "sing us one of the songs of Zion;" as if they had said, Now, see what your religion has availed you! This was your favourite employ, and these were the songs wherewith you addressed your Deity, in whom you confided to deliver you out of our hands; what think you now? Poor Zion! "She spreadeth forth her hands, but there is none to comfort her. The Lord hath commanded that her adversaries should be round about her:"[76] her captive sons can only remember Jerusalem and weep! Alas, "how can they sing the Lord's song in a strange land!"[77]

But is there no help from above? Is there no physician there? Yes, the God whom Babel derides, but Judah adores, looks down, and sees their affliction. To his disheartened friends, in this situation, he addresses himself, saying, "Who is among you that feareth the Lord, that obeyeth the voice of his servant, that walketh in darkness, and hath no light? Let him trust in the name of the Lord, and stay upon his God."[78] As if he should say, "For a season you must walk by faith, and not by sight; but, trust me, that season shall soon be over." Seventy years, and Babylon shall fall, and Judah return! By these declarations the church was encouraged in her captivity, and furnished with an answer to her insulting foes; yea, and, what is wonderful, breaks forth into one of the Lord's songs in a strange land! (Hearken, O Babel, to "one of the songs of Zion!") "Rejoice not against me, O mine enemy; when I fall, I shall arise; when I sit in darkness, the Lord shall be a light unto me. I will bear the indignation of the Lord, because I have sinned against him, until he plead my cause, and execute judgment for me. He will bring me forth to the light, and I shall behold his righteousness. Then she that is mine enemy shall see it,

---

[76] Lamentations 1:17.
[77] Psalm 137:4.
[78] Isaiah 50:10.

and shame shall cover her which said unto me, Where is the Lord thy God?"[79]

This is encouraging to us as churches and as ministers. We have, in many cases, to walk in darkness, and have no light, and to go on in our ministrations, in a great degree, like the prophet Isaiah, lamenting that there are so few who have believed our report, so few to whom the arm of the Lord has been revealed. When death removes worthy characters, we must sometimes live, and lament to see their places unoccupied by others of the like character; and, what is worse, instead of increase by Christ's conquests, we must sometimes live to see a decrease by the conquests of the evil one! Many a faithful minister has had to preach, year after year, till, either by public scandals or private disgusts, many of his people have gone off, and walked no more with him. But let him then remember the testimony of God: "Him that honoureth me I will honour."[80] Let him go on, and faithfully discharge his duty, whether they will hear or whether they will forbear; let him, and those that are with him, walk by faith, and not by sight. It often proves that, after such a night of weeping, comes a morning of rejoicing. Let us not be discouraged; better breath than ours has been spent apparently in vain. Our Lord himself seemed to labour in vain, and to spend his strength for nought; but he comforted himself in this, (herein leaving us an example): "Though Israel be not gathered, yet shall I be glorious in the eyes of the Lord, and my God shall be my strength."[81]

This may encourage and direct us in larger concerns; concerns which respect the whole interest of Christ in the world. If we compare the present state of things, or even the past, with the glorious prophecies of the word of God, we cannot think, surely, that all is yet accomplished. By these prophecies the Christian church is encouraged to look for great things at some period or other of her existence. She is taught to look for a time when "the earth shall be full of the knowledge of the Lord, as the waters cover the sea;"[82] when "a nation shall be born at once;"[83] when "the kingdoms of this world shall become the kingdoms of our Lord, and

---

[79] Micah 7:8–10.
[80] 1 Samuel 2:30.
[81] Isaiah 49:5.
[82] Habakkuk 2:14.
[83] Isaiah 66:8.

of his Christ;"[84] and he "shall reign from sea to sea, and from the river unto the ends of the earth."[85] But surely, for the present, though great things, upon the whole, have been done in the world, yet nothing like this has ever come to pass. Instead of the world being conquered, what a great part yet continues to stand out against him! Heathenism, Mahomedism, popery, and infidelity, how extensive still their influence! In all probability, not a single country, city, town, village, or congregation has ever yet been brought wholly to submit to Christ! Nay, is it not very rare to find, in any one of these, so many real friends as to make even a majority in his favour? May not the Christian church then, for the present, adopt that language, "We have been with child, we have as it were brought forth wind, we have not wrought any deliverance in the earth, neither have the inhabitants of the world fallen?"[86] What then, shall we despair? God forbid! "The vision is yet for an appointed time, but at the end it shall speak, and not lie: though it tarry, wait for it, because it will surely come, it will not tarry;"[87] and, meanwhile, "the just shall live by faith."[88]

Let us take encouragement, in the present day of small things, by looking forward, and hoping for better days. Let this be attended with earnest and united prayer to him by whom Jacob must arise. A life of faith will ever be a life of prayer. O brethren, let us pray much for an outpouring of God's Spirit upon our ministers and churches, and not upon those only of our own connection and denomination, but upon "all that in every place call upon the name of Jesus Christ our Lord, both theirs and ours!"

Our hope of a better state, when this is over, is built on faith in God's testimony. We have no sort of evidence but that any such state exists. We cannot see anything of the kind, or aught from which we can infer it. We cannot learn it from any of our senses. Reason itself could never have found it out. Reason might have taught us the idea of a future state, but not of a future state of bliss. Though much might be argued from the fitness of things, to prove that man is not made barely for the present life,

---

[84] Revelation 11:15.
[85] Psalm 72:8.
[86] Isaiah 26:18.
[87] Habakkuk 2:3.
[88] Romans 1:17; Galatians 3:11; Hebrews 10:38.

yet nothing could thence be drawn to prove that rebels against the Supreme Being should live in a state of eternal felicity; no, for this we are wholly indebted to the word of promise. Hence faith is said to be "the substance, ground, or foundation of things hoped for."[89] Supported by that, we sustain our heaviest losses; and, attracted by these, we come up out of great tribulations, following the Lamb whithersoever he goes, till we shall overcome, and "sit down with him in his throne, as he also hath overcome, and is set down with his Father in his throne."[90]

The importance of walking by faith

We will now add a few words on the importance of such a life. If, all things considered, it would have been best for us to have always seen our way before us—to have been guided, so to speak, with our own eyes, and not to have implicitly followed the directions of God—no doubt so it would have been ordered. But he who perfectly, and at once, saw the beginning and end of all things, judged otherwise. With the highest wisdom, no doubt, he formed the resolution, "the just shall live by faith."[91] It may be impossible for us, in the present state, to find out all the reasons for this resolution; but two or three seem to present themselves to our view.

Such a life brings great glory to God
Confidence is universally a medium of honour. To confide in a fellow creature puts honour upon him in the account of others, and affords a pleasure to himself; especially if he be a wise and upright character, as it gives him an opportunity of proving his wisdom and fidelity. Though the great God cannot be made more honourable than he is by anything we can do, yet his honour may, by this, be made more apparent. We honour him, so far as we form just conceptions of him in our own minds, and act so as to give just representations of him to others. God is graciously pleased to declare that "he takes pleasure in those that hope in his mercy;"[92] and why? Surely among other things, because it gives him occasion to display the glory of his grace. And as he takes pleasure in those that hope in his mercy and rely upon it, so he takes pleasure in ordering

---

[89] Hebrews 11:1.
[90] Revelation 3:21.
[91] Romans 1:17; Galatians 3:11; Hebrews 10:38.
[92] Psalm 147:11.

things so that we may be put to the trial, whether we will rely on him or not. It was this which induced him to lead Israel through the wilderness, rather than by the ready road to Canaan. He knew they would be, in fact, dependent upon him, let them be where they would; but they would not be sensible of that dependence, nor have so much opportunity of entirely trusting him, in any way as in this; and so it would not be so much for the glory of his great name. He therefore would lead a nation, with all their little ones, into an inhospitable desert, where was scarcely a morsel of meat to eat, and, in many places, not a drop of water to drink; "a land of deserts and of pits, of scorpions and fiery flying serpents."[93] Here, if anywhere, they must be sensibly dependent on God. They must be fed and preserved immediately from heaven itself, and that by miracle, or all perish in a few days. Here God must appear to be what he was—here mercy and truth must appear to go with them indeed!

What an opportunity was afforded them to have walked these forty years by faith. What grounds for an entire confidence. But, alas, their faithless hearts perverted their way, and, in the end, proved their ruin! Ten times they tempted God in the desert, till at length he swore, concerning that generation, that, for their unbelief, they should die in the wilderness, and never enter his rest. Few, if any, besides Joshua and Caleb, would dare to trust him, notwithstanding all his wonders and all his mercies! They, however, for their part, took hold of his strength, and thought themselves able, having God on their side, to encounter anything. Their spirit was to walk by faith and not by sight, and herein it is easy to see how they glorified God.

O brethren, let the glory of God lie near our hearts! Let it be dearer to us than our dearest delights! Herein consists the criterion of true love to him. Let us, after the noble example of Joshua and Caleb, "follow the Lord fully."[94] Let us approve of everything that tends to glorify him. Let us be reconciled to his conduct, who "suffers us to hunger, that we may know that man lives not by bread alone, but by every word that proceedeth out of the mouth of God."[95] If he should bring us into hard and difficult situations, situations to an eye of sense impossible to be endured, let us remember that it is that he may give us an opportunity of glorifying

---

[93] Deuteronomy 8:15.
[94] Numbers 14:24.
[95] Deuteronomy 8:3.

him, by trusting him in the dark. The more difficult the trial, the more glory to him that bears us through, and the greater opportunity is afforded us for proving that we can indeed trust him with all our concerns—that we can trust him when we cannot see the end of his present dispensations.

Those very much dishonour God who profess to trust him for another world, but in the common difficulties of this are perpetually murmuring, peevish, and distrustful. How different was it with Abraham, in offering up his son Isaac. What, offer up Isaac! My son, my only son of promise! Why, is not the Messiah to spring out of his loins? What are to become of all the nations of the earth, who are to be blessed in him? How natural and excusable might such questions have seemed. Much more so than most of our objections to the divine conduct. Sense, in this case, had it been consulted, must have entered a thousand protests. But the father of the faithful consulted not with flesh and blood, not doubting but God knew what he was about, if he himself did not (O that we may prove ourselves the children of faithful Abraham!). Against hope, in appearance, he believed in hope of divine all-sufficiency. Fully persuaded that what God had promised he was able to perform, he stretched forth his obedient arm; nor had he recalled it, had not heaven interposed: he was "strong in faith, giving glory to God."[96]

Such a life is productive of great good to us
The glory of God and the good of those that love him (thanks be to his name!) always go together. It is equally to their benefit as to his honour, for instance, to lie low before him, and to feel their entire dependence upon him. It is essential to the real happiness of an intelligent creature to be in its proper place, and to take a complacency in being so. But nothing tends more to cultivate these dispositions than God's determining that, at present, we should walk by faith and not by sight. Faith, in the whole of it, tends more than a little to abase the fallen creature; and to walk by faith (which is as much as to acknowledge that we are blind, and must see with the eyes of another) is very humbling. The objects of our desire being frequently for a time withheld, and our being at such times reduced to situations wherein we can see no help, and thus obliged to repose our

---

[96] Romans 4:20.

PREPARING SERMONS

trust in God, contribute more than a little to make us feel our dependence upon him. Agur saw that a constant fullness of this world was unfriendly to a spirit of entire dependence upon God; therefore, he prayed, "Give me not riches: lest I be full, and deny thee."[97] Whatever tends to humble and try us, tends to "do us good in the latter end."[98]

Great and wonderful is the consolation that such a life affords. In all the vicissitudes of life and horrors of death, nothing can cheer and fortify the mind like this. By faith in an unseen world we can endure injuries without revenge, afflictions without fainting, and losses without despair. Let the nations of the earth dash, like potsherds, one against another; yea, let nature herself approach towards her final dissolution; let her groan as being ready to expire, and sink into her primitive nothing; still the believer lives! His all is not on board that vessel! His chief inheritance lies in another soil!

His hand the good man fastens on the skies,
And bids earth roll, nor feels her idle whirl![99]

It will make vision the sweeter
It affords a great pleasure, when we make a venture of any kind, to find ourselves at last not disappointed. If a considerate man embark his all on board a vessel, and himself with it, he may have a thousand fears, before he reaches the end of his voyage; yet should he, after numberless dangers, safely arrive, and find it not only answer, but far exceed his expectations, his joy will then be greater than if he had run no hazard at all. What he has gained will seem much sweeter than if it had fallen to him in a way that had cost him nothing. Thus believers venture their all in the hands of Christ, persuaded that he is able to keep that which they have committed to him against that day. To find at last that they have not confided in him in vain—yea, that their expectations are not only answered, but infinitely outdone—will surely enhance the bliss of heaven. The remembrance of our dangers, fears, and sorrows will enable us to enjoy the

---

[97] Proverbs 30:8–9.
[98] Job 8:7.
[99] Edward Young, *The Poetical Works of Milton, Young, Gray, Beattie, and Collins*, "The complaint; or Night-thoughts on life, death, and immortality" (Philadelphia: J.B. Lippincott and Co., 1859), 91.

heavenly state with a degree of happiness impossible to have been felt, if those dangers, fears, and sorrows had never existed.

My hearers! All of us live either by faith or by sight; either upon things heavenly or things earthly. If on the former, let us go on, upon the word of God; everlasting glory is before us. But if on the latter, alas, our store will be soon exhausted. All these dear delights are but the brood of time, a brood that will soon take to themselves wings, and, with her that cherished them, fly away. O my hearers! Is it not common for many of you to suppose that those who live by faith in the enjoyments of a world to come live upon mere imaginations? But are you not mistaken? It is your enjoyments, and not theirs, that are imaginary. Pleasures, profits, honours, what are they? The whole form only a kind of ideal world, a sort of splendid show, like that in a dream, which, when you wake, all is gone! At most it is a fashion, and a fashion that passes away. To grasp it is to grasp a shadow; and to feed upon it is to feed upon the wind. Oh, that you may turn away your eyes from beholding these vanities, and look to the Lord Jesus Christ, and the substantial realities beyond the grave, for your never-failing portion!

But if not, if you still prefer this world, with its enjoyments, to those which are heavenly, how just will it be for the Lord Jesus to say to you, at the last great day, "Depart!"[100] Depart, you have had your reward! you have had your choice; what would you have? You never chose me for your portion: you, in effect, said, of me and my interest, "We will have no part in David, nor inheritance in the son of Jesse: see to thyself, David."[101] Ah, now, see to yourself, sinner!

Christians, ministers, brethren, all of us! Let us realize the subject. Let us pray, and preach, and hear, and do everything we do with eternity in view. Let us deal much with Christ and invisible realities. Let us, whenever called, freely deny ourselves for his sake, and trust him to make up the loss. Let us not faint under present difficulties, but consider them as opportunities afforded us to glorify God. Let us be ashamed that we derive our happiness so much from things below, and so little from things above. In one word, let us fight the good fight of faith and lay hold on eternal life!

---

[100] Matthew 7:23.
[101] 1 Kings 12:16.

4
Preparing the Preacher to Preach Christ

"His humility and godly jealousy appear continually," John Ryland wrote about his close ministry friend, Andrew Fuller. Ryland added, "While others admired his zeal and diligence, he was perpetually bewailing his lukewarmness, inconstancy, and inactivity; and dreading lest he should prove an 'idol shepherd,' who fed not the flock."[1] Fuller's ministerial courage and pervasive influence were rooted in his consistent fight to think of himself first and foremost as a Christian who was in daily need of the gospel, and not as a pastor, evangelist, theologian, apologist, missions advocate, or strategist. In Fuller's understanding, there was no room for a ceremonial pastor who had learned how to perform the duties of the ministry but did not feel daily his own need of the gospel.

A letter that Ryland found among Fuller's papers as he was writing his biography, shortly after Fuller's death on May 7, 1815, provides a helpful window into the affectionate Christian outlook he fought so hard to personally maintain. The letter was to a friend to whom Fuller had been complaining regarding some of his ministry struggles. Fuller had dated the letter October 5, 1783, and written on it, "O may I never forget the hints in this letter!" His friend had written,

> I love you, but I do not greatly pity you: I am glad you feel as you do—"when I am weak, then I am strong." God Almighty keep us from ever being great men, or, rather, from thinking ourselves so! Oh! It requires numberless miracles to get any man to heaven; perhaps, I might say, especially a minister! You will do, as long as you feel vile, and foolish, and weak. I had rather preach at your funeral, than live to see you good, and wise, and great, and strong, in your own estimation.[2]

---

[1] John Ryland, *The Work of Faith, the Labor of Love, and the Patience of Hope Illustrated in the Life and Death of the Rev. Andrew Fuller* (London: Button and Son, 1818), 95.

[2] Ryland, *Work of Faith, Labor of Love*, 95.

Fuller was committed to a genuine, gut-level, and felt Christianity, which meant as a pastor, he must live as a Christian first, if he was to have a faithful ministry in the sight of God.

A Christian with gospel friendships

The kind of friendships Fuller had with John Sutcliff, Samuel Pearce, and John Ryland are best described as gospel friendships. Some so-called friendships never rise beyond superficial compliments and flattery but Fuller valued and maintained the kind of longstanding friendships that eventuated in mutual accountability and spurring one another on toward spiritual growth because the gospel was valued more than one's temporal feelings. Preaching the funeral sermon of his pastor friend John Sutcliff on June 28, 1814, Fuller said, "There was a gentleness in his reproofs that distinguished them." [3] John Ryland wrote about the intimacy and accountability of his almost four-decade long friendship with Andrew Fuller in the preface to his memoirs of Fuller,

> Most of our common acquaintance are well aware that I was his oldest and most intimate friend; and though my removal to Bristol, above twenty years ago, placed us at a distance from each other, yet a constant correspondence was all long maintained; and, to me at least, it seemed a tedious interval, if more than a fortnight elapsed without my receiving a letter from him. ... But, as I affirmed at his funeral, so I again avow my persuasion, that our intimate friendship did not blind either of us to the defects of the other; but, rather, showed itself in the freedom of affectionate remark on whatever appeared to be wrong.[4]

Michael Haykin described Fuller as having the "ability to nurture and sustain deep, long-lasting and satisfying friendships."[5] These satisfying gospel friendships were not forged from absolute unanimity of views on all theological, ecclesiological, and practical issues. Fuller sometimes had exegetical disagreements with his closest friends, yet their friendship was

---

[3] Fuller, "Principles and Prospects of a Servant of Christ," *Complete Works*, 1:354.
[4] Fuller, "Principles and Prospects of a Servant of Christ," *Complete Works*, 1:viii–ix.
[5] Michael Haykin, *The Armies of the Lamb: The Spirituality of Andrew Fuller* (Dundas: Joshua Press, 2001), 42.

based upon a oneness of soul regarding fundamental and essential matters. Even among his Arminian and High Calvinist theological opponents, of whom Fuller had foundational disagreements, he noted, "I saw those whom I thought to be godly men," because he said "we may profess an erroneous creed, and yet our spirit and conduct may be formed nearly irrespective of it; in short, that there is a difference between principles and opinions."[6] Fuller's deep and abiding gospel friendships provided personal and ministerial accountability and influenced every aspect of his theological and ministry decisions, as well as providing vital support amidst the theological firestorm produced by the publication of *The Gospel Worthy of All Acceptation*.

One of the important things Fuller shared with his friends was the blessing of Christian books. Fuller was determined "to take up no principle second hand"[7] because according to him the Bible is "the book by way of eminence, the book of books," which is preeminent, authoritative, without error, and that book by which all else will be judged.[8] Nevertheless, Fuller was a reader, and as a young man he testified to reading John Bunyan's *Grace abounding to the Chief of Sinners* and *Pilgrim's Progress*, and Ralph Erskine's *Gospel Sonnets* and *Christ All in All in our Complete Redemption*. Fuller states that while these books had some impact upon him at the time, the conviction they produced was momentary.[9]

Once Fuller assumed the pastorate of the church at Soham in 1775, Robert Hall of Arnsby recommended Fuller read Jonathan Edwards' book *Freedom of the Will*, which he eventually acquired and read by 1777. Fuller wrote to Jonathan Edwards' grandson, stating that Edwards' writings "have been food to me and many others."[10] Particularly, Edwards' distinction between natural inability and moral inability regarding faith provided Fuller the biblical ground for the free offer of the gospel. According to Fuller (following Edwards), "the inability ascribed to man, with respect to believing, arises from the aversion of his heart," it is moral and not natural inability.[11] Fuller explains the influence and connection in his life of gospel friends and gospel books,

---

[6] Ryland, *Work of Faith*, 35.
[7] Fuller, "Memoir," *Complete Works*, 1:20.
[8] Fuller, "The Apostolic Office," *Complete Works*, 3:499.
[9] Fuller, "Memoir," *Complete Works*, 1:3.
[10] Fuller, "Memoirs," *Complete Works*, 1:85.
[11] Fuller, "The Gospel Worthy of All Acceptation," *Complete Works*, 2:330.

In 1776 I became acquainted with Mr. Sutcliff, who had lately come to Olney, and soon after with Mr. John Ryland, jun., then of Northampton. In them I found familiar and faithful brethren; and who, partly by reflection, and partly by reading the writings of Edwards, Bellamy, Brainerd, &c., had begun to doubt of the system of false Calvinism to which they had been inclined when they first entered on the ministry, or rather to be decided against it. But as I lived sixty or seventy miles from them, I seldom saw them, and did not correspond upon the subject. I therefore pursued my inquiries by myself, and wrote out the substance of what I afterwards published under the title of *The Gospel worthy of all Acceptation; or the Obligations of Men cordially to believe whatever God makes known*.[12]

At the end of his life Fuller wrote to his friend Ryland asking him to preach his funeral sermon. In the correspondence, Fuller defends his friend John Sutcliff and his favorite writer, Jonathan Edwards, from criticism,

We have some who have been giving out, of late, that "If Sutcliff and some others had preached more of Christ, and less of Jonathan Edwards, they would have been more useful." If those who talked thus preached Christ half as much as Jonathan Edwards did, and were half as useful as he was, their usefulness would be double what it is. It is very singular that the mission to the east should have originated with men of these principles; and, without pretending to be a prophet, I may say, if ever it falls into the hands of men who talk in this strain, it will soon come to nothing.

If I should never see your face in the flesh, I could wish one last testimony of brotherly love, and of the truth of the gospel, to be expressed by your coming over and preaching my funeral sermon, if it can be, from Rom. 8:10. I can dictate no more, but am ever yours.[13]

A passionate love for Christ's church to the ends of the earth

When Fuller was laboring over whether or not he should leave the Soham Church for the Baptist Church in Kettering his friend John Ryland said, "Men who fear not God, would risk the welfare of a nation with fewer searchings of heart than it cost him to determine whether he should leave

---

[12] Fuller, "Memoirs," *Complete Works*, 1:16.
[13] Fuller, "Memoirs," *Complete Works*, 1:101–102.

a little dissenting church, scarcely containing forty members besides himself and his wife."[14] Fuller's commitment to preach the gospel to all men without exception, calling them to repent of their sin and trust in Christ, had already proven costly in his ministry at Soham. As his ministry at Soham had become more heart-searching, applicatory, practical, and directly evangelistic some church members responded by withholding tithes and offerings. His salary was already meager and he was forced to try to earn money in other ways. Fuller could hardly afford his tiny piece of property but he was so reluctant to leave because he believed God used Christian suffering to advance the gospel.

Eventually, in 1782, Fuller moved to Kettering to become the pastor, but even then, his love and burden for the flock in Soham was evident. He believed it was the right decision because he believed that the necessary mutual "bond of affection was dissolved," which Fuller described as "a painful event to me."[15] Nevertheless, his heart was anything but cold toward the Soham church, he wrote a letter on December 4, 1782 after arriving at Kettering,

> Since I have been here, I have had various exercises of mind; but the state of the church at Soham has laid nearest of anything! Such has been the union of affection between them and me that I suppose no events in time, and I hope none in eternity, will ever dissolve it. ... But, alas, poor people! They are destitute! Oh! This, after all, wounds me. O may he whose name is Jehovan-jireh, see and provide for them![16]

After a twelve-month trial period, Fuller was formally inducted as the pastor of the Baptist Church in Kettering on October 7, 1783. Fuller committed himself to "the welfare of Christ's kingdom" as the pastor in Kettering but acknowledged the difficulty of the transition because "union with the one church cannot be effected but by disunion with the other."[17] In the end, every ounce of Fuller's strength at Kettering would be used to live out his conviction that the gospel must be preached to every creature. It was in his first year as pastor at Kettering that Fuller, along with

---

[14] Fuller, "Memoirs," *Complete* Works, 1:19.
[15] Ryland, *Work of Faith, Labor of Love*, 63.
[16] Ryland, *Work of Faith, the Labor of Love*, 59–60.
[17] Ryland, *Work of Faith, the Labor of Love*, 63.

PREPARING THE PREACHER

friends John Sutcliff and John Ryland Jr., called the local Baptist association to meet "the first Monday evening in every month for prayer for the extension of the gospel."[18]

His son, Andrew Gunton Fuller, wrote about those prayer meetings, "It is, perhaps, not too much to say that these gave the impetus to that missionary spirit which afterward extended itself successively through every denomination of the Christian world."[19] The simple prayer meetings, among a small group of people with a burden for the spread of the gospel were powerful enough to transform the entire world. In 1785, the theological shot that would eventually be heard round the world, *The Gospel Worthy of All Acceptation*, was published. It is doubtful whether it would have ever been published without the encouragement of his friends and these prayer meetings. On May 11, 1874, Fuller wrote in his diary, "Devoted this day to fasting and prayer, in conjunction with several other ministers, who have agreed thus to spend the second Tuesday in every other month, to seek the revival of real religion, and the extension of Christ's kingdom in the world."[20]

Fuller recounted the moment when the decision was finally made by the Baptist Missionary Society to send William Carey as a missionary to India,

> Our undertaking to India really appeared to me, on its commencement, to be somewhat like a few men, who were deliberating about the importance of penetrating into a deep mine, which had never before been explored. We had no one to guide us; and, while we were thus deliberating, Carey, as it were, said, "Well, I will go down if you will hold the rope." But, before he went down, he, as it seemed to me, took an oath from each of us at the mouth of the pit to this effect, that while we lived we should never let go the rope. You understand me. There was great responsibility attached to us who began the business.[21]

According to Fuller, there was no disassociation between the responsibility of those who would go and those who would stay. The burden was

---

[18] Fuller, "Memoirs," *Complete Works*, 1:35.
[19] Fuller, "Memoirs," *Complete Works*, 1:35.
[20] Fuller, "Memoirs," *Complete Works*, 1:36.
[21] Fuller, "Memoir," *Complete Works*, 1:68.

great for both because both would sacrifice and suffer for the Great Cause. Fuller never let go of the rope and worked tirelessly to get others to hold the rope as well. He explained, "We take for granted that the spread of the gospel is the great object of your desire. Without this it will be hard to prove that you are Christian churches."[22] For Fuller, pastors were to lead churches in mirroring the mission of Jesus by seeking the salvation of sinners, locally and globally.

A Christian first and then a minister

When Fuller discussed pastoral ministry, preaching, and gave ordination charges to other ministers, one of his most frequent admonitions is that the minister must have a genuine, personal, and vibrant gospel-spirituality. He was fearful of the deadening effects of ceremonial ministry where the minister becomes merely a religious professional who knows what to say and when to say it. Fuller feared approaching ministry in a functional and formulaic way as if it were merely a skill learned in an ecclesial trade school. Fuller's thinking was in line with that of his later admirer, Charles Haddon Spurgeon, when he warned young ministry students, "We must never preach to others with a counterfeit voice, narrating an experience which we have not ourselves enjoyed."[23]

According to Fuller, "eminent spirituality in a minister is usually attended with eminent usefulness," not in an automatic sense, that disregards the sovereignty of God, but in a way that recognizes our spirituality is more important than our giftedness.[24] Fuller writes, "God has frequently been known to succeed men of inferior abilities, when they have been eminent for holiness, while he has blasted others of much superior talents, when that quality has been wanting."[25] He argues that eminency in grace will: "fire your souls with a holy love to Christ and the souls of men," "direct your ends to the glory of God, and the welfare of men's souls," and "will enable you to bear prosperity in your ministry without

---

[22] Fuller, "The Promise of the Spirit," *Complete Works*, 3:359.

[23] Charles Haddon Spurgeon, *An All-Around Ministry: Addresses to Ministers and Students* (Bellingham: Logos Bible Software, 2009), 64.

[24] Fuller, "The Qualifications and Encouragement of a Faithful Minister," *Complete Works*, 1:143.

[25] Fuller, "The Qualifications and Encouragement of a Faithful Minister" *Complete Works*, 1:143.

being lifted up with it." Fuller calls on ministers, like the angels, to be perpetual gospel students (1 Pet. 1:10–12).[26]

For Fuller, the Christian can never move past the gospel and his unalterable and constant need of grace, and the minister must always consider himself a needy Christian before he thinks of himself as a minister. Consider how frequently this theme reoccurs in the Fuller corpus through the representative quotes below:

Study divine truths as a Christian

> The studying of divine truth as preachers rather than as Christians, or, in other words, studying it for the sake of finding out something to say to others, without so much as thinking of profiting our own souls, is a temptation to which we are more than ordinarily exposed. If we studied divine truths as Christians, our being constantly engaged in the service of God would be friendly to our growth in grace. We should be "like trees planted by the rivers of waters, that bring forth fruit in their season," and all that we did would be likely to "prosper." But if we study it only as preachers, it will be the reverse. Our being conversant with the Bible will be like surgeons and soldiers being conversant with the shedding of human blood, till they lose all sensibility concerning it. I believe it is a fact that, where a preacher is wicked, he is generally the most hardened against conviction of any character whatever. Happy will it be for us if, like Barnabas, we are "full of faith" in that Saviour whom we recommend—in that gospel which it is our employment to proclaim.[27]

> Such preparation of heart is not only necessary for your entrance into the pastoral office, but also for your continuance in it. You will find that every exercise requires it. You do not need being, guarded against that erroneous notion of so trusting to the Spirit as to neglect personal preparation for your public labours. But this preparedness is not only requisite for speaking the truth in public, but as well for seeking it in private. Let all your private meditations be mingled with prayer. You will study your Bible to wonderful advantage, if you go to it spiritually-minded. It is this which causes

---

[26] Fuller, "Ministers Fellow Laborers with God," *Complete Works*, 1:492.
[27] Fuller, "The Qualifications and Encouragement of a Faithful Minister," *Complete Works*, 1:142.

us to see the beauty and to feel the force of many parts of Scripture, to which, in a carnal state of mind, we are blind and stupid. If we go to the study of the Bible wise in our own conceits, and self-sufficient, we shall get no good. When we would be taught from God's word, we must learn as little children. Again, if we go to the Bible merely, or chiefly, to find something to say to the people, without respect to our own souls, we shall make but poor progress. My brother, study divine truth as a Christian, and not merely as a minister. Consider your own soul as deeply interested; and dread the thought of cultivating others, while you suffer your own heart to remain uncultivated. If you study divine truth as a Christian, your being constantly engaged in the study will promote your growth in grace; you will be like "a tree planted by rivers of water;" you will not only bring forth fruit for the people, but your leaf shall not wither, and whatever you do shall prosper. But if merely as a minister, the reverse. I believe it is a fact, that where a minister is wicked, he is the most hardened against conviction of any character.[28]

Live upon the truth as a Christian

Live the life of a Christian, as well as of a minister. Read as one, preach as one, converse as one—to be profited, as well as to profit others. One of the greatest temptations of a ministerial life is to handle divine truth as ministers, rather than as Christians—for others, rather than for ourselves. But the word will not profit them that preach it, any more than it will them that hear it, unless it be "mixed with faith." If we study the Scriptures as Christians, the more familiar we are with them, the more we shall feel their importance; but if our object be only to find out something to say to others, our familiarity with them will prove a snare. It will resemble that of soldiers, and doctors, and undertakers with death; the more familiar we are with them, the less we shall feel their importance (See Ps. 1:2, 3; Prov. 22:17, 18).[29]

The best way to hold fast the truth as a minister is to live upon it as a Christian. Attempt to keep it anywhere but in your heart, and it will go. If it be merely in the memory, it is not safe. He that is

---

[28] Fuller, "On an Intimate and Practical Acquaintance with the Word of God," *Complete Works*, 1:484.

[29] Fuller, "Spiritual Knowledge and Love necessary for the Ministry," *Complete Works*, 1:482.

reasoned into the truth may be reasoned out of it. It is living upon the truth as a Christian that will cause the heart to be established with grace.[30]

Study, pray, and preach as a Christian

It is a blessing which you shall enjoy in common with your Christian brethren. It is not peculiar to you as a minister, but common to all Christians. And is it the better (you may ask) for this? Yes, it is. The best blessings, are those common to Christians (Ps. 27:4; Phil. 3:8). The Romish priests have contrived to secure the cup exclusively to themselves: but it was not so from the beginning: "Drink ye all of it." And not only the cup, but the thing signified, is common to all Christians. And the blessings which are common to Christians as such are of the greatest importance to us as ministers. If we study, and pray, and preach merely as ministers, we shall make poor work of it; but if as Christians, we shall prosper.[31]

Read and think as a Christian

Do not be content with general truth. Study the Scriptures minutely, and for yourself, and pray over your study. This will make it your own; and it will be doubly interesting to yourself and your people, than if you adopt it at second hand. Read and think, not merely as a minister, but as a Christian.[32]

Taste truth as a Christian before we preach it

This is the only motive that will render preaching a delight. How can we discourse on subjects which we do not believe? If we have not tasted the grace of God, we shall feel no pleasure in proclaiming it to others. Is it any wonder that faithless preachers call preaching "doing duty?" or that they peach other men's sermons? And that in delivering them they are uninterested by them? But if

---

[30] Fuller, "The Work and Encouragements of the Christian Minister," *Complete Works*, 1:498.

[31] Fuller, "The Influence of the Presence of Christ on a Minister," *Complete Works*, 1:505.

[32] Fuller, "Habitual Devotedness to the Ministry," *Complete Works*, 1:507.

we speak because we believe, our preaching will be the utterance of a full heart, and our work its own reward. We must taste of truth as Christians, before we preach it. Studying it merely as ministers will never do. Believing belongs to us as Christians.[33]

Busy, joyful, gospel spirituality

Most Christian spirituality authors focus nearly exclusively on solitude with God, private devotions, and an individualistic pursuit of spirituality. However, in my reading of church history, many heroic Christian figures describe their pursuit of spirituality in quite a different manner. In fact, they often describe the right kind of busyness as a catalyst to spiritual growth. Andrew Fuller is one such figure, and credited busyness in the cause of Christ as a key factor in his cultivation of Christian joy. For Fuller, busyness was not always to be perceived as an enemy of spirituality. According to him, we must spend and be spent for the sake of the Gospel with an energetic and rugged spirituality.

Of course, he was often guilty of taking on too much and felt overwhelmed by responsibilities pressing in on him. His schedule was so demanding that at times his pastoral friends worried about his health.[34] Fuller wrote in his diary,

> My wife looks at me, with a tear ready to drop, and says, "My dear, you have hardly time to speak to me." My friends at home are kind, but they also say, "You have no time to see or know us, and you will soon be worn out." Amidst all this, there is "Come again to Scotland—come to Portsmouth—come to Plymouth—come to Bristol."

> Excuse this effusion of melancholy. My heart is willing to do everything you desire that I can do, but my hands fail me. Dear brother Ryland complains of old age coming upon him, and I expect old

---

[33] Fuller, "Faith in the Gospel a Necessary Prerequisite to Preaching It," *Complete Works*, 1: 517.

[34] "Robert Hall Jr, having heard that Fuller had indeed recently visited Plymouth and Bristol, expressed his fears for Fuller's health in a letter to Ryland, 'If he is not more careful he will be in danger of wearing himself out before his time. His journeys, his studies, his correspondencies [sic] must be too much for any man.'" See, Peter Morden, *The Life and Thought of Andrew Fuller (1754–1815)* (Milton Keynes: Paternoster, 2015), 169.

age will come upon me before I am really old. Under this complicated load my heart has often of late groaned for rest, longing to finish my days in comparative retirement.[35]

Nevertheless, Fuller was self-consciously active in the cause of Christ. John Ryland wrote of Fuller, "as fast as some of his labours had been accomplished, his active mind would have been devising fresh measures for advancing the divine glory, and extending the kingdom of Christ." Ryland adds, "As it was, he certainly did more for God than most men could have effected in a life longer by twenty years."[36] Biographer J.W. Morris explains that Fuller "was generally regular in his hours of rest" and he was "the determined enemy of procrastination." He adds, "He had no idea of ease or rest, but seemed to contemplate life only as a scene of perpetual activity, in which he was to serve his generation by the will of God."[37] As Baptist historian Thomas J. Nettles described, Fuller had a "vigorous and useful spirituality."[38]

The importance of missional activity for Christian spirituality is not a point often developed. Peter J. Morden's journal article, "So valuable a life ... A biographical sketch of Andrew Fuller (1754-1815)," explains how Fuller's commitment to the newly founded Baptist Missionary Society in England led to a rigorous schedule of writing in defense of the society and traveling great distances to raise awareness and financial support of the society, and all of this was in addition to his pastoral responsibilities. According to Morden, as a result of Fuller's newfound gospel busyness, he "became less introspective" and discovered that "activity in the cause of Christ led to joy."[39] We usually think about spirituality in terms of reflection that strengthens us and is ultimately lived out. We almost never think of the equally vital inverse: activity in the cause of Christ that, when lived out and reflected upon, strengthens us.

---

[35] Fuller, "Memoirs," *Complete* Works, 1:69-70.

[36] Ryland, *Work of Faith, the Labor of Love*, 384.

[37] Morris, *Memoirs of the Life and Writings of the Rev. Andrew Fuller*, 308-309.

[38] Thomas J. Nettles as quoted in Michael A.G. Haykin, ed., *The Armies of the Lamb: The Spirituality of Andrew Fuller*, 15.

[39] Peter Morden, "'So valuable a life...' A biographical sketch of Andrew Fuller, (1754-1815)," *SBJT* 17.1 (2013): 4-14.

David E. Prince

It was Fuller's busyness in a cause that he knew was biblically right that helped reorient his thinking and helped him reclaim joy in his personal devotion and ministry service. Fuller wrote, "Christian experience clings to Christ and his gospel. The religion of some, who talk of experience, goes to idolize their own feelings and admire their supposed graces. But true Christian experience thinks little of self, and much of Christ."[40] The problem with the way some Christians pursue spirituality is that they think too much on the self and make an idol of one's feelings and emotions. Often, it is the action of living out the implications of the gospel that feeds our soul and ensures that our meditative spirituality is not self-centered but Christ-centered and gospel-focused.

A warning about ministry callousness

Fuller revered pastoral ministry as a high and holy calling but he did not romanticize it and constantly spoke of its inherent dangers. Pastors are always in danger of getting by on the mere image that they are spiritual men while actually being little more than ceremonial ministers adept at ceremonial responsibilities. In other words, pastors can learn how to fake it. Fuller approvingly quotes Abraham Booth saying, "I fear, there will be found a larger proportion of wicked ministers than of any other order of professing Christians!"

> It did not appear to me at the time, nor has it ever appeared since, that this remark proceeded from a want of charity, but rather from a deep knowledge of the nature of Christianity, and an impartial observation of men and things. It behooves us, not only as professing Christians, but as ministers, to "examine ourselves, whether we be in the faith." It certainly is possible, after we have preached to others, that we ourselves should be cast away! I believe it is very common for the personal religion of a minister to be taken for granted; and this may prove a temptation to him to take it for granted too. Ministers, being wholly devoted to the service of God, are supposed to have considerable advantages for spiritual improvement. These they certainly have; and if their minds be spiritual, they may be expected to make greater proficiency in the divine life than their brethren. But it should be remembered, that if they are not spiritual, those things which would otherwise be a

---

[40] Fuller, "Faith in the Gospel a Necessary Prerequisite to Preaching It," *Complete Works*, 1:516–517.

help would prove a hinderance. If we study divine subjects merely as ministers, they will produce no salutary effect. We may converse with the most impressive truths, as soldiers and surgeons do with blood, till they cease to make any impression upon us. We must meditate on these things as Christians, first feeding our own souls upon them, and then imparting that which we have believed and felt to others; or, whatever good we may do to them, we shall receive none ourselves. Unless we mix faith with what we preach, as well as with what we hear, the word will not profit us. It may be on these accounts that ministers, while employed in watching over others, are so solemnly warned against neglecting themselves: "Take heed unto yourselves and to all the flock," &c.—"Take heed unto thyself, and unto the doctrine; continue in them; for in doing this thou shalt both save thyself and them that hear thee."[41]

Fuller believed in the importance of a living ministry and warned of the real possibility of a barren one. Horatius Bonar's warning in *Words to Winners of Souls* was in step with Fuller's burden. Bonar writes,

> Even when sound in faith, through unbelief, lukewarmness and slothful formality, they may do irreparable injury to the cause of Christ, freezing and withering up all spiritual life around them. The lukewarm ministry of one who is theoretically orthodox is often more extensively and fatally ruinous to souls than that of one grossly inconsistent or flagrantly heretical. ... The true minister must be a true Christian.[42]

In an ordination sermon delivered in 1787, Fuller warned against "assumed earnestness or forced zeal in the pulpit," warning it would create "disgust" before men and God. Fuller explains, the preacher can "put on violent emotions" and "stamp with the foot" while being "destitute of a genuine feeling sense of what we deliver." He further exhorts,

> Prove by your spirit and conduct that you are a lover of all mankind. To men in general, but especially to the poor and the afflicted, be pitiful, be courteous. It is this, my brother, that will recommend the gospel you proclaim. Without this, could you preach

---

[41] Fuller, "The Work and Encouragements of the Christian Minister," *Complete Works*, 1:501.

[42] Horatius Bonar, *Words to Winners of Souls* (Phillipsburg: P&R, 1995), 1-2, 9.

with the eloquence of an angel, you may expect that no good end will be answered.[43]

In another ordination sermon titled, "Ministers Should Be Concerned Not to Be Despised," Fuller's headings reveal his burden for authentic ministry:

1. Avoid all affectation in your manner.
2. Avoid self-seeking in your ends.
3. Avoid vulgarity and low wit.
4. Do not advance sentiments without being able to support them by Scripture evidence.
5. Beware that you do not preach an unfelt gospel.
6. Let not the fear of man deter you from declaring the whole counsel of God.
7. Never degrade the pulpit by indulging in personalities. [Personal rebukes should be private. To do so, Fuller says would be "unmanly."][44]

He continues to urge pastors to consistently have character marked by living out the truth as it is in Jesus,

> Let your conduct correspond with your preaching. Men will watch you. You may put off the preacher in mixed company; but you must never put off the man of God—the Christian. Whatever you may be in the pulpit, if in the world you be frothy, vain, contentious, captious, unfeeling, unjust, or make engagements you cannot fulfill, you will be despised. On the contrary, consistency of character will wear, and live down opposition.[45]

The remainder of this chapter contains readings from Fuller pertaining to the preacher's responsibility to "train yourself for godliness" and to "keep a close watch on yourself" (1 Tim. 4:6, 16), as Paul admonishes.

---

[43] Fuller, "Memoirs," *Complete Works*, 1: 137-138.
[44] Fuller, "Ministers Should Be Concerned Not to Be Despised," *Complete Works*, 1:489-490.
[45] Fuller, "Ministers Should Be Concerned Not to Be Despised," *Complete Works*, 1:491.

Preparing the Preacher

For Fuller, this "training" and "watching" was not a matter of legalistic spiritual performance, but rather the grace-fueled "obedience of faith" (Rom. 1:5; 16:26). A Christ-centered walking in line with the gospel (Gal. 2:14), living out truth as it is in Jesus (Eph. 4:21), was for the sake of the church and the spread of the gospel in the world. As a leading and influential pastor, Fuller was in great demand for ordination services or church special occasions. All of the readings are for these occasions: "The Influence of the Presence of Christ on a Minister (2 Tim. 4:22)," "Habitual Devotedness to the Ministry (1 Tim. 4:15-16)," "Affectionate Concern of a Minister for the Salvation of His Hearers (1 Thess. 2:7-8)," "Ministers Should be Concerned Not to be Despised (Titus 2:15)," "Churches Walking in the Truth and the Joy of Ministers (3 John 4)," "Christian Churches Fellow Helpers with their Pastors to the Truth (3 John 8)," "Churches Should Exhibit the Light of the Gospel" (Rev. 2:1)," "On an Intimate and Practical Acquaintance with the Word of God (Ezra 7:10)," "The Promise of the Spirit the Grand Encouragement in Promoting the Gospel."

The Influence of the Presence of Christ on a Minister[1]

"The Lord Jesus Christ be with thy spirit." 2 Timothy 4:22

In addressing you, my brother, on this interesting portion of Scripture, I shall simply offer a few remarks on the blessing desired, and consider its influence on the discharge of the Christian ministry.

The blessing desired

Let us offer a few remarks on the blessing desired. If we were addressing ourselves to persons who were strangers to experimental religion, we might despair of being understood on this part of the subject; and even among Christians it is more easily felt than accurately described. We know nothing of divine influence but by its effects. We know we are created, but we know nothing of creative power. We know we are supported, but we can only feel ourselves upheld. We know Christ promised to be with his servants to the end of the world, and I hope we have felt the effects of it. We feel our wants hitherto supplied, our strength renewed, and our work in some measure succeeded; and we are taught to what to ascribe it. ... But more particularly,

1. The blessing here desired is something different from gifts. God has favoured you with gifts, but so he did Judas. Many shine and figure away with these, with whose spirits the Lord Jesus Christ holds no communion. Gifts are the gold of the temple, but communion with Christ is that which sanctifies the gold. Without this, gifts will be injurious both to you and to your people.

2. This blessing is more than grace itself, considered as inherent. I need not tell you that our graces have no separate subsistence. We are the branches living on the vine. Paul said, "I live" (and surely he had a right to say so, if any man had!) and yet he checks himself, and adds, "yet

---

[1] Fuller, "The Influence and Presence of Christ on a Minister," *Complete Works*, 1:504–505.

not I, but Christ liveth in me, and the life which I now live in the flesh I live by the faith of the Son of God."[2]

3. It is a blessing which you shall enjoy in common with your Christian brethren. It is not peculiar to you as a minister, but common to all Christians. And is it the better (you may ask) for this? Yes, it is. The best blessings are those common to Christians (Ps. 27:4; Phil. 3:8). The Romish priests have contrived to secure the cup exclusively to themselves, but it was not so from the beginning: "Drink ye all of it." And not only the cup, but the thing signified, is common to all Christians. And the blessings which are common to Christians as such are of the greatest importance to us as ministers. If we study, and pray, and preach merely as ministers, we shall make poor work of it; but if as Christians, we shall prosper. We proceed,

The influence of this blessing on the discharge of the Christian

To consider the influence of this blessing on the discharge of the Christian. Knowing that without him we could do nothing, our Lord has assured us, "Lo! I am with you always, to the end of the world." And now, by his strengthening us, we can do all things. Observe,

1. It is this that will render the doctrine of Christ familiar to us, and our favourite theme. The Spirit of prophecy is called the Spirit of Christ, because it testified of his sufferings (1 Pet. 1:11). And if Christ be with our spirit, though only in an ordinary way, it will lead us to delight in the doctrine of Christ (Eph. 3:17–18). When Christ dwells in the heart, see what follows. This is the unction by which we know all things. And this is the doctrine which God blesses to the building of his church.

2. It is that which gives a divine energy to our preaching. It imparts a much greater energy than the greatest eloquence, natural or artificial. And though it will not in itself convert sinners, yet God usually honours such preaching. And it is a means of conversion. The apostle "so spoke that a great multitude believed."[3] And where such preaching does not convert, it yet commends itself to the conscience. "They were not able to resist the wisdom and the Spirit by which he (Stephen) spoke."[4] Apol-

---

[2] Galatians 2:20.
[3] Acts 14:1.
[4] Acts 6:10.

los, who was "fervent in the Spirit," by his preaching "mightily convinced the Jews."[5] The preaching of Paul was "not with enticing words of man's wisdom, but in demonstration of the Spirit, and of power."[6]

3. It is this that will render our visits profitable. It is difficult to turn conversation into a savoury and useful channel. But if the Lord Jesus Christ be with our spirit, all difficulty will vanish. Without this everything will be forced and constrained; and we shall feel especially at a loss in our directions to inquirers.

4. It is this that will sustain your heart under trials. You are aware you must expect these. You will see things in your people towards God that will grieve you. This will enable you to reprove them in love. You will see things in them towards each other that are decidedly wrong. This spirit will cause you to be a peacemaker. You will experience painful things towards yourself, some will not receive your doctrine. Some will misconstrue your conduct and pervert your statements, but if the Lord Jesus Christ be with your spirit, you will not sink under the heaviest trials. You may have to lament your want of success. But go on and be of good cheer. If the Lord Jesus Christ be with your spirit, though Israel be not gathered, you shall not go unrewarded.

---

[5] Acts 18:25, 28
[6] 1 Corinthians 2:4

Habitual Devotedness to the Ministry[1]

"Meditate upon these things; give thyself wholly to them; that thy profiting may appear to all. Take heed unto thyself, and unto the doctrine; continue in them: for in doing this thou shalt both save thyself, and them that hear thee." 1 Timothy 4:15-16

My dear brother,

You will find many things in these Epistles worthy of your attention. With a view of showing the connection of the text, let us notice what is said in the preceding verses.

Verse 12. Timothy was a young man, and was charged to let no man despise his youth. But how could he prevent that? By being "an example of the believers, in word, in conversation, in charity, in spirit, in faith, in purity." Then, whoever might dislike him, no one could despise him.

Verse 13. It is supposed that Paul expected shortly to see Timothy, when he would have many things to say. Meanwhile he directed him how to spend his time to good purpose. In reading. God knows all things, but we must receive before we impart. Exhortation. He was not to hide, but to communicate his knowledge of divine things, as he received it: the reading of a minister should be for his people, that he may be furnished with sentiments suited to their cases. Exhortation seems to be that kind of teaching which is from house to house, consisting of counsels, cautions, &c. Doctrine. He was to dig in this mine, that he might enrich others.

Verse 14. He was supposed to have a gift, an extraordinary gift, foretold in prophecy by some of the New Testament prophets and imparted by the laying on of hands. Yet even this was a talent to be improved, and not neglected. Then how much more ordinary gifts!

Verse 15. This verse expresses how his gift was to be improved. It is a shameful abuse of the doctrine of divine influence to allege it as a reason for neglecting diligent study for the pulpit. Yet such things are; and the

---

[1] Fuller, "Habitual Devotedness to the Ministry," *Complete Works*, 1:506-508.

advocates of this perversion can quote Scripture for it; as "Take no thought beforehand what ye shall speak, neither premeditate; but whatsoever shall be given to you in that hour, that speak ye; for it is not ye that speak, but the Holy Ghost."[2] But this has no application to pulpit exercises, or ordinary ministrations. It was very suitable for the persecuted Christians; for how could they know what to answer before they were questioned by their persecutors. It was therefore greatly calculated to encourage them, and relieve them from all anxiety. But to apply this direction to our ordinary ministrations is a shameful perversion (See Eccl. 12:9–11).

Give me your attention, my dear brother, while I endeavour to illustrate the different branches of the exhortation of the text, and consider the motives held up to enforce it.

Let us endeavour to illustrate the exhortation

The things on which you are called to meditate are what you "read," the things to which you "exhort," and the "doctrine" of Christ. Or on the Scriptures—on the precepts contained in them, and on the doctrines to be deduced from them.

"Meditate on these things"

There is a depth in them that requires it. You may read the Scriptures a hundred times over, and yet be only on the surface, far from having fathomed them. They are able to make us wise through faith, but to believe without searching argues great indifference, and is building without a foundation. The Scriptures were always considered a deep mine, even when they consisted of only the five Books of Moses. David meditated in the law of the Lord "day and night."[3] It was to his spiritual growth as water is to a tree.

Do not imagine you understand enough of the Bible; or because you have assented to a few truths, therefore you are in possession of all. Paul desired to know yet more. Angels desire to look into the things revealed there.[4] David intimates that the law contains "wondrous things,"[5] and

---

[2] Mark 13:11.
[3] Psalm 1:2.
[4] 1 Peter 1:12.
[5] Psalm 119:18.

prays that his mind might be enlightened to comprehend them. A spiritual state of mind is the best expositor, and more is discovered with it, in a few verses, than in whole chapters without it.

Do not be content with general truth. Study the Scriptures minutely, and for yourself, and pray over your study. This will make it your own; and it will be doubly interesting to yourself and your people than if you adopt it at second hand. Read and think, not merely as a minister, but as a Christian.

"Give yourself wholly to them"
No man can excel in any art or science, but by giving himself wholly to it. Why is it one understands law? Because he gives himself wholly to it. Why is it another understands physic? Because he gives himself wholly to it. Why do rulers understand government? Because "they attend continually upon this very thing." And though divine knowledge differs in some things from that which is natural and worldly, yet not in this. It is by constant application and use that our senses discern truth from error, and good from evil (Heb. 5:14). And you must not only give your whole time to this study, but your whole heart.

"Be thou in them"
It is a shocking thing to be engaged in a work which is against the heart. It is not what we think officially, but spontaneously that proves what we are. Not what we do at certain appointed seasons, but the bent of our minds in common, in our leisure hours, when we sit in the house, or walk by the way. Engaging in the work without the heart is the forerunner and cause of many scandals. Time hangs heavy on their hands—they saunter and gossip from place to place—scandalize and listen to scandal—and not seldom terminate their career by impurity.

"Take heed to thyself"
It were an awful thing to guide others to the right way, and not walk in it ourselves. See that all is right between God and your own soul. Public religion, without that which is private and personal, is worse than no religion. We had better be anything than preachers of the gospel, unless we be personally interested in it.

"And to thy doctrine"
There is great danger of going off from the gospel—perhaps in submission to great authorities, or to please the people. That minister who makes the taste of his hearers the standard of his preaching may go on, and succeed in pleasing them and himself; but, at the coming of his Lord, it will be said to him, thou hast had thy reward!

There is also danger of going off from the gospel by leaning to our own understanding. Consult your own understanding; but remember you are liable to err; therefore do not lean to it, in opposition to the Scriptures.

Finally, "Continue in these things"
That only is true religion which endures to the end.

Let us consider the motives by which the exhortations are enforced

Your growth in gifts and graces will be hereby apparent
"That thy profiting may appear to all." The meaning is much the same as the parable of the talents—five, by improvement, gaining other five. It holds true in temporal things even (Prov. 22:29). There is, however, this difference between their pursuits and yours: they labour to obtain an earthly good; you a heavenly, spiritual, and eternal one. If worldly profit or honour were your object, you might study the embellishments of style, or the arts of the partisan; but if you would be the servant of God, your heart must be in your work. A diligent minister will be a useful one.

Your own salvation is involved in it
"Thou shalt save thyself." This language does not denote that we are the cause of our own salvation any more than of the salvation of others. But as we may be instrumental in the latter, so we may be active in the former (Acts 2:40). Take refuge in the Saviour you recommend to others. The expression may also have reference to that particular kind of salvation which consists in being delivered from the blood of souls.

The salvation of your people may be involved in it
A spiritual, diligent minister is commonly a fruitful one, and a blessing to his people. Consider these exhortations, and the motives by which they are enforced, and may the Lord give you understanding in all things.

David E. Prince

Thus thou shall both save yourself and them that hear you.

Affectionate Concern of a Minister for the Salvation of His Hearers[1]

"We were gentle among you, even as a nurse cherisheth her children: so, being affectionately desirous of you, we were willing to have imparted unto you, not the gospel of God only, but also our own souls, because ye were dear unto us." 1 Thessalonians 2:7–8

My dear brother,

You have requested me to address you on your appointment to the important office of pastor over this people; and I know of nothing more impressive on the subject of the Christian ministry than this whole chapter, both as to what a minister should not be, and as to what he should be. Not of deceit, nor of uncleanness, nor in guile, nor as pleasing men, but gentle, affectionate, laborious, disinterested, holy. Let us, however, confine ourselves to the words we have selected as a text, in which the apostle compares his own ministrations and those of his colleagues to the gentle solicitude of a nurse, whose concern is to impart warmth and strength to her children. "So we, being affectionately desirous," &c. Three things here require your attention: the feeling of a true minister of Christ towards the people of his charge—the subject-matter of his ministry—and the manner in which he must dispense it.

The feeling of a true minister towards the people of his charge

This is an affectionate concern after their salvation, one of the most important qualifications for the ministry. True, it is not the only one. There are gifts, both natural and acquired, which are necessary, since, without them, we cannot be said to be "apt to teach."[2] But this qualification is that without which the greatest gifts, natural and acquired, are nothing as to real usefulness. Genius may amuse, but "love edifieth." A strong mind and a brilliant imagination may excite their admiration, but this will

---

[1] Fuller, "Affectionate Concern of a Minister for the Salvation of His Hearers," *Complete Works*, 1:508–510.

[2] 2 Timothy 2:24.

attract the hearts of the people. Look at the men who have been the most honoured and you will find that they are not the brightest geniuses, but the humble and affectionate.

Look at the example of Paul. Observe how he felt towards his poor, unbelieving countrymen who sought his life: "Brethren, my heart's desire and prayer to God for Israel is that they may be saved."[3] Even his zeal for the conversion of the Gentiles bore an aspect towards his brethren after the flesh: "I speak to you Gentiles, inasmuch as I am the apostle of the Gentiles, I magnify my office; if by any means I may provoke to emulation them which are my flesh, and might save some of them."[4] He speaks as a humane seaman would in a wreck, who, when he found he could not save all, would do what he could, plunging into the sea and saving at least some of them. Here, my brother, is an example for your imitation, towards the unbelieving part of your hearers.

See also how he felt toward those Christians who had sinned. Witness his Epistles to the Corinthians. How anxious he was to reclaim them. How dissatisfied with anything short of their restoration, looking upon them as lost children (2 Cor. 2; 13:2).

Look at the example of John towards the rising generation: "I rejoiced greatly that I found of thy children walking in the truth."[5] And look at the example of our apostle, in connection with the text, towards all to whom he wrote. He could not be satisfied with any reward short of their eternal salvation. All other hope, all other joy connected with them, he considered as of small account; and he looked forward to them as constituting the brightest jewels in his future crown.

Most of all, look at the example of your Lord and Saviour. How did the kindness and love of God our Saviour appear. What did he not forego, and do, and suffer. May the love of Christ constrain you!

Consider the subject-matter of his ministry: "The gospel of God"
1. It is a blessed errand to go on. Good news to a lost world. Angels were visited with wrath, but men with the cup of salvation. There is a pleasure in being an almoner, even of earthly blessings: but you have the unsearchable riches of Christ to impart; you are the herald of peace, and pardon,

---

[3] Romans 10:1.
[4] Romans 11:3.
[5] 2 John 1:4.

and reconciliation. How a man, bearing such tidings from an earthly sovereign, would be hailed by a number of convicts!

2. But what is the gospel? It is not merely the privilege of believers; for then it would not be for every creature. It is a declaration of what Christ has done and suffered, and of the effects; exhibiting a way in which God can be "just and the justifier of the ungodly."[6] It is not merely to convince of sin, but also to point to the remedy.

3. Make a point, then, of distinctly and habitually preaching the gospel. Do not suppose your people are so good, and so well informed, as not to need this. Visit the sick, and you will be astonished how little they know compared with what it might reasonably be expected they should know. Many sermons are ingenious essays, but if they bear not on this great object, they are not the gospel. Woe to you if you preach not the gospel! Do not suppose I have any particular suspicion that you will not. But I feel the importance of the exhortation, "Preach the gospel."[7] Study the gospel—what it implies, what it includes, and what consequences it involves. I have heard complaints of some of our young ministers, that though they are not heterodox, yet they are not evangelical; that though they do not propagate error, yet the grand, essential, distinguishing truths of the gospel do not form the prevailing theme of their discourses.

I love a sermon well laden with Christian doctrine. I love to find young ministers well learned in the Scriptures. Then their preaching will not be dry, but good news and glad tidings. Complaints have been made of some preaching as too doctrinal, and a preference has been manifested for experimental and practical preaching; but that doctrinal preaching which I would recommend should include both. The doctrines of the Scriptures, scripturally stated, are calculated to interest the heart, and to produce genuine evangelical obedience. You need not fear that you shall be limited. You may take a wide range. There is a great variety of subjects which may be introduced: the purity and spirituality of the law, the evil of sin, the wrath of God against it, and many others; but then all these naturally lead to an explicit declaration of "the glorious gospel of the blessed God."[8]

---

[6] Romans 3:26.
[7] Mark 16:15.
[8] 1 Timothy 1:11.

Preparing the preacher

Consider the manner of the gospel minister: "willingly"

And so as, while imparting the gospel, to impart their own souls with it. Some have supposed that it is the matter, and not the manner of preaching, that God blesses. But I see no ground for this distinction. I allow that the matter is of the first importance; but the manner is not of small account. For example: the apostle prays that he might make the gospel manifest, "as he ought to speak" (Col. 4:4). And this relates to manner, not to matter. You may preach even the gospel dryly. It must be preached faithfully, firmly, earnestly, affectionately. The apostle so spoke that many believed. Manner is a means of conveying truth. A cold manner disgraces important truth.

"Willingly." Where the ministration of the word is connected with external honours and great temporal advantage, there is no test of this; but where it is attended with self-denial, there is ... "Our own souls."[9] This is expressive of the deep interest the apostles and their colleagues took in the gospel, and their earnest desire that their hearers should embrace it. Hence, we speak of pouring out our souls in prayer. How would you feel in throwing out a rope to a drowning man, or in lighting a fire in a wilderness to attract the attention of one who was dear to you, and who was lost? How did Aaron feel during the plague, when he stood between the dead and the living? O my brother, enter into these feelings. Realize them. Let them inspire you with holy, affectionate zeal. Souls are perishing around you, and though you cannot "make an atonement for the people's sins,"[10] yet you can publish one, made by our great high priest; and, receiving and exhibiting this atonement, you may hope to save yourself and them that hear you.

---

[9] 1 Thessalonians 2:8.
[10] Hebrews 2:17.

Ministers Should Be Concerned Not to Be Despised[1]

"Let no man despise thee." Titus 2:15

My brother,

I feel a pleasure in the work of this day, partly from the love I bear to you, and partly from the love I feel towards the church. I trust you will receive a word of advice on this solemn occasion with candour and attention.

You will observe the passage is not an address to the people, not to despise their minister; but to the minister, not to be despised by the people. If you ask how you are to prevent this, I answer, contempt is not a voluntary feeling. It is not in the power of men to despise some characters. They may dislike them, they may affect to ridicule them, but they cannot in their hearts despise them. If a minister conducts himself in character, no man will be able to despise him. This, then, is the sentiment which I wish to impress upon you.

Your work as a pastor may be distinguished into three departments—the pulpit, the church, and the world—in each of which I hope you will so conduct yourself as that no man shall be able to despise you. Let me offer to your consideration a few particulars under each.

What concerns you in the pulpit or in the preaching the gospel

1. Avoid all affectation in your manner. Do not affect the man of learning by useless criticisms. Many do this only to display their knowledge. Nor yet the orator, by high-sounding words, or airs, or gestures. Useful learning and an impressive delivery should by no means be slighted, but they must not be affected, or men will be sure to despise you.

2. Avoid self-seeking in your ends. Preach not yourself, but Christ Jesus. Seek not the approbation of men for yourself, but for your doctrine.

---

[1] Fuller, "Ministers Should be Concerned Not to Be Despised," *Complete Works*, 1:489–491.

Study to commend the gospel to the consciences of your hearers, rather than your own orthodoxy, or ingenuity, or zeal, to their admiration. If, instead of endeavouring to secure their reception of the gospel message, you are concerned to recommend yourself to their applause, you will be sure to be despised.

3. Avoid vulgarity and low wit. Though the pulpit is not the place for affected pomposity, neither is it the place for mean and low language. Few men are more contemptible than those who study to introduce vulgar nonsense and jocose anecdotes, to make people laugh. Sound speech, sound sense, and the greatest seriousness adorn the pulpit. Without these, you will be despised.

4. Do not advance sentiments without being able to support them by Scripture evidence. Many content themselves with assertions without proof, and make vehemence supply the place of evidence. But this will cause you to be despised by men of understanding.

5. Beware that you do not preach an unfelt gospel. If you do, it will be seen, and you will be despised. It will be seen that, though you affect to be in earnest, you do not feel; and that you scarcely believe your own doctrine. We may get into a habit of talking for the truth, and pleading for holiness, and yet be dead ourselves; and if so, we shall be sure to be despised.

6. Let not the fear of man deter you from declaring the whole counsel of God. Insist on every divine truth and duty. Where interest or friendship stand in the way, it may be trying; but if you yield, the very parties to whom you yield will despise you. Speak but the truth in love, and speak the whole truth, and you will commend yourself to every man's conscience when you can do no more.

7. Never degrade the pulpit by indulging in personalities. These are for private admonition. "Rebuke with all authority;"[2] but let your personal rebukes be private. To introduce them in the pulpit is unmanly, and would render you despicable. Let us apply the language,

To your behaviour in the church and among your fellow Christians

1. Do not lord it over God's heritage. You will have to preside in the

---

[2] Titus 2:15.

church, and direct its measures; but never assume the lordly priest. Expect your judgment, in some cases, to be overruled, and learn to yield with cheerfulness when the measures you wish to introduce appear to be opposed to the opinion and desires of the majority of your brethren. It is not with a minister of the gospel as with a minister of state—that he must have a majority, or he cannot stand his ground. If we "look on the things of others,"[3] we may, in non-essentials, after speaking our minds, yield and be happy. But if we are determined to carry every point which appears to us desirable, in spite of the opinion of our brethren, though we may not always succeed, we shall invariably be despised for the attempt.

2. Yet have a judgment of your own. This will become you on every subject, and where it is of importance you ought to be firm and resolute. A minister must not be borne down by the capriciousness of a few. He who is easily turned aside from a good object, and will bear insult without a proper manifestation of his displeasure will be despised as much as a lordly high priest. If a minister be not firm, discipline will, in many cases, be neglected. People have their friends, and relatives, and favourites; and very few, though the operation be bloodless, have sufficient regard for rectitude to act upon the principle of the sons of Levi (See Exod. 32:17-29). But you must, or you will be despised.

3. Do not affect the gentleman in your visits. Do not assume airs of consequence, and take liberties in families, as if, because you are a minister, you are therefore superior as a man. I do not say, do not be a gentleman; but do not affect the great man. Real gentility, and urbanity, and politeness are no mean or despicable attainments. There was much Christian politeness in the apostle Paul. But the affectation of the fine gentleman is great folly; and no men are more despised than those who strut about with lordly dignity and give themselves consequential airs. You had much better feel yourself a Christian and consider that you are associating with your fellow Christians, or with those who expect you to exhibit a pattern for their imitation.

4. Yet preserve a dignity of manner and demeanour. There is no occasion for you, in order to avoid the affectation of gentility, to sink into low buffoonery, vulgarity, or drollery. My brother, the fear of God, and a deep sense of religion will effectually preserve you from these extremes,

---

[3] Philippians 2:4.

and render you respectable, instead of contemptible.

5. Beware of being a loiterer. Do not acquire a habit of wandering about and doing nothing. Visit, and visit "from house to house."[4] But look well to your visits: "preach from house to house." There is work enough in a congregation for a minister to do; but nothing renders him more contemptible and despised than a habit of religious gossiping. Let us apply the text,

To your general deportment in the world

1. Let your conduct correspond with your preaching. Men will watch you. You may put off the preacher in mixed company, but you must never put off the man of God—the Christian. Whatever you may be in the pulpit, if in the world you be frothy, vain, contentious, captious, unfeeling, unjust, or make engagements you cannot fulfil, you will be despised. On the contrary, consistency of character will wear, and live down opposition.

2. Never be ashamed of religion in any company. There is no need to introduce it on all occasions, and in all companies. This would render you despised one way. But be not the subject of cowardly timidity. That would render you equally, if not more, despicable. There is nothing in true religion but what admits of a rational defence. There wants nothing to defend religion but firmness of mind. But if you are ashamed of the cause you have espoused, its opponents will heartily despise you.

Conclusion

If the contempt of men be such a matter of dread, how much more the contempt of God! Then so conduct yourself that you may not be ashamed, and not be despised, at his coming!

---

[4] Acts 2:46

Churches Walking in the Truth and Joy of Ministers[1]

"I have no greater joy than to hear that my children walk in truth."
3 John 4

The connection of pastor and people in dissenting churches is altogether voluntary. There are no bonds to bring them together, or to keep them together, but love. The great point, therefore, in this connection, is the maintaining of brotherly love and to render each other holy and happy. You wish to render your minister happy, or you can expect no religious happiness yourselves. I have selected the text as pointing out the course of conduct that will accomplish this end. "Walk in the truth."

I take it for granted that your minister can adopt the language of the text. If, indeed, he were a mercenary or an ambitious man, many other things would afford him much greater pleasure. But I trust, in this respect, his heart is one with the apostle's. In pursuing this subject, I shall,

Observations on the duty of walking in the truth

In order to this, we may observe that the truth is of a practical nature; other truths may be speculative, but not this. But what is truth? To this question I would reply generally and particularly.

General truths about truth

In general—(1.) The truth is a system of love and goodness—an overflow of divine blessedness. Then walk in love to the church, and bear goodwill even to enemies. (2.) The truth is a system full of joy—"good news, and glad tidings of great joy."[2] Then be cheerful and happy, not morose and gloomy. (3.) The truth is a system of reconciliation. Then let it be your concern to live peaceably, and to exercise forgiveness. (4.) The truth is a system of amazing condescension. Then "let the same mind be

---

[1] Fuller, "Churches Walking in the Truth and the Joy of Ministers," *Complete Works*, 1:529–531.
[2] Luke 2:10.

in you that was in Christ Jesus."³ (5.) The truth is a system of purity—"a highway of holiness."⁴ Then "be ye holy, in all manner of conversation."⁵ (6.) The truth is a system full of importance. Then be you in earnest. "Strive earnestly for the faith once delivered to the saints."⁶

Particular truths about truth
More particularly—(1.) Divine truth includes the existence of God, as a Being of infinite excellence and glory; "holy, just, and good."⁷ Then live in the love and fear of God. (2.) It includes the divine authority of the Holy Scriptures. Then make them, and not interest, or inclination, or fashion, the rule of your faith and practice. (3.) It includes the guilty and lost condition of men as sinners. Then, in all your dealings with God, approach him in that character—as ill and hell-deserving. (4.) It includes the doctrine of redemption by the blood of Christ. Then remember that you are "not your own,"⁸ but his. (5.) Divine truth teaches us, that if we are saved, it is in consequence of sovereign and discriminating grace. It traces our salvation to electing love, and informs us that the great end that Christ had, in laying down his life, was "that he might redeem us from all iniquity, and purify unto himself a peculiar people, zealous of good works."⁹ And to walk in this truth is to be such people, to be distinguished by zeal and uprightness. Let it never be asked concerning us, "What do ye more than others?" (6.) It includes the doctrine of efficacious grace: "My people shall be willing in the day of my power."¹⁰ "The righteous shall hold on his way."¹¹ Then to walk in this truth is to prove that grace is efficacious by a perseverance in all holy conversation and godliness. (7.) It includes the doctrine of eternal life, as infinitely outweighing all the pleasures and all the ills of the present life: "I reckon that the sufferings of this present life are not worthy to be compared with the glory that shall be revealed."¹² Then be dead to the world, and alive to

---

³ Philippians 2:5.
⁴ Isaiah 35:8.
⁵ Isaiah 35:8; 1 Peter 1:15.
⁶ Jude 1:3.
⁷ Romans 7:12.
⁸ 1 Corinthians 6:19.
⁹ Titus 2:14.
¹⁰ Psalm 110:3.
¹¹ Job 17:9.
¹² Romans 8:18.

God. Look not at the things that are seen and are temporal; but at those which are unseen and eternal.

My brethren, if the truth thus dwell in you, and operate, you will naturally be attentive to all relative duties; you will love your *pastor*, for the truth's sake which he preaches; and if you love him, you will make a point of attending his ministry, of contributing to his support, and of consulting his peace and happiness in every possible way. And if the truth dwell in you, you will also love *one another*, for the truth's sake. You will watch over one another in the Lord, and follow the things that make for peace.

Connection between the conduct of a people and the joy of a minister
I proceed to notice the connection between such a course of conduct in a people, and the joy and happiness of a minister.

1. If he be an upright man, it will be the great object of his life that the people of his charge should be conformed to Christ; and it must needs be a matter of joy to see this great end answered. He must needs rejoice over the prosperity of those with whom he travailed in birth, till Christ was formed in them.

2. Such a course of conduct in a people would greatly assist a minister in his public work. It recommends his preaching to the world. It speaks louder than language when he can say of his people, "Ye are my epistles, known and read of all men."[13] It enables him to be bold in declaring the holy efficacy of truth; and to answer the enemies in the gate, who would reproach the grace of God as tending to licentiousness.

3. Your sanctification and salvation are his great reward: "For what is our hope, or joy, or crown of rejoicing? Are not even ye in the presence of our Lord Jesus Christ, at his coming?"[14] As to any other reward, you well know that the prospects of dissenting ministers, generally speaking, are anything but inviting. And if his pecuniary reward were ten times greater, if he be a Christian, it would not satisfy him. It is not yours, but you, that must make him happy. He will long to present you before the throne, and to be able to say, "Here, Lord, am I, and the children which thou hast given me."[15]

Young people, your minister longs also for your salvation. He looks

---
[13] 2 Corinthians 3:2.
[14] 1 Thessalonians 2:19.
[15] Isaiah 8:18.

upon you as rising plants, destined, he hopes, to occupy the places of those who must soon die. You have no conception how much you can add to his joy. He can have no greater joy than to see you walking in the truth. Then do not disappoint him. Remember that his joy and your joy are involved in the same course of conduct. Then, while others wander in the mazes of error, be it your concern to walk in the truth.

Christian Churches Fellow Helpers with their Pastors to the Truth[1]

> "We therefore ought to receive such,
> that we might be fellow helpers to the truth."
> 3 John 8

The ordination of elders over the churches was a practice among the primitive Christians (Acts 14:23). And I hope it will never be dispensed with in our churches. Besides being sanctioned by apostolical example, it is a guard against the introduction of improper characters, who, by getting an artificial majority in a church, may intrude themselves on a people to their great injury. Hence the exhortation, "Lay hands suddenly on no man."[2] It also furnishes an opportunity of solemnly addressing both parties on the intimate relation into which they have entered. In compliance with this custom, I would affectionately address the members of this church on the present interesting occasion.

The language of the text, I allow, has respect to Christian missionaries; but that which is said of them, and the treatment due to them, will in a great degree apply to settled pastors; for,

1. They went forth, taking nothing of the Gentiles; and these give up all worldly prospects and pursuits for Christ's name's sake, and to serve your spiritual interests.

2. They were engaged in a great work, even the evangelization of the world; and so are these. God promised Canaan to Abraham, but Israel must take it; and the world to Christ, but Christians must conquer it. "Go ye into all the world,"[3] &c. Of this army, Christian missionaries and ministers are the leaders.

3. They wanted help from their brethren, and it was to the honour of private Christians to help them; for in so doing they became fellow-helpers, not to them only, but also "to the truth." And so do these need help,

---

[1] Fuller, "Christian Churches Fellow Helpers," *Complete Works*, 1:524–526.
[2] 1 Timothy 5:22.
[3] Mark 16:15.

and it is for you, by helping them, to be fellow helpers to the truth.

To illustrate and enforce the duty which is here enjoined upon you, we shall take a view of the work of a pastor, and observe, as we go along, how you are to be fellow helpers in it.

In general, it is spreading the truth. This is a name by which the religion of the Bible is very properly designated, since it is not only true, but emphatically the truth; being the only true doctrine ever given to the world under the name of religion. All that went before it were false, and tended to mislead and destroy the souls of men, on the true character of God and of men, and on the true way of salvation.

The apostle spoke not the language of conjecture, but of assurance; as one having been in a mine, coming to the light of day: "We believe and are sure."[4]

It is the work of your pastor to spread the heavenly truth, and yours to be fellow helpers to the truth. Particularly,

Ways to be fellow helpers in his preaching the gospel
It is his work to preach the gospel to you. There are many ways in which you may be his fellow helpers.

1. In your prayers to God for him. I have lately read of a man who despised the prayers of a people. But so did not Paul. "Brethren, pray for us."[5] "Now I beseech you, brethren, for the Lord Jesus Christ's sake, and for the love of the Spirit, that ye strive together with me in your prayers to God for me."[6] Prepare the way to God's house by prayer. Do not expect to profit else. It is a great mercy that God sends to us by men like ourselves; men whose everlasting interests are involved in their doctrine. But they are sinful creatures, subject to temptations in common with others, and to some peculiar to themselves; they therefore need your prayers.

2. By an early and constant attendance, and spiritual attentiveness to the word, you may be fellow helpers. What an effect do empty pews, and yawning, sleepy hearers, produce! How delightful for a minister to enter his pulpit, as Paul speaks of coming to Rome—in the hope of being com-

---

[4] John 6:69.
[5] 1 Thessalonians 5:25; 2 Thessalonians 3:1.
[6] Romans 15:30.

forted by the faith of his hearers (Rom. 1:12). Where faith is seen to glisten in the eyes of an attentive audience, it produces feelings and thoughts more interesting and affecting than could ever have been produced in the study; while the contrary has a tendency to chill and freeze the feelings of the soul, and to reduce a minister to a situation resembling a ship locked in by islands of ice near the poles.

3. By rendering his circumstances as easy as possible, so that his mind may not be harassed by worldly cares, you may be fellow helpers. I never felt it a hardship to be dependent on a people who loved me. I have thought it an honour to be so supported. The expressions of love are sweet. But if love be wanting, all goes wrong. Little is done, and that little is not done heartily.

4. By enabling him by your habitual deportment to speak strongly is to the holy effects of religion, you may be fellow helpers. He will wish to be able to point the world to the people of his charge, and say "There are my epistles of commendation, known and read of all men!"[7] And to address you boldly in their hearing, in the language of the apostle: "Such *were* some of you; but ye are washed, but ye are sanctified, but ye are justified, in the name of the Lord Jesus, and by the Spirit of our God."[8] But if your conduct does not answer the description, who will believe him?

Ways to be fellow helpers in his visitations

Another part of your pastor's work is visiting his people from house to house and encouraging hopeful characters to stand forward on the Lord's side. And in this you may be fellow helpers.

1. By welcoming him, and teaching your children and servants to respect him. Much depends on this. They will form their opinion of him by the sentiments they hear you express towards him; and if they do not think highly of him, it cannot be expected they should profit under his ministrations. On the contrary, if they witness in you a high esteem for his character and his talents, they will attend his ministry greatly prepossessed in his favour, and with minds prepared to receive his instructions.

2. By noticing those in the congregation who are inquiring after the way of salvation, and directing them to the good old way, you may be

---

[7] 2 Corinthians 3:2.
[8] 1 Corinthians 6:11.

fellow helpers. There are some who, like Barnabas with Saul, get acquainted with and assist converts in the divine life, and introduce them to the church (Acts 9:27). Such persons are great blessings in a church, and great helpers to the pastor. Be friendly with the poor; encourage the modest and timid; visit the sick, and converse and pray with them. This will strengthen the hands and cheer the heart of your pastor, and greatly promote the interests of the truth.

Ways to be fellow helpers in his discipline
Another part of his duty is the maintenance of a strict and faithful discipline. And in this you may be fellow helpers. He must reprove, and rebuke, and sometimes separate from the church some of whom he once thought well. This is a painful duty. But it is a duty, and it is your duty to stand by him. Say to him, as the people said to Ezra, "Arise; for this matter belongeth unto thee: we also will be with thee: be of good courage, and do it."[9] Do not consult relationship, or worldly interests, or private friendships. Do not weaken his reproofs by siding with the sinner. Act in unison. "Have no fellowship with such a one, no, not to eat!"[10]

You especially who are deacons, you must be fellow helpers. You must be to your pastor as Aaron and Hur were to Moses. Encourage him to advise with you. It is customary in some of our churches, and I wish it were in all, for the pastor and deacons to meet and consult on the affairs of the church an hour or two, some evening immediately preceding the monthly meeting of the church. These meetings, in connection with the stated meetings of the church, constitute a happy union of Christian wisdom with Christian liberty.

Thus, my dear brethren, I have pointed out, very briefly and plainly, a few ways in which you and your pastor may be fellow helpers to the truth. Consider what I have said as dictated by love and a desire for your own welfare, and for the promotion of the cause of our common Lord; and may the Lord give you understanding in all things.

---

[9] Ezra 10:4.
[10] 1 Corinthians 5:11.

Churches Should Exhibit the Light of the Gospel[1]

> "These things saith he ... who walketh in the midst of the seven golden candlesticks." Revelation 2:1

My dear brethren,

That part of the solemn exercises of this day which you have allotted to me is to give a word of advice to you as a church of Christ. I confess it is with pleasure I accept of this service, partly because I see you once more happily united in the choice of a pastor, and partly because I believe you will receive the word of exhortation with candour and attention.

The language of the text, though figurative, is sufficiently explained in the preceding verse: "The seven stars are the angels of the seven churches, and the seven candlesticks which thou sawest are the seven churches." The allusion in the latter figure is doubtless to the candlestick in the Jewish tabernacle, which was made of solid gold (Exod. 25:31-37; Zech. 4:2). It is described as a candlestick with a bowl, or fountain, from which oil was conveyed, through pipes, to the several lamps which branched out from it.

It is observable, that, under the Old Testament dispensation, the church is represented as one candlestick, though with diverse branches, but under the New as seven distinct candlesticks, which may denote the different kinds of church government under the different dispensations. Under the first the church was national, and so was represented by one candlestick. Under the last the churches were congregational, and the seven churches are represented by seven distinct candlesticks.

The gospel is "a light shining in a dark place." To view God as having lighted up a candle to a benighted world is a cheering thought, and to consider yourselves as instrumental in holding it forth—as being that to the gospel which a candlestick is to the candle—is as interesting as the other is cheering.

You may consider yourselves therefore, brethren, as instruments in

---

[1] Fuller, "Churches Should Exhibit the Light of the Gospel," *Complete Works*, 1:531-534.

holding forth the light of the gospel to a benighted world. This is the thought I propose to dwell upon, and this only.

The end of your existence, as a church of Christ, is to "hold forth the word of life."[2] There are two ways of doing this, to both which I hope you will religiously attend: firstly, by supporting the preaching of the gospel and, secondly, by recommending it in your spirit and practice.

By supporting the preaching of the gospel

I scarcely need inform you that to do this you must support him that preaches it. And now give me your attention while I mention a few different ways in which it is your duty, interest, and honour to support your pastor:

1. By a diligent and constant attendance on his ministry—if possible, at all the services of the sabbath, and in the week. And those who live in neighbouring places may support the cause essentially by receiving them minister at their houses, for the purpose of village preaching.

2. By a free and affectionate carriage towards him. Treat him as a friend and a brother. If in his preaching he should occasionally make a mistake, do not magnify it. Do not make him an offender for a word. You are as likely to mistake in judging as he is in advancing a sentiment. If you perceive faults in his deportment, do not whisper them about but kindly mention them to him. Do not give ear to every report concerning him. He has a right to expect this as a brother, but especially as an elder. "Rebuke not an elder, but entreat him as a father."[3] That is, an elder in office. And though your pastor may be your junior in years, he is your elder in office, and as such has an especial claim on your forbearance and protection. Ministers are the objects of envy, and if every report against them were encouraged, they would be unable to stand their ground. Under trials and afflictions, especially, you should manifest great tenderness towards them. God often afflicts ministers for the good of the people—that they may be able to comfort those who are afflicted. Surely then it becomes the people to be very affectionate towards them under their trials. You that are officers in the church should especially be concerned to bear up his hands, as Aaron and Hur stayed the hands of Moses.[4]

---

[2] Philippians 2:16.
[3] 1 Timothy 5:1.
[4] Exodus 17:12.

3. By treating him with becoming respect, and teaching your children and servants to do the same. This will conduce to your own advantage. So long as he deserves your respect, you ought to show it; and no longer ought he to continue to be your pastor.

4. By acknowledging his instrumentality in your edification. There is great danger of extremes here. Some are always feeding a minister's vanity by telling him how well he preached at this time and that; and, by the by, at the same time displaying their own vanity, by wishing him to consider what good judges they are of an ingenious discourse. Others, to avoid this extreme, will never speak to him in the language of encouragement. Surely there is a way of acknowledging ourselves to have been edified and profited, which does not tend to feed a minister's vanity, but to encourage him in his work.

5. By giving him a place in your prayers. Think much on the greatness of his work. It is to enlighten a benighted world. Pray that he himself may be enlightened. It is to "feed you with knowledge and understanding."[5] Pray that he himself may be fed. It is to stand between God and men. Pray that he may be kept humble. It is to disturb the carnal security of men. Pray that he himself may be kept awake. It is to break the hard heart. Pray that he may be tender-hearted. It is to rouse the listless soul to action. Pray that he may be alive himself. It is to trace the windings of the human heart, and to describe the genuine operations of grace in the true believer. Pray that he himself may increase in Christian experience. From what your pastor has this day heard, methinks I hear him sigh and say to himself "Who is sufficient for these things?"[6] Think of this, my brethren, and you will not forget him in your near addresses to God.

6. By not hindering, but helping him, in the exercises of his pastoral office. Be not of a touchy temper, so as to prevent him from freely giving you advice and caution, and even reproof. It would be to his dishonour to deal in personal reflections in the pulpit; but out of it, it will be to your dishonour to be offended with plain and close dealing. If you are of such a temper that you cannot bear to be told of your faults, you will hinder him in the discharge of his office. Be at the same time also willing to take your share in the exercise of discipline. In cases of personal offence, it

---

[5] Jeremiah 3:15.
[6] 2 Corinthians 2:16.

may be well for your pastor in some instances to be excused, lest the parties contract a prejudice against him, and so prevent the success of his ministrations. But where he cannot be excused, be you always ready to join him, to stand by him, to sanction and encourage him in the execution of the laws of Christ; even though the offenders be among your relatives and acquaintance. Let the deacons in particular stand by him; and never let a church censure have so much as the appearance of being passed by the influence of the minister. The address of the elders of Israel to Ezra, in a most painful case of discipline, will furnish you with a good example: "Arise, for this matter belongeth unto thee: we also will be with thee: be of good courage, and do it."[7]

7. By liberally contributing to the support of his family. It is to the honour of Protestant Dissenters that what they contribute to their ministers they contribute freely, without constraint; but it is greater honour still, if they contribute liberally. Consider your minister's salary, not as a gift, but as a debt; and not as done to him, but to Christ. Give liberally, or you will lose the liberal reward. Give it as due to the cause of Christ, or Christ will take no favourable notice of it. A generous and punctilious regard to God's servants, even in their temporal character, was a feature of the great reformation in the days of Nehemiah (Neh. 12:43-47).

"Hold forth the word of life" in spirit and practice

We proceed to observe, that the end of your existence as a church of Christ, is to "hold forth the word of life" by recommending it in your spirit and practice. "Be blameless and harmless, the sons of God, without rebuke, in the midst of a crooked and perverse nation, among whom ye shine as lights in the world; holding forth the word of life; that I may rejoice in the day of Christ that I have not run in vain, neither laboured in vain."[8] This is a powerful way of preaching the gospel. It speaks louder than words—louder than thunder. Your ministers may assure those who are strangers to religion that religion is a matter of infinite importance, and you may say so too; but if they see you light and frothy in your conversation, indifferent and negligent in your duties, do you think they will believe you? No (say they), they don't believe it themselves! Again, you

---

[7] Ezra 10:4.
[8] Philippians 2:15-16.

may tell them what an evil and bitter thing sin is, but if they see you loose and vain in your deportment, you cannot expect them to believe you. You may dilate upon the vanity of the world; but if you are covetous and oppressive, what will your servants and workmen say? You may assure the gay and thoughtless that religion is the happiest life; but what can they think, if they see you melancholy in the service of God, and cheerful only when engaged in other pursuits?

There are various divine truths, besides the above, which you believe, and which you wish others to believe. For instance, justification by the imputed righteousness of Christ—then disprove the calumny that this doctrine leads to licentiousness, by letting them see that your personal righteousness exceeds the righteousness of the scribes and the Pharisees. The near relation of Christians to God as their Father—then be of a child-like disposition. The work of the Holy Spirit—then bear its fruits. Efficacious grace—then prove it by your perseverance.

There are three things I would here recommend as to your spirit, and then draw to a close.

1. Cultivate a humble, savoury spirit, rather than a censorious or a curious one. A curious and censorious temper is almost always the mark of a little mind, and has no tendency to recommend the gospel. A humble, savoury Christian will speak the loudest.

2. Cultivate a peaceful, sincere, affectionate spirit to each other. "Be ye all of one mind."[9] All of a piece, like the golden candlestick. If jarring, and strife, and contention be kindled among you, the scandal will not be confined to you, but will extend to the whole body, yea, to religion itself. It is in a time of peace that a people are prosperous. The heavenly Dove "flies from the abode of noise and strife."[10] Let me especially recommend you,

3. To cultivate godly sincerity. If there is any one leading idea held forth in your being compared to a golden candlestick, it seems to be this. The candlestick was to be all gold—no washing, no deception; yea, of

---

[9] 1 Peter 3:8.
[10] Issac Watts, "Hymn CXXX. [L. M.] Love and hatred," in *The Works of the Rev. Isaac Watts*, 3 volumes (Leeds: Edward Baines, 1813), 9:155. The first line of the hymn is, "Now by the bowels of my God!" The third stanza of the hymn Fuller references reads, "The Spirit, like a peaceful dove, Flies from the realms of noise and strife; Why should we vex and grieve his love, Who seals our souls to heav'nly life?" The words are probably an allusion to Psalm 55:6 and James 3:16.

beaten gold—that no part should be hollow. It was what it appeared to be—the same within as without. Let this be your character. The great art of church government is to love in sincerity.

My brethren, Christ walks among you! This should: (1.) impress you with fear—his eye is upon you! (2.) inspire you with courage—what could you do without him? (3.) induce you to imbibe his spirit—a meek and benevolent spirit to all mankind.

On an Intimate and Practical Acquaintance with the Word of God[1]

"Ezra had prepared his heart to seek the law of the Lord, and to do it, and to teach in Israel statutes and judgments." Ezra 7:10

My dear brother,

The long and intimate friendship which has subsisted between us will, I hope, render any apology unnecessary for my occupying this situation upon this solemn occasion. I should certainly have felt a pleasure in hearing some senior minister; but with your desire, on the ground of intimate friendship, I feel disposed to comply. I feel a peculiar pleasure in addressing you, for I can speak to you as a friend—a brother—an equal—an acquaintance, with whom I have often taken sweet counsel, and walked to the house of God. You will not, I am sure, misinterpret my freedom, or suppose that I wish to assume any superiority over you, or to dictate to you. You expect me to insist upon the importance of the work in which you are engaged; and for this purpose I have directed my attention to the passage I have read, and would recommend to you the example of Ezra.

Example has a strong tendency to excite us to emulation, and in Ezra the scribe you have the character of an eminent servant of the most high God held up to your admiration and imitation. Ministers in the New Testament are called "scribes, instructed unto the kingdom of heaven;"[2] and in Ezra you have the character of "a ready scribe."[3] There are four things in his character upon which I shall discourse, and which I would recommend to you.

Seek the law, or will, of God

I need not inform you, my brother, that the law, in the Old Testament

---

[1] Fuller, "On an Intimate and Practical Acquaintance with the Word of God," *Complete Works*, 1:483–486.
[2] Matthew 13:52.
[3] Ezra 7:6.

especially, is commonly to be understood as synonymous with the Scriptures, the word, or the revealed will of God. The Scriptures were then as commonly called "the law of the Lord"[4] as they are now called "the word of God."[5] So the term is to be understood here. To "seek the law of the Lord" is the same as to ascertain his mind and will in his sacred word.

You are to "feed the people with knowledge and understanding,"[6] but you cannot do this without understanding yourself. Your lips are to "keep knowledge,"[7] and the people are to "seek the law at your mouth;" but, in order to communicate it to them, you must seek it at the mouth of God.

1. Seek it, my brother. It will never be found without. It is a mine, in which you will have to dig. And it is a precious mine, which will well repay all your labour.

2. Seek it at the fountainhead. You feel, I doubt not, a great esteem for many of your brethren now living, and admire the writings of some who are now no more; and you will read their productions with attention and pleasure. But whatever excellence your brethren possess, it is all borrowed, and it is mingled with error. Learn your religion from the Bible. Let that be your decisive rule. Adopt not a body of sentiments, or even a single sentiment, solely on the authority of any man—however great, however respected. Dare to think for yourself. Human compositions are fallible. But the Scriptures were written by men who wrote as they were inspired by the Holy Spirit. Human writings on religion resemble preaching—they are useful only so far as they illustrate the Scriptures and induce us to search them for ourselves.

3. Seek the will of God in every part of the Bible. It is very true that

---

[4] 2 Kings 10:31; 1 Chronicles 16:40; 22:12; 2 Chronicles 12:1; 17:9; 31:3, 4; 34:14; 36:26; Ezra 7:10; Nehemiah 9:3; Psalm 1:2; 19:7; 119:1; Isaiah 5:24; 30:9; Jeremiah 8:8; Amos 2:4; Luke 2:23, 24, 39.

[5] 1 Samuel 9:27; 1 Kings 12:22; 1 Chronicles 17:3; Mark 7:13; Luke 3:2; 5:1; 8:11; 8:21; 11:26; John 10:35; Acts 4:31; 6:2, 7; 8:14; 11:1; 12:24; 13:5, 7; 13:44, 46; 17:13; 18:11; 19:20; Romans 9:6; 10:17; 1 Corinthians 14:36; 2 Corinthians 4:2; Ephesians 6:7; Colossians 1:25; 1 Thessalonians 2:13; 1 Timothy 4:5; 2 Timothy 2:9; Titus 2:5; Hebrews 4:12; 11:3; 13:7; 1 Peter 1:23, 3:5; 1 John 2:14; Revelation 1:2, 9; 6:9; 19:13; 20:4.

[6] Jeremiah 3:15.

[7] Malachi 2:7.

some parts of the Bible are more interesting than others. But "all Scripture is profitable"[8] and necessary. Do not take this part and leave that. Some people foolishly talk of Arminian texts, and Calvinistic texts, as if Scripture were repugnant to itself! That system, whatever it be called, cannot be the right one that rejects any one part of Scripture whatever.

4. Seek it perseveringly. Do not reckon yourself so to have found it as to be self-sufficient. Be open to conviction from every quarter. Seek it by reading, by meditation, by prayer, by conversation—by all the means that offer. Do not reject information from an inferior, or even an enemy. In the study of the Scriptures you will always be a learner.

Prepare your heart to seek the law of the Lord

There is a preparation of heart in which we are wholly passive, which is, in the strictest sense, the work of God; and, without this, woe be to any of us that should dare to set up for teachers of his law and gospel! But there is also a preparation of heart in which we are active, and this is the preparedness intended in the text. In this even, God is the cause: he actuates, but then we act. Of this preparation we have to speak, and it consists in prayer, and self-examination, and meditation. Your work is a course, and for this you must prepare by "girding up the loins of your mind"[9] a fight, and you must "put on the whole armour of God."[10] The work of God should not be entered upon rashly. God frequently brings his servants through a train of instructions and trials, that they may be fitted for it. Moses was forty years at court, and forty years a shepherd. These were his days of preparation. Christ prepared his disciples by his instructions during his life, and previous to their great work they prepared themselves (Acts 1).

Such preparation of heart is not only necessary for your entrance into the pastoral office, but also for your continuance in it. You will find that every exercise requires it. You do not need being, guarded against that erroneous notion of so trusting to the Spirit as to neglect personal preparation for your public labours. But this preparedness is not only requisite for speaking the truth in public, but as well for seeking it in private. Let all your private meditations be mingled with prayer. You will study your

---

[8] 2 Timothy 3:16.
[9] 1 Peter 1:13.
[10] Ephesians 6:11.

Bible to wonderful advantage, if you go to it spiritually-minded. It is this which causes us to see the beauty and to feel the force of many parts of Scripture, to which, in a carnal state of mind, we are blind and stupid. If we go to the study of the Bible wise in our own conceits, and self-sufficient, we shall get no good. When we would be taught from God's word, we must learn as little children. Again, if we go to the Bible merely, or chiefly, to find something to say to the people, without respect to our own souls, we shall make but poor progress. My brother, study divine truth as a Christian, and not merely as a minister. Consider your own soul as deeply interested, and dread the thought of cultivating others while you suffer your own heart to remain uncultivated. If you study divine truth as a Christian, your being constantly engaged in the study will promote your growth in grace. You will be like "a tree planted by rivers of water."[11] You will not only bring forth fruit for the people, but your leaf shall not wither, and whatever you do shall prosper. But if merely as a minister, the reverse. I believe it is a fact that where a minister is wicked, he is the most hardened against conviction of any character.

Keep the law
"Do it." The apostle Paul, in writing to Timothy, is very particular as to personal religion, in a bishop, or pastor: "Take heed to thyself, and to the doctrine." — "Keep thyself pure."[12] — "Be thou an example of the believers, in word, in conversation, in charity, in spirit, in faith, in purity."[13] Observe, too, the connection in which this exhortation stands: "Let no man despise thy youth;"[14] plainly intimating that a holy example will render even youth respectable. Your Lord and Master both did and taught the will of God.

1. Dread nothing more than recommending that to your people to which you do not attend yourself. You may preach with the fervour of an angel; but if your practice, your habitual deportment, be inconsistent, all you do will be in vain.

2. More is expected from you than from others. A wicked preacher is of all characters the most contemptible. Even the profane despise him.

---

[11] Psalm 1:3.
[12] 1 Timothy 5:22.
[13] 1 Timothy 4:12.
[14] 1 Timothy 4:12.

3. You will attend to practical preaching. But how can you either exhort or reprove, if your people should ever have it in their power to say, "Physician, heal thyself?"[15]—"Thou that teachest another, teachest thou not thyself?"[16]

4. Attend not only to such duties as fall under the eye of man, but walk with God—in your family, and in your closet. It will require all your wisdom to bring up your children "in the nurture and admonition of the Lord;"[17] and if you rule not well in your own house, you cannot expect to maintain a proper influence in the church of God. Beware also of omitting secret devotions. Conversing with men and things may brighten your gifts, but communion with God is necessary to improve your graces.

Teach in Israel the statutes and judgements of God
It is not for me to dictate to you what doctrines you are to teach, or what precepts you should enforce. But I hope you will evince your sincerity by preaching in the main such things as, in your confession of faith, you have just avowed; not however to the neglect of other points, which could scarcely be expected to be introduced in such a document. The more you are acquainted with the word of God, the more you will find it abounds with truths, reviving truths too, which seldom or never have a place in confessions of faith. But, passing this, allow me to give you a few general hints on the subject of teaching.

1. Let Christ and his apostles be your examples. Teach as they taught. It would be worthwhile to read over the Gospels, and the Acts of the Apostles, if it were only to discover their manner of teaching. Dare to avow every truth which they avowed; and address your audience in such language as they addressed to theirs, and that without softening it down, or explaining it away.

2. Give every part of the truth its due proportion. Preach every truth in the proportion in which it is introduced by God in his word. You will find some people attached to one class of truths, and others to another class; but be you attached to all. If you are habitually dwelling upon one truth, it must be to the neglect of others; and it is at your peril to keep back any part of the counsel of God! If you preach not the great doctrines

---
[15] Luke 4:23.
[16] Romans 2:21.
[17] Ephesians 6:4.

of the gospel, such as the entire depravity of our nature, the atonement of Christ, the work of the Spirit, &c., the people of God will be famished. If you preach these doctrines, to the neglect of close practical addresses, they will be in danger of a religious surfeit. If you preach doctrinally, some may call you an Antinomian. If you preach practically, others may call you a legalist. But go on, my brother: this is a kind of dirt that won't stick. Preach the law evangelically, and the gospel practically, and God will bless you and make you a blessing.

3. Dare to teach unwelcome truths. The Christian ministry must be exercised with affection and fidelity. Study not to offend any man; yet keep not back important truth, even if it does offend. You must not enter the pulpit to indulge your own temper, but neither are you at liberty to indulge the humour of others. Be more concerned to commend yourself to the consciences of your people than to their good opinion.

4. Give Scriptural proof of what you teach. Do not imagine that mere assertion will do. Evidence ought to form the body of your discourses. Such expressions as "I say," uttered in the most magisterial tone, will, after all, prove nothing—except the unwarrantable confidence of the preacher.

5. Consider yourself as standing engaged to teach all that hear you—rich and poor, young and old, godly and ungodly—"warning the wicked, lest his blood be required at your hands."[18] Seek the salvation of every man's soul. This was the apostolic method; "warning every man, and teaching every man in all wisdom."[19] Whether every individual of your congregation will accept your message is another question. Your concern should be, not to intermeddle with what is not revealed, but to "preach the gospel to every creature;" and to pray for all, as Paul did for Agrippa and his court, without distinction: "I would that—all that hear me this day were—altogether such as I am."[20]

6. Teach privately as well as publicly. Make your visits among your people subservient to instruction and edification. Take the example of Paul (Acts 20:20). Let a savour of Christ accompany you in your intercourse with your flock. This will greatly contribute to your public usefulness.

---

[18] Ezekiel 3:18.
[19] Colossians 1:28.
[20] Acts 26:29.

My brother, seek the law of God—seek it with a prepared heart—reduce it to practice—and teach it diligently; and you will be, not only, like Ezra, a "ready" scribe; but "a scribe well-instructed in the kingdom of God."[21]

---

[21] Matthew 13:52.

The Promise of the Spirit the Grand Encouragement in Promoting the Gospel[1]

Dear Brethren,

In our last public letter, we addressed you on the work of the Holy Spirit; in this we would direct your attention to the promise of the Spirit as the grand encouragement in promoting the spread of the gospel.

We take for granted that the spread of the gospel is the great object of your desire. Without this it will be hard to prove that you are Christian churches. An agreement in a few favourite opinions, or on one side of a disputed subject, or even a disagreement with others, will often induce men to form themselves into religious societies, and to expend much zeal and much property in accomplishing their objects; but this is not Christianity. We may be of what is called a sect, but we must not be of a sectarian spirit, seeking only the promotion of a party. The true churches of Jesus Christ travail in birth for the salvation of men. They are the armies of the lamb, the grand object of whose existence is to extend the redeemer's kingdom.

About eighteen years ago God put it into the hearts of a number of your ministers and members to do something for his name among the heathen; the effect of which has been to give an impulse to those labours for the attainment of the same object in our several stations at home. The success which has followed is sufficient to induce us to press forward in the work, and to search after every direction and every consideration that may aid our progress.

The influence of the Holy Spirit is by some disowned, by others abused; and even those who are the subjects of it, from various causes, enjoy much less of it than might be expected.

Those who disown it apply all that is said in the Scriptures on the subject to the communication of miraculous and extraordinary gifts, as though the Lord had long since forsaken the earth, and men were now to be converted by the mere influence of moral suasion. It is on this principle that writers, according to the leaning which they have felt towards the

---

[1] Fuller, "The Promise of the Spirit," *Complete Works*, 3:359–363.

opinions of this or that political party, have represented the work of converting the heathen as either extremely easy or absolutely impossible. It is not for us to acquiesce in either; but, while we despair of success from mere human efforts, to trust in him who, when sending forth his servants to teach all nations, promised to be with them "to the end of the world."[2]

There are those, on the other hand, who abuse the doctrine by converting it into an argument for sloth and avarice. God can convert sinners, say they, when he pleases, and without any exertions or contributions of ours. Yes, he can, and probably he will. Deliverance will arise from other quarters, and they who continue in this spirit will be destroyed.

Even those in whom the Spirit of God is enjoy much less of it than might be expected, and this principally for want of the things which were stated in our letter of last year; namely, setting a proper value upon it, seeking it with fervent prayer, placing an entire dependence upon it, and maintaining a deportment suitable to it. In proving, therefore, that the promise of the Holy Spirit is the grand encouragement in promoting the spread of the gospel, we have not merely to oppose the adversaries of the doctrine, but to instruct and impress the minds of its friends. With these ends in view, let us recommend to your consideration the following remarks.

The gospel cause of God in the Old Testament

First, the success of God's cause under the Old Testament was considered by believers in those days as depending entirely upon God. God had a cause in the world from the earliest ages, and this it was which interested the hearts of his servants. It was for the setting up of his spiritual kingdom in the world that he blessed the seed of Abraham, and formed them into a people. This was the work that he carried on from generation to generation among them. When, therefore, sentence was passed on the people who came up out of Egypt, that they should die in the wilderness, Moses, who seems on that occasion to have written the 90th Psalm, was deeply concerned, lest, in addition to temporal judgments, the Lord should withdraw from them his Holy Spirit. "Let thy work," said he, "appear unto thy servants, and thy glory unto their children; and let the

---

[2] Matthew 28:20.

beauty of Jehovah our God be upon us: and establish thou the work of our hands upon us; the work of our hands establish thou it."[3] It is worthy of notice that this prayer was answered. Though the first generation fell in the wilderness, yet the labours of Moses and his companions were blessed to the second. These were the most devoted to God of any generation that Israel ever saw. It was of them that the Lord said, "I remember thee, the kindness of thy youth, the love of thine espousals, when thou wentest after me in the wilderness, in a land that was not sown. Israel was holiness unto the Lord, and the first-fruits of his increase."[4] It was then that Balaam could not curse, but, though desirous of the wages of unrighteousness, was compelled to forego them, and his curse was turned into a blessing. We are taught by this case, amidst temporal calamities and judgments, in which our earthly hopes may be in a manner extinguished, to seek to have the loss repaired by spiritual blessings. If God's work does but appear to us, and our posterity after us, we need not be dismayed at the evils which afflict the earth.

Similar remarks might be made on the state of the church at the captivity. When the temple was burnt, and the people reduced to slavery in a foreign land, it must seem as if the cause of God in the world would go to ruin. Hence the prayer of Habakkuk, "O Lord, I have heard thy speech, and was afraid. O Lord, revive (or preserve alive) thy work in the midst of the years: in the midst of the years make known; in wrath remember mercy."[5] This prayer also was answered. The work of God did not suffer, but was promoted by the captivity. The church was purified, and the world, beholding the divine interposition, acknowledged, "The Lord hath done great things for them."[6]

After the return of the captives, they went about to rebuild the temple, but they had many adversaries and no military force to protect them. On this occasion the prophet Zechariah (who with Haggai stood to strengthen the builders) had a vision. He saw, and behold "a candlestick, all of gold, with a bowl upon the top of it; and his seven lamps therein; and seven pipes to the seven lamps; and two olive trees on each side of the bowl, which, through the golden pipes, emptied the golden oil out of

---

[3] Psalm 90:16–17.
[4] Jeremiah 2:2–3.
[5] Habakkuk 3:2.
[6] Psalm 126:3.

themselves."[7] On inquiry of the angel what these meant, he was answered, "This is the word of the Lord unto Zerubbabel, saying, 'Not by might, nor by power, but by my Spirit,' saith the Lord of hosts."[8] As if he had said, this vision contains a message of encouragement to Zerubbabel, the purport of which is, "Not by army or by power," &c. For, like as the candlestick is supplied without the hand of man, so God will prosper his cause, nor by worldly power or armies, but by his gracious influence and superintending providence. Here, also, a lesson is taught us not to wait for legal protection, or even toleration, before we endeavour to introduce the gospel into a country, but to engage in the work, trusting in God, not only to succeed our labours, but, while acting on Christian principles, either to give us favour in the eyes of those with whom we have to do or strength to endure the contrary.

The Holy Spirit and the apostolic witness

Further, the success of the gospel in the times of the apostles is ascribed to the influence of the Holy Spirit, as its first or primary cause. That the truth of the doctrine, and even the manner in which it was delivered, contributed as second causes to its success, is allowed. Such appears to be the meaning of Acts 14:1: "They so spoke that a great multitude believed." But if we look to either of these as the first cause, we shall be unable to account for the little success of our Lord's preaching when compared with that of his apostles. He spoke as never man spoke; yet compared with them he laboured in vain and spent his strength for nought and in vain. It is the Holy Spirit to which the difference is ascribed. They did greater works than he, because, as he said, "I go to the Father."[9]

In promising to "be with his disciples to the end of the world,"[10] he could refer to no other than his spiritual presence; to this, therefore, he taught them to look for encouragement. To this cause the success of the apostles is uniformly ascribed:

---

[7] Zechariah 4:2–3.
[8] Zechariah 4:6.
[9] John 14:28.
[10] Matthew 28:20,

- "The hand of the Lord was with them, and a great number believed, and turned to the Lord."[11]
- "God always causeth us to triumph in Christ, and maketh manifest the savour of his knowledge by us in every place."[12]
- "The Lord opened the heart of Lydia, and she attended unto the things which were spoken of Paul."[13]
- "The weapons of our warfare are mighty through God to the pulling down of strong holds."[14]

The great success which prophecy gives us to expect in the latter days is ascribed to the same cause. Upon the land of my people shall be thorns and briers "until the Spirit be poured upon us from on high."[15] Then the wilderness would be a fruitful field, and that which had been hitherto considered as a fruitful field would be counted a forest.

If the success of the gospel were owing to the pliability of the people, or to any preparedness, natural or acquired, for receiving it, we might have expected it to prevail most in those places which were the most distinguished by their morality, and most cultivated in their minds and manners. But the fact was, that in Corinth, a sink of debauchery, God had "much people;"[16] whereas in Athens, the seat of polite literature, there were only a few individuals who embraced the truth. Nor was this the greatest display of the freeness of the Spirit. Jerusalem, which had not only withstood the preaching and miracles of the Lord, but had actually put him to death—Jerusalem bows at the pouring out of his Spirit; and not merely the common people, but "a great company of the priests, were obedient to the faith."[17]

All our help be in God

To the above may be added, the experience of those whose ministry has been most blessed to the turning of sinners to God. Men of light and speculative minds, whose preaching produces scarcely any fruit, will go about

---

[11] Acts 11:21.
[12] 2 Corinthians 2:14.
[13] Acts 16:14.
[14] 2 Corinthians 10:4.
[15] Isaiah 32:15.
[16] Acts 18:10.
[17] Acts 6:7.

to account for the renewal of the mind by the established laws of nature; but they who see most of this change among their hearers see most of God in it, and have been always ready to subscribe to the truth of our Lord's words to Peter, "Flesh and blood hath not revealed it unto thee, but my Father who is in heaven."[18]

To this brief statement of the evidence of the doctrine, we shall only add a few remarks to enforce "the prayer of faith"[19] in your endeavours to propagate the gospel both at home and abroad. This is the natural consequence of the doctrine. If all our help be in God, to him it becomes us to look for success. It was from a prayer-meeting, held in an upper room, that the first Christians descended, and commenced that notable attack on Satan's kingdom in which three thousand fell before them. When Peter was imprisoned, prayer was made without ceasing of the church unto God for him. When liberated by the angel, in the dead of night, he found his brethren engaged in this exercise. It was in prayer that the late undertakings for spreading the gospel among the heathen originated. We have seen success enough attend them to encourage us to go forward; and probably if we had been more sensible of our dependence on the Holy Spirit, and more importunate in our prayers, we should have seen much more. The prayer of faith falls not to the ground. If "we have not," it is "because we ask not;" or, if "we ask and receive not,"[20] it is "because we ask amiss."[21] Joash smote thrice upon the ground and stayed, by which he cut short his victories.[22] Something analogous to this may be the cause of our having no more success than we have.

The kingdom of the Messiah

Consider, brethren, the dispensation under which we live. We are under the kingdom of the Messiah, fitly called "the ministration of the Spirit,"[23] because the richest effusions of the Holy Spirit are reserved for his reign, and great accessions to the church from among the Gentiles ordained to grace his triumphs. It was fit that the death of Christ should be followed by the outpouring of the Spirit, that it might appear to be

---

[18] Matthew 16:17.
[19] James 5:15.
[20] James 4:2-3.
[21] James 4:3.
[22] 2 Kings 13:18.
[23] 2 Corinthians 3:8.

what it was, its proper effect; and that which was seen in the days of Pentecost was but an earnest of what is yet to come. To pray under such a dispensation is coming to God in a good time. In asking for the success of the gospel, we ask that of the Father of heaven and earth in which his soul delights, and to which he has pledged his every perfection; namely, to glorify his Son.

The progress of the gospel of the Kingdom

Finally, compare the current language of prophecy with the state of things in the world, and in the church. In whatever obscurity the minutiae of future events may be involved, the events themselves are plainly revealed. We have seen the four monarchies, or preponderating powers, described by Daniel as successively ruling the world; namely, the Babylonian, the Persian, the Macedonian, and the Roman. We have seen the last subdivided into ten kingdoms, and the little papal horn growing up among them. We have seen the saints of the most high "worn out" for more than a thousand years by his persecutions. We have seen his rise, his reign, and, in a considerable degree, his downfall. "The judgment is set,"[24] and they have begun to "take away his dominion;"[25] and will go on "to consume and to destroy it unto the end." And when this is accomplished, "the kingdom and dominion, and the greatness of the kingdom under the whole heaven, will be given to the people of the saints of the most high."[26] It is not improbable that "the days of the voice of the seventh angel, when he shall begin to sound," have already commenced; which voice, while it ushers in the vials or seven last plagues upon the antichristian powers, is to the church a signal of prosperity. For the seventh angel having sounded, voices are heard in heaven, saying, "The kingdoms of this world are become the kingdoms of our Lord and of his Christ, and he shall reign for ever and ever."[27] The glorious things spoken of the church are not all confined to the days of the millennium. Many of them will go before it in like manner as the victorious days of David went before the rest, or pacific reign, of Solomon, and prepared its way. Previous to the fall of Babylon, an angel is seen flying in the midst

---

[24] Daniel 7:26.
[25] Daniel 7:26.
[26] Daniel 7:27.
[27] Revelation 11:15.

of heaven, having the everlasting gospel to preach to them that dwell on the earth; and before that terrible conflict in which the beast and the false prophet are taken, the Son of God is described as riding forth on a white horse, and the armies of heaven as following him. The final ruin of the antichristian cause will be brought upon itself by its opposition to the progress of the gospel.

The sum is, that the time for the promulgation of the gospel is come; and, if attended to in a full dependence on the promise of the Spirit, it will, no doubt, be successful. The rough places in its way are smoothing, that all flesh may see the salvation of God. The greatest events pertaining to the kingdom of heaven have occurred in such a way as to escape the observation of the unbelieving world, and, it may be, of some believers. It was so at the coming of our Lord, and probably will be so in much that is before us. If we look at events only with respect to instruments, second causes, and political bearings, we shall be filled with vexation and disquietude, and shall come within the sweep of that awful threatening, "Because they regard not the works of the Lord, nor the operations of his hands, he will destroy them, and not build them up."[28] But if we keep our eye on the kingdom of God, whatever becomes of the kingdoms of this world, we shall reap advantage from everything that passes before us. God in our times is shaking the heavens and the earth: but there are things which cannot be shaken. "Wherefore we, receiving a kingdom which cannot be moved, let us have grace whereby we may serve God acceptably, with reverence and godly fear."[29]

---

[28] Psalm 28:5.
[29] Hebrews 12:28.

Acknowledgements

Every book is a community project, even when only one person is listed as the author. I am thankful for all who have helped launch the resurgence of Andrew Fuller studies in recent years, especially those scholars I have had the privilege of knowing and directly learning from; Tom Nettles, Michael Haykin, and Nathan Finn. Also, I am indebted to pastoral ministry partners who have been conversation partners with me about Fuller's life and ministry as we do ministry together today; Jeremy Haskins, Nate BeVier, Casey McCall, Todd Martin, Thomas Walters, Jon Canler, and Adam York. Every student I have taught over the years at The Southern Baptist Theological Seminary has heard about Andrew Fuller and your questions and dialogue have sharpened my understanding. I cannot even remember all who have read some portion of this manuscript and offered helpful advice over the years but a few stand out; Russell Moore, Josh Wester, Jon Canler, Thomas Walters, and Dustin Bruce. Their thoughts, advice, and encouragement improved this work and all of its shortcomings lie at my feet. Chance Faulkner and the fine team at H&E publishing have been an absolute joy with which to work. Their advice and push for greater clarity in my writing, and willingness to bear with my shortcoming have been a blessing to me. Finally, I'd like to acknowledge my outstanding Administrative Assistant Michelle Manning who has typed her fair share of Fuller writings for me through the years. To all, I am in your debt, thank you.

Scripture Index

Old Testament

Genesis
1:1	15
1:13	141
1:17	141
3:15.	158
6:7	89
14:18	16
14:19	63
25:29–34	16
32:12	162, 163
37:32	163
42:36	163

Exodus
14:13	164
14:15	164
17:12	222
25:31–37	221
32:17–29	211

Numbers
10:29	16
14:24	174

Deuteronomy
6:5	138
8:3	174
8:15	174
15:11	140
33:16	133, 139

Ruth
2:12	167

1 Samuel
2:30	171
9:27	228
18:22	33

2 Samuel
7:19	160
18:22	127

1 Kings
12:16	177
12:22	228

2 Kings
4:23	163
10:31	228
13:18	240

1 Chronicles
16:22	228
16:40	228
17:3	228

2 Chronicles
12:1	228
12:17	228

Ezra
6:10	68
7:6	229
7:10	194, 227, 228
10:4	220, 224

Nehemiah
9:3	228
12:43–47	224

Job
4:4–5	163
8:7	176
17:9	214
23:14	83

Psalms
1:2	187, 200, 228
1:3	187, 230
1:19	228
2:12	84
19:1–11	141
27:4	188, 196
28:5	242
34:10	139

Scripture Index

37:3	139, 162	66:8	171
40:6–7	89	Jeremiah	
41:9	139	2:2–3	237
55:6	225	3:15	223, 228
72:8	172	8:8	228
73:1	164	8:20	86
73:10	163	23:28	149
90:16–17	237	29:4-7	60
110:3	214	29:7	59, 60
119:18	17, 200	31:3	154
122:8	62	Lamentations	
126:3	237	1:17	170
137:4	170	3:24	165
147:11	173	Ezekiel	
Proverbs		3:18	232
6:10	84	3:16–21	54
22:17	187	Daniel	
22:18	187	4:35	68
22:29	202	6:1–13	68
24:33	84	7:26	241
30:8–9	176	7:27	241
Ecclesiastes		Amos	
9:10	82	2:4	228
12:9–11	200	Micah	
Isaiah		5:2	18
5:24	228	7:8–10	171
5:30	228	Habakkuk	
8:18	215	2:3	172
26:18	172	2:14	171
30:26	142	3:2	237
32:15	239	3:17–18	151, 165
35:8	24, 214, 216	Haggai	
41:8	154	1:2	73, 74
41:10	154	Zechariah	
42:3	18	4:2	221
45:5	68	4:6	238
49:5	171	4:2–3	238
49:6	17	9:17	133
50:10	151, 170	14:4	18
55:6	83	Malachi	
56:11	78	2:7	228
58:6	69		

New Testament

Matthew		7:13	228
3:1–2	130	8:34	82, 167
4:9	25	9:7	165
4:23	25	10:29	25
5:39	64	10:45	20
5:44	91	13:10	25
7:23	177	13:11	200
8:8	153	13:37	81
8:5–13	66	14:9	25
11:25	56	16:15	25, 32, 126, 207, 217
11:28	166	16:16	55, 116
11:29	153	16:15–16	77
12:20	18	Luke	
13:11	56	2:10	213
13:52	20, 229, 233	2:23	228
13:1–23	145	2:24	228
15:27	153	2:39	228
16:17	240	3:2	228
16:18	4	3:5	228
16:24	82, 167	3:14	66
19:29	167	4:18	126
22:21	71	4:23	231
22:37	138	5:11	167
23:10	19	5:32	123
24:13	36	8:4–15	145
24:44	81	9:6	25, 32
26:28	28	9:20	32
26:52	63, 64	9:23	82, 167
27:46	91	9:35	165
27:54	66	9:61–62	80
28:18	162	13:25	83
28:20	236, 238	16:16	129
28:18–20	77	19:10	25
Mark		20:1	25
1:1	25	22:27	19
1:15	51	23:34	92
1:14–15	130	24:25	125
4:1–20	145	24:47	32
5:19	94	24:46–47	126

Scripture Index

John
1:1 15
1:17 17
3:16 25, 51, 56, 165
3:18 51
4:38 16
5:39 18
5:46 102
6:29 50
6:33 17
6:37 156
6:51 17
6:68 43
6:69 220
6:53–56 4
8:43 25
9:4 82
10:35 6, 228
12:36 82
12:27–28 91
14:6 25
14:28 238
18:23 64
18:36 65
20:29 151, 159
21:15 52
21:15–17 20

Acts
2:40 202
2:46 212
3:19 38
4:6 228
4:12 26, 55, 116
4:31 228
6:7 239
6:10 196
7 16
8:25 32
8:26 25
8:40 32
9:27 220
10:43 17, 25
11:21 239

13 16
13:34 18
14:1 196, 238
14:7 25, 32
14:16 32
14:21 32
14:23 217
15:7 25
16:10 25, 126
16:14 239
16:17 36
18:10 239
18:25 197
18:28 197
20:17-38 147
20:20 33, 232
20:24 25
20:27 85
20:28 20, 43, 48, 52, 132, 147
20:30 49
20:20–21 127
24:25 75
26 63
26:29 232

Romans
1:5 194
1:9 25
1:10 126
1:12 219
1:15 32, 126
1:17 149, 172, 173
1:28 141
1:15–16 25
2:21 231
3:26 207
3:28 149
4:18 151
4:20 177
5:1 149
7:12 214
8:10 182
8:18 214

8:28	162	16:13	150
9:6	228	2 Corinthians	
9:10	228	2:12	25
10:1	206	2:14	239
10:9	27	2:16	223
10:16	25	3:2	215, 221
10:13–15	78	3:8	242
11:13	208	3:18	152
11:28	25	4:2	228
13:4	65	4:4	25
15:16	25	4:5	47
15:30	218	4:13	2, 41, 129
15:19–20	25	4:17	162
16:26	194	4:8–10	93
1 Corinthians		5:6	161
1:9	32, 126	5:7	149
1:17	25, 32, 126	5:19	41
1:23	26, 33, 41, 126	5:20	33
2:2	26, 33, 34, 85, 126	5:21	33
2:4	197	5:18–20	130
2:7	56	5:20–21	127
2:9	142	6:17	56
2:10	147	8:9	43, 86
3:3	146	8:18	25
3:18	124	9:13	25
4:15	25	9:15	86
4:12–13	92	10:4	239
5:11	220	10:14	25
6:19	216	10:16	25
6:11	219	13:2	206
6:19–20	86	13:5	153
8:2	124	Galatians	
9:12	25	1:3	32
9:16	50	1:7	25
9:23	25	1:8	32
13:12	161	1:9	32
14:36	228	1:11	25, 32
14:38	50	1:23	41
15:1	25	2:2	25
15:1-3	33	2:5	25
15:3	3	2:14	194
15:1–3	26	2:16	149
15:1–4	42, 126	2:20	196

Scripture Index

3:4	25	3:10	85, 87
3:8	25	3:8–9	87
3:11	149, 172, 173	4:3	25
5:2	101	4:15	25
5:6	152	Colossians	
5:12	23	1:5	25
5:13	19	1:23	25
Ephesians		1:25	228
1:7	132	1:28	232
1:10	5	3:3	168
1:11	83	3:16	120
1:13	25	4:4	56, 208
1:22	162	4:3–4	53
2:10	4	1 Thessalonians	
3:5	56	2:2	25
3:6	25	2:3	49
3:8	56	2:5	49
3:17–18	196	2:8	208
4:1	4	2:13	228
4:20	5	2:19	215
4:21	3, 5, 25, 41, 194	2:7–8	194, 205
4:24	87	3:2	25
4:32	43, 86	5:25	220
4:17–24	4	2 Thessalonians	
4:17–6	4	1:8	25
5:2	17, 93	3:1	220
5:25	43, 86	1 Timothy	
6:4	231	1:11	25, 56, 207
6:7	228	1:15	26, 51
6:11	229	2:7	41
6:15	25	3:16	3, 56
6:19	25, 54	4:5	228
Philippians		4:6	194
1:5	25	4:12	21, 230
1:7	25	4:15	20
2:4	211	4:16	48, 55, 194
2:5	43, 216	4:15–16	194, 199
2:12	94	5:1	222
2:22	25	5:22	217, 230
2:15–16	224	6:4	124
2:16.	222	2 Timothy	
2:5–8	85	1:8	25
3:8	188, 196	1:10	25

1:12	166	11:14	169
2:8	32	11:26	167
2:9	228	11:27	166
2:12	92	11:24–26	16, 168
2:17	101	11:26–27	168
2:24	205	12:2	92
3:5	2	12:15	45
3:16	229	12:28	242
4:2	20, 32, 126, 129	12:16–17	16
4:22	194, 195	13:17	52
Titus		James	
1:4	25	2:14	153
2:5	228	2:17	153
2:14	214	3:16	225
2:15	194, 209, 210	4:3	240
Philemon		4:8	153
1:13	25	4:2–3	240
Hebrews		5:15	240
1:2	15	5:16	69
1:3	90	1 Peter	
1:4	153	1:3	228
2:14	42	1:8	166
2:15	42	1:11	18, 196
2:17	210	1:12	85, 200
3:15	82	1:13	229
4:11	228	1:15	214
4:12	228	1:17	153
4:14	90	1:23	228
4:14–16	51	1:18–19	132
5:14	201	3:8	225
6:18	17	4:6	25, 32
7:25	166	4:17	25
10:4	89	2 Peter	
10:29	51	1:19	142, 163
10:38	149, 172, 173	1 John	
10:30–31	90	1:1	124
11:1	173, 152	1:7	51, 90
11:4	157	2:14	228
11:7	158	2:20	119
11:9	169	2:23	28
11:10	169	3:.16	43
11:11	159	3:8	93
		4:10–11	86

Scripture index

5:1	4, 27	1:9	228
5:5	4, 27	2:1	194, 221
5:11	4, 26, 28, 126	2:2	23
5:12	27	3:21	95, 173
2 John		6:16	84
1	4	11:15	172, 241
4	206	12:11	65
Jude		13:8	93
3	214	19:10	17
Revelation		21:8	76
1:2	228	21:23	161
1:5	93	21:25	161
1:6	228	22:11	83

About the Author

David Prince has served as the senior pastor at Ashland Avenue Baptist Church in Lexington, Kentucky, since 2003. In addition, he served as an adjunct instructor of Christian preaching and pastoral ministry at The Southern Baptist Theological Seminary in Louisville, Kentucky, from 2006-2011. Since 2012, he serves as Assistant Professor of Christian Preaching.

David is the author of *In the Arena: The Promise of Sports for Christian Discipleship* (September 2016, Broadman and Holman). In addition, he was the general editor of *The Church with Jesus as the Hero* (Ashland Publishing, 2015) and the *Jesus the Hero Family Devotional* (Ashland Publishing, 2016). David is also currently working on *Exalting Jesus in Numbers: Christ-Centered Exposition*, eds., Daniel Akin, David Platt, and Tony Merida (Broadman and Holman, forthcoming). He has also contributed chapters in many books and articles for a variety of theological journals.

David's ministry is extended through his Prince on Preaching blog (davidprince.com) and media ministries. He is also a regular writer for The Ethics and Religious Liberty Commission of the Southern Baptist Convention (erlc.com), For the Church (ftc.co), Servants of Grace (servanstofgrace.org), and Reformation 21 (Reformation21.org).

David is a graduate of Huntingdon College in Montgomery, Alabama, where he received a B.A. (1991) and played college baseball. He received an M.Div. from Southwestern Baptist Theological Seminary in Fort Worth, Texas (1997). He completed his Ph.D. at The Southern Baptist Theological Seminary in Louisville, Kentucky (2011). His dissertation was *Developing a Christocentric, Kingdom-Focused Model of Expository Preaching*. The central labor and passion of David's life and ministry is preaching Christ.

David has been married to Judi since 1992, and God has blessed them with eight children and five grandchildren.

www.ingramcontent.com/pod-product-compliance
Lightning Source LLC
Chambersburg PA
CBHW030903080526
44589CB00010B/129